A BRASS POLE IN BANGKOK

A Brass Pole in Bangkok

❀

A Thing I Aspire to Be

Fred Reed

iUniverse, Inc.

New York Lincoln Shanghai

A Brass Pole in Bangkok
A Thing I Aspire to Be

iUniverse books may be ordered through booksellers or by contacting:

iUniverse
2021 Pine Lake Road, Suite 100
Lincoln, NE 68512
www.iuniverse.com
1-800-Authors (1-800-288-4677)

ISBN-13: 978-0-595-39390-9 (pbk)
ISBN-13: 978-0-595-83789-2 (ebk)
ISBN-10: 0-595-39390-X (pbk)
ISBN-10: 0-595-83789-1 (ebk)

Printed in the United States of America

For Violeta de Jesús González Munguía
Everything that a woman should be
Nothing that she shouldn't
And always an everlovin' delight

Introduction

If there's any hope, I figure it will come from outer space. The human race grows like mutant crabgrass, like over-sexed hamsters, like the trade deficit, like slime on a wet rock. Soon we'll be infesting other planets. Nothing has helped, not even the luminous columns collected in this indispensable book. I figure our best shot is a really big asteroid that smashes into the earth at about eight bazillion miles an hour. The cultural improvement alone argues for it. Think: Such a salutary rock would get rid of singing commercials for toilet paper: "*Ooooh*, it's *squee*zable!" (Get me that asteroid. Quick. Two. One might miss.) And it would vaporize Oprah—at least if it happened in one of those periods when she wasn't bigger than the asteroid.

The poorly informed underestimate the curative potency of planetary collisions. Imagine towering tidal waves, quakes measuring Richter whole bunches, and impenetrable dust clouds lasting for centuries. These would forever do away with Washington, and with babble-blonde news-anchoresses nattering on the lobotomy box like concussed parrots, and with mangy passive-aggressive psychotherapists gnawing on the raw psyches of unhappy women. I'm for it. And, blessedly, the tidal waves would everywhere drown the crowds on lovely Asian beaches. I want to contemplate the ocean instead of mounds of sordid flesh sagging in folds like adipose theater curtains.

Thing is, I don't know how to start an asteroid.

OK, I grant you that I have here a large bottle of Padre Kino red in front of me. You will see that I often consult with the good Padre.

Anyway, for a while I opposed the advent of this scary civilizational twilight that creeps over the planet. In fact, I have earnestly tried to redeem the world, without even being asked. At the time it seemed the least I could do in my role as principal moral gyroscope to this weary blue ball we live on. More specifically, I wrote the columns contained herein, sometimes while sober, explaining how the species might mend its ways, and save the ragged shreds remaining to us of worthwhile human endeavor. If the government can tell people how to run their lives, I thought, why can't I?

I failed. Inexplicably the peoples of the earth have taken no notice of me. Still, I regard the following literary droppings as, if not curative, at least diagnostic. It is more fun having leprosy if you know why your fingers are falling off.

As for remedies, more drastic measures than columns clearly are needed. Failing the asteroid, maybe a universal nuclear exchange would serve, after which cockroaches might take over the earth. The little buggers would constitute a needed jolt of moral uplift, a social advance of historic magnitude. Think about it. No cockroach has ever been a talking head. Show me a single cockroach that ever read a Harlequin romance or bumped into people while bellowing inarticulately on a skate board. They do not mangle English grammar. True, they may live in sewage outflows, but housing is scarce today at reasonable prices. Anyway the better drains are more dignified than dolorous suburbs named Brookdale Mews or Meadowbrook Dales.

I suspect the human race is really just some space-alien kid's science project gone bad in his mother's refrigerator, and one day she'll decide to throw it out. The sooner the better. Ever look down on cities at night from an airplane? They look like colonies of malign luminescent bacteria spreading in a Petri dish, with green tendrils migrating through the darkness to outlying colonies.

Actually, I can't imagine why God ever let us out of that garden. Maybe he liked the garden. Maybe Adam began singing karaoke, or Eve wanted to talk about her feelings, and He just couldn't take it any more.

Everything suggests that the time is ripe for our extinction. Literacy is down, illegitimacy up, housing developments spread like concrete scabs through any remaining countryside. Everything is regulated till it squeals. You can't drive drunk anymore, or shoot at cats from a car window with a twelve-gauge. The world will probably be overrun by cats. We won't be able to walk across the yard without stepping on several of them. What kind of life is that?

The onrushing florescence of unlivability has two sources. (If florescence can rush. Who knows what it might do? I'm not its mother. This Padre Kino is good stuff.) One source is women. They got political power, and used it to make everybody secure. Men naturally want to go fast, crash into things, kill themselves and each other, dangle from high objects, put cities to the sword, and leave camshafts in the kitchen sink. This is only reasonable. Why dangle from a low object? If the camshaft wasn't in the sink, how could you find it?

By contrast, women want everybody to wear helmets and life-preservers and don't go swimming after you eat. They're intolerant about it. A man is perfectly willing to let a woman be as safe as she wants, as long as he doesn't have to. He doesn't want to force her to shoot cats, as long as he can shoot them. But no. Women want everybody to be safe and not shoot cats. They're natural totalitarians, as well as too damned reasonable.

The second problem was Henry Ford. He started paying the lower orders a living wage. Pretty soon they had the money to dominate the culture. This brought snowmobiles and dune buggies to tear up the outlying solitude and make unending wretched noise. These newly empowered proles watched really stupid movies, so Hollywood stopped making anything else, and of course the whole mess engendered witless rap music among the gorrilloids, and low College Boards and trashy kids on snowboards with no manners. The whole world will soon be in the hands of dirtballs. And cats.

I sense that I'm losing coherence. What the hell. It's overrated anyway.

Bringing back serfdom would be a good idea. Then our aggregate loutdom couldn't pollute the worthy with reality TV. Or fat women like Rosy O'Donnell, who looks like a refrigerator with eyes. Poisoning selected water supplies would help.

Maybe bird flu. I'm willing to be flexible, though. Failing the arrival from Mars of carnivorous garden slugs full of radioactive cyanide, (*Sclurp!* "Mommy! Where did Daddy *go?*") we could get rid of antibiotics, clean water, and doctors, and distribute dirty water in lead pipes. We could grow locusts.

The world is twirling strangely. Maybe someone put something in the Padre Kino. Perhaps the solar system is in some sort of gravitational flux.

Another reason why the world is going to hell is the economy. It works too well. Used to be, nobody had squat, so there was more demand than supply. People starved colorfully but without a lot of noise in ramshackle cabins in the South, so that Depression-era photographers could take pictures of them. We got nice coffee-table books out of it.

Now we have more supply than demand, much more, usually of things we'd be better off without. Profligately fecund factories furiously spit out useless gunch, such as electric toothbrushes with seven speeds and a little miracle rubber thingy on the end that does something or other. Everybody has to consume stuff at a bitch of a rate, twenty-four hours a day, so it doesn't pile up. I mean, it could upset the balance of the earth. Think about it: A million tons of powered toothbrushes, probably with two-cycle engines, just sitting there and attracting nearby masses.

Yet we keep building this stuff. Why? Nobody who can read really needs a fifty-horsepower riding mower with harrow attachment, GPS nav, and an adjustable manure spreader to cultivate the grass on a quarter-acre lot. It just serves to prevent exercise. The driver's arteries clog and he porks up like a garbage bag full of cow liver and then gets diabetes. Gangrene comes, they cut his legs off, and then he *needs* a fifty-horsepower…. We ought to cut production, especially of food, illegalize the internal combustion engine, put a tax on fat, and impose a death sentence for possession of a credit card.

But we won't. We need an asteroid, I tell you. Let us pray….

CHAPTER 1

A Brass Pole in Bangkok

In the windy darkness beyond my window a brawling thunderstorm rages over Guadalajara. Lightning arcs sideways across the horizon, cloud to cloud, and rain sluices down like an outburst from an incontinent cow. For a day crumbling streets will be clean, the air breathable.

For me, storms encourage contemplation, lend themselves to thoughts of whence and whither and why. Maybe Guad is just a third-world city like many I have known, but it is where I live now. Looking backward over a lengthening life, I wonder how I ended up here. I am not sure why anyone might care. On the other hand, we all end up somewhere, and perhaps wonder why.

Granted, (as I warned you in the introduction that I might) I'm watering introspection with another bottle of Padre Kino red. Reality occasionally needs a little help.

Perhaps it is because I have made only unwise choices, thank God, that I seem to be permanently here. Ages ago, setting out into the world, I almost did prudent things and made sensible decisions, but something always stayed my hand. Consistently I have taken the wrong turn. Almost I applied to graduate school in chemistry, almost I became a federal programmer and, while in Washington applying, was almost hit by a bus. Better the bus, I soon decided, than programming.

In the middle of college I joined the Marines, later drifted around the world like a bottle bobbing in the Pacific, washed up on various of the beaches of life as so much spindrift, fell into journalism, covered minor wars and ran the Asian alleys. It was behavior most unwise. I recommend it. Along the way I met the underflow of the world, the freelances and bar owners in Manila and the whores and the ingenious flotsam who lived by their wits in the wilder places of the earth. I became one of them. For this I will be forever grateful.

We who live thus have our critics. They say that we have dark moods, that we drink too much, that we do not behave as we ought. (Ah, but they read us, those of us who became mercenaries of the keyboard.) And perhaps they do not drink enough. The virtue of virtue is everywhere exaggerated. Something is wrong with those who are always proper, careful, and as they should be. I would rather talk to a bourbon-swilling correspondent in a hooch chute in Manila, with a cigarette in his hand and a barmaid on his knee, than to the cleverest chemist at Yale, tamer of ketones.

We, the useless of the earth, may in our varying ways and degrees be besotted, or bedrugged, or have teeth yellowed by nicotine—live hand-to-mouth, work for unsavory magazines, or serve in the Foreign Legion. We may indeed, and many of us do. We may not be orderly or admirable. But we have seen the mortar flares hanging in the monsoon clouds over Danang. We have known the back alleys of Phnom Penh late at night, blind drunk on cheap gin, when Chicom 122s whistled in from the swamps. We have heard the ice cracking when spring comes to the far North.

We are not always a happy lot, being restless, easily bored, and unable to bear routine. We have our good days when we sense the rightness of things on a sunny morning in God knows where—for that is where we have spent much of our time. We have passed days without end in roadside diners, atop boxcars late at night on the seaboard rails, in honky-tonks in Austin. We have heard the Greezy Wheels. We knew BC Street in Koza, and the street of the snake butchers in Wan Wha, in Taipei where the workers brothels were. We have hobnobbed with hookers, drunks, geniuses, psychopaths, mercenaries, transvestites, and the men of the fishing fleets. We have seen fresh squid draped like glistening pink gloves on fish carts in Hong Kong.

Some will say that our lives constitute a sordid cohabitation with the ungodly. I do not see any objection to this. Detritus we are, and detritus we will be. It suits us. The world, the part worth knowing, lives in the alleys. We have known the smoke and dimness of a thousand Asian bars, known them till they run together in the mind, and found the hookers morally preferable to the expensively suited criminals of good society, more engaging than the liars of the press conferences. There is more of life and humanity in the driver of a battered Ford who picks up a hitchhiker in the darkling valleys of Tennessee than in the moral fetor and vanity of Washington.

We are not entirely without ambition. Often I have seen a young lovely in Bangkok, on Patpong or Nana Plaza or Soi Cowboy, revolving without excessive clothing around a brass pole in a dim club, with disco thumping in the murk, almond eyes watching for a flicker of interest. I do not want to be president, nor a Rothschild nor a computer magnate. But a brass pole in Bangkok, that I could be.

We are what we are. We can't help it. In moments of desperation we have taken jobs in places with names like *Federal Computer Week*, and sat in horror, muscles tensing in uncontrollable despair, waiting for lunch and a drink or a joint or something to get us through four more hours of federal contracts. I did that. A friend tried graduate school, another was a mortgage broker for a bit. He couldn't take it, bailed, and opened a dive shop in Mexico.

One day it hits, boom: fuggit-I'm-outta-here. We buy a ticket to Mexico City, or Kuala Lumpur, or Istanbul. Decide on the way to the airport. What the hell's in Mexico City? Find out when we get there. Somebody will know.

The literary among us found that sociopathy is a saleable commodity in the magazine racket. A press card, as a great man said, is a ticket to ride. We spent years patrolling with the Marines in Lebanon, stalking through remote Africa with guerilla bands, being cat-shot from carrier decks. For those who do these things worlds open like gorgeous orchids unknown to science and swallow you. Not all are pleasant worlds. When you get to know the cops, ride with them, you see things you can't write about, things dark and strange, drug pads with walls moving in roaches. A friend spent weeks in Tibet, at the expense of a television network. She loved it. It is how we are.

The life changes you, and starts to be a closed club. We talk to each other because we can't talk to anyone else. Outside of Washington you can't say you're a writer without people saying, "Oh. And have you been published?" Well, yeah, lady, actually. So you shut up. To another scribe, you can speak of the unlikely and distant and not entirely believable, and it is just shop talk.

A strange life, I suppose, and not much to show for it. I don't think we care. If this rain doesn't stop, there will be three feet of water in the low streets.

CHAPTER 2

Doing the D.C. Bob

In Washington, it's everywhere, like God and mendacity: The DC Bob. As people talk, in fern bars, in eateries, on the sidewalk, an incorrect thought occurs—something that might upset Them. You know who They are: The racial, sexual, religious, and political groups that One Doesn't Offend, the ideas and policies one mustn't mention, the simple observations of fact that one may not make. We all know where trouble lies. And we are careful.

The incipient malefactor leans forward. He's getting closer to his hearers to avoid eavesdroppers. Next he drops his chin and looks furtively over each shoulder in turn to see who might be listening. This is the DC Bob. It is routine. People don't even notice that they are doing it.

The heretic whispers, "I'm sick of affirmative-action hires. We can't get anything done in my office...."

The DC Bob. You have to watch what you say in America.

A while back I attended a party of people in government. I didn't know them. They knew me indirectly from this column. We clutched Heinekens in the kitchen and chewed cheesy stuff on crackers. Pretending we weren't, we felt each other out to be sure none of us was with the thought police (another ritual in Washington). The conversation came around to the deterioration of American society. The subject is common. In fact, it is close to inevitable.

One fellow finally said approximately, "I don't get it. We all know what's going on. Why can't we even talk about it? This isn't the Soviet Union."

Ah, but, yes, actually, it *is* the Soviet Union. When people have to look over their shoulders before speaking in public places—when they are afraid to utter reasonable criticism of very questionable governmental policies—we've reached the suburbs of Moscow. I'm not trying to be cute about this. Ours is very much the same system of social control, but without the truncheons. It's cleverly done, so that we have no way of revolting and nothing really to revolt against.

Yes, the penalties for political transgression are here lighter than in the USSR, but methods vary little. If you criticized Stalin, you got a bullet in the nape of the neck. Rubber hoses served their soothing purpose, and there were the Gulag and psychiatric committal. We don't do these things here.

They aren't necessary. To enforce conformity, the threat need not be extreme, merely adequate. Here, if you say the wrong thing, you lose your job. The years toward retirement vanish. The press savages you. You don't get tenure or, if you have it, you are shunned by the rest of the faculty—including those who secretly agree with you but are afraid of the same treatment. This is enough. We don't need thumbscrews.

Intimidation depends not just on penalties but upon the certainty, or near certainty, of their application. In the Soviet Union, people knew they would lose if they transgressed. They couldn't run. The police were faster. They couldn't hide. The police would find them. They couldn't even die gloriously to make a statement. The government wouldn't broadcast it. Hopelessness breeds passivity. People may rebel against long odds. They seldom rebel when they know that they can accomplish nothing.

The same is true here. We can't win, although the penalties are not grisly, and do not always come from the formal government. If we take the wrong position on the wrong subject, the federal EEO apparatus will crush us. The feds know they can drag a case out for a decade and spend us into submission. Institutions—companies, universities—will force us to apologize and publicly humiliate us. If we go to another university, apply for another job, the word will have gotten around and we won't be hired.

The fewer the people you can trust, the greater the intimidation. In the Soviet Union, children were encouraged to rat out their parents. Under Stalin, the ratting could be fatal. Things aren't so bad here. Our kids are only occasionally asked to inform. ("Do your parents have guns?") But in school, children are steeped unendingly in Appropriate Thought. In communist countries, it was more openly done, being honestly called Marxism-Leninism or Mao Thought. In our schools it's packaged as immanent self-evident Goodness. The effect is to erect a police wall between parents and children.

Do I exaggerate? Try telling your kid that Sojourner Truth and Harriet Tubman (whoever she was) were perhaps not the central achievements of Western Civilization, that there is an astronomical lopsidedness by race in commission of crime, or that universal illegitimacy may involve both immorality and irresponsibility. The tad will likely be horrified that you are such a racist. Don't her teachers and the telescreen say so?

And so many parents speak carefully at home, checking to see that the children aren't listening. As in the Soviet Union, indoctrination is the unspoken purpose of schooling.

Here, as in the USSR, the press—in particular the ever-whispering screen, half-ignored, babbling like a brook, slowly depositing assumptions, views, unnoticed beliefs—is the key to social control. Russians knew they were being lied to, but they didn't know how much. Our telescreens lie more subtly, and thus more effectively. The principle is that if people absorb one lie in two, tell them three. Soon they will believe…enough. That is all it takes.

American journalism isn't as controlled as that of the Soviet Union, but it is controlled enough. In the media the punishment for deviationist thought is swift and sure. We in the trade know exactly what we can and cannot say. Criticize the wrong things and you will lose your job and be, for practical purposes, blacklisted.

Many journalists of course know what is going on, assuredly including editors of major publications. But, being intimidated, they intimidate. Thus what we know we don't write, and what we write we don't believe. Editorialists and columnists argue pointlessly within understood constraints, like ping-pong balls bouncing between two walls. The walls are there. One doesn't step beyond.

Yet there is more to it. Editors do not control the content of publications. Advertisers do—advertisers and the owners. If you buy important amounts of advertising, you have veto power.

Sometimes the influence is quietly explicit. A major upper-middle-brow magazine once assigned me a story that might have involved criticism of defense contractors. The editor asked me to go easy on McDonnell-Douglas because it advertised. This is not uncommon. But usually writers just know what They don't want. And they don't write it. They are afraid.

Looking over our shoulders, dealing cautiously with strangers, doing the DC Bob....

CHAPTER 3

Route 301: A Report from the Which There Ain't No More

Three a.m. in August of 1962, on US 301, still two-lane, through rural Virginia. The night was humid with vapor from the nearby Potomac River. Bugs shrieked and keened in the woods, like bearings that needed lubrication. Gus's Esso glowed in the night, brash and red as a Budweiser sign. Route 301 was still the freight route to Florida. Interstate 95 had not yet gone through Fredericksburg, stealing the long-haul north-south traffic and killing businesses on the highway.

After midnight, traffic was mostly big trucks. They roared past the dark forest, roadside trash blowing in the blast, tires whining as mournful as lost dogs. Miles away, they coughed, downshifted, gathered themselves to blatt their way up the grade to Edge Hill. Hour after hour they sailed by.

The country boys worked shifts in the county's gas stations, six days a week at seventy-five cents an hour. For the most part we were wiry, slightly crazy, with bad complexions and the empty minds of thirteenth-century peasants. At night we worked alone. Crime had not yet engulfed America. For a stripling of sixteen the night shift was a big feeling. The great roads at night were not a kid's world. We liked that.

I'd sit in the office, door open, and listen to the radio or just to the silence. Outside, above the fluorescent lights of the pump islands, insects swirled and jittered. The forest brooded dark around. Once a green luna moth landed on the outside of the plate glass. It was about the size of Batman. I walked over and peered into bulging dark eyes inches away. A bug like that can make you think the world is stranger than they tell us, with maybe more to it.

It was another time and a smaller world. The Sixties hadn't started. We kids lived in rural isolation, knowing nothing of the growing tumult in the Middle East, of which we had never heard, or of the coming war in Asia, where some of us would die, or anything beyond the bounds of King George County. Drugs didn't exist. There were as many malls in the county as there were Bactrian camels. We knew only what we saw, what we did—the woods, creeks, fishing, crabbing on the river, guns, sock hops, innocent attempts at lechery and, especially, cars.

In a dispersed land, with people living in remote farms and tiny towns, some of them not even wide spots on the roads, cars were important. We lived and dreamed them, craved the forged pistons we couldn't afford, the milled heads and magneto ignition. A boy automatically cataloged cars that streamed by on the highway: fitty-six Fly-mouth, '48 Chev, *ba-a-ad*-ass 61 'Vette, exotic confections like the Studebaker Avanti.

It was funny how a kid could bond to his car almost as he might to a favorite pooch. Your mo-sheen was part of who you were. Butch wasn't Butch. He was, for all time in memory, Butch of the '53 Ford painted white with barn paint. When you parked (the term invariably connoted "with your girlfriend") in some deserted lane in the darkness of Saturday night, you had a fond appreciation for what your crumbling rust bucket could do, such as, usually, start.

A gas station was a natural home for us.

You learned funny things: where the gas cap was on every car ever made. (Try a fitty-six Chevy.) Mostly it was just "Fillerup? Check y'awl?" squeegee the windshield, maybe check the trans fluid, tires. Self-service stations were in the future. People were courteous.

In the late hours a seriousness fell over the highway. At four a.m. we got travelers who meant it, running on caffeine and maybe no choice, faces blank with a dozen hours on the road. They'd slow from a steady eighty—past midnight the cops were sparse and didn't care anyway—get fuel, hit the rest rooms, and blow on out in five minutes. At the pumps the mufflers ticked and creaked as they cooled and there was sometimes a momentary camaraderie between people out in the lonely night when nobody with sense was. I've felt the same thing on the bridge of a carrier on a late watch.

Strange things happened. Others were said to have happened. A tall skinny senior we called Gopher worked shift at Gus's. Gopher was a bright but odd country kid with a perpetually puzzled expression. You had a feeling he wasn't always sure where he was. Being immensely tall and wearing a Norfolk and Western cap, he looked like a lighthouse disguised as a railroad engineer.

One day (I was told, and hope it is true) a woman pulled up to the island in a Corvair—a car, now extinct, that was shaped like a bar of soap and low to the ground. The car was as short as Gopher was tall. From altitude Gopher asked, "Can I help you, Ma'am?

"Do you have a rest room?"

The distance was too great. Gopher thought she had said, "Whisk broom," and responded, "No, Ma'am, but we could blow it out for you with the air hose." In the resulting turmoil, Gopher had no idea why she was yelling at him.

The roads were a course in humanity. We picked up a jack-leg sociology that, later, years of thumbing the continent would verify. The better the car, the worse the people in it. Owners of Cadillacs were awful snots, but people in old pickups would go out of their way for you. That sounds too cute, but it's true. Cadillacs didn't impress us anyway. There was just something wrong with those people. Now if they'd had a huge Chrysler hemi with pistons like buckets and cross-bolted bearing journals....

One night a smoking, rattling wreck of a former school bus pulled in. Migrant workers. Fabric showed on the tires. They were going north to harvest some crop or other. They were not Latinos, as we had not yet opened the southern border. I could tell they were down on their luck. They were ragged, wore bandannas and crumbling jeans, and just looked tired. Two dollars gas. The driver politely asked if they could use the rest room as if he thought I might say no.

I gave them a couple of quarts of used oil. More correctly, reprocessed oil. Kids didn't steal from their employers as they do now, and it was the only time I did it, but, well, those folk needed oil, and they didn't have money. It was thirty-five cents a can.

A different place.

CHAPTER 4

The Suicide of Marlboro Man

The other days I was reading G. Gordon Liddy's book of conservative nostalgia, *When I Was a Kid, This Was a Free Country*. He paints a sunset picture of former times when America was free, farmers could fill in swamps without violating wetland laws, and guns were just guns. People were independent and had character, and made their own economic decisions. The market ruled as it ought, and governmental intrusion was minimal.

The picture is accurate. I lived it. I wish it would come back, which it won't. It was a world certain to kill itself.

What happens is that, in an independent-minded rural county full of hardy yeomen, the density of population grows, either nearby or at distant points on each side. A highway comes through because the truckers lobby in Washington wants it. Building a highway is A Good Thing, because it represents Progress, and provides jobs for a year.

It also makes the country accessible to the big city fifty miles away. A real-estate developer buys 500 acres along the river from the self-reliant character-filled owner. He does this by offering sums of money that water the farmer's eyes.

First, 500 houses go up in a bedroom suburb called Brook Dale Manor. A year later, 500 more go up at Dale View Estates. This is A Good Thing, because the character-filled independent now-former farmer is exercising his property rights, and because building the suburb creates jobs. The river now looks ugly as the devil, but this matters only to environmental wackos.

At Safeway corporate headquarters, way off in God knows where, the new population shows up as a denser shade of green on a computer screen. A new Safeway goes in along the highway. This is A Good Thing, exemplifying free enterprise in action and creating jobs in construction. Further, Safeway sells cheaper, more varied and, truth be known, better food than the half-dozen mom-and-pop stores in the county, which go out of business.

Soon the mall men in the big city hear of the county. A billion-dollar company has no difficulty in buying out a character-filled, self-reliant farmer who makes less than forty thousand dollars a year. A shopping center arrives with a Wal-Mart. This is A Good Thing, etc. Wal-Mart sells almost everything cheaply.

It also puts most of the stores in the country seat out of business. With them go the restaurants, which no longer have the walk-by traffic previously generated by the stores. With the restaurants goes the sense of community that flourishes in a town with eateries and stores and a town square. But this is granola philosophy, appealing only to meddlesome lefties.

K-Mart arrives, along with, beside the highway, McDonald's, Arby's, Roy Rogers, and the other way stations on the road to coronary occlusion. Strip development is A Good Thing because it represents the exercise of economic freedom. The county's commerce is now controlled by distant behemoths to · whom the place is the equivalent of a pin on a map.

This is A Good Thing. The jobs in these outlets are secure and comfortable. The independent, character-filled frontiersmen are now low-level chain employees, no longer independent because they can be fired.

A third suburb, Brook Manor View Downs, appears. The displaced urbanites in these eyesores now outnumber the character-filled etcs. They are also smarter, have lawyers among their ranks, and co-operate. They quickly come to control the government of the county.

They want city sewerage, more roads, schools, and zoning. The latter isn't unreasonable. In a sparsely settled county, a few hogs penned out back and a crumbling Merc on blocks don't matter. In a quarter-acre yuppie ghetto, they do. Next come leash laws and dog licenses. The boisterous clouds of floppy-eared hounds turn illegal.

Prices go up, as do taxes. The profits of farming and commercial crabbing in the river do not go up. The farmers and fishermen are gradually forced to sell their land to developers, and to go into eight-to-fiving. Unfortunately you cannot simultaneously be character-filled and independent and be afraid of your boss. A hardy self-reliant farmer, when he becomes a security guard at the Gap, is a rented peon. The difference between an independent yeoman and a second-rate handyman is independence.

People make more money, and buy houses in Manor Dale Mews, but have less control over their time, and so no longer build their own barns, wire their houses, and change their own clutch-plates. Prosperity is A Good Thing. Its effect is that the children of the hardy yeoman become dependent on others to change their oil, fix their furnaces, and repair their boats.

The new urban majority are frightened by guns. They don't hunt, knowing that food comes from Safeway and its newly-arrived competitor, Giant. They do not like independent countrymen, whom they refer to as rednecks, grits, and hillbillies. Hunting makes no sense to them anyway, since the migratory flocks are vanishing with the wetlands.

Truth be told, it isn't safe to have people firing rifles and shotguns in what is increasingly an appendage of the city. The clout of the newcomers makes it harder for the independent whatevers to let their weapons even be seen in public. The dump is closed to rat-shooting.

The children of the hardy rustics do not do as well in school as the offspring of the commuting infestation, and become slowly marginalized. Crime goes up as social bonds break down. Before, everyone pretty much knew everyone and what his car looked like. Strangers stood out. Teenagers raised hell, but there were limits. Now the anonymity of numbers sets in and, anyway, there's no community any longer.

And so the rural character-filled county becomes another squishy suburb of pallid yups who can't put air in their own tires. The rugged rural individualists become cogs in somebody else's gear train. Their children grow up as libidinous mall monkeys drugging themselves to escape boredom. The county itself is a hideous expanse of garish low-end development. People's lives are run from afar.

What it comes to is that the self-reliant yeoman's inalienable right to dispose of his property as he sees fit (which I do not dispute) will generally lead to a developer's possession of it. The inalienable right to reproduce will result in crowding, which leads to dependency, intrusive government, and loss of local control.

I'd like to live again in Mr. Liddy's world. Unfortunately it is self-eliminating. Freedom is in the long run inconsistent with freedom, because it is inevitably exercised in ways that engender control. And as a species, we just can't keep our pants up. But it was nice for a while.

CHAPTER 5

Reflections on a Confederate Education

Yesterday I listened to a discussion, aired by the radio station of the University of Guadalajara, on how to get Mexican children to read more, which it seems theirs don't either. A group concerned with the question had compiled a solid list of suggested reading for Mexican students (including Dumas and Robert Louis Stevenson). I wish them well.

What caught my attention was that, as Mexico tries to raise its standards, we have sought to lower ours, with notable success. It seems a perverse thing to do. My daughters recently graduated from high school (and do read) so I have an idea of the state of bookish affairs. By all reports, even smart children today read little, and still less that is worth reading. I have seen the works of science fiction and political correctness required as literature. It is sorry stuff. Our kids have missed, I think, an important boat.

The wonderful children's books of the past were not merely for children, and were not in the least dumbed down (I prefer "enstupidated") or unsophisticated. *Winnie the Pooh* and *The House at Pooh Corner* are delightful things, notable for the sheer quality of the writing. Through the *Looking Glass* and *Alice's Adventures in Wonderland* are not easy books, unsurprising since Dodgson was a mathematician, and swim in deep philosophical waters. *The Wind in the Willows* likewise bears rereading by grownups and, may I emphasize, isn't easy reading unless a child has truly learned to read. These books required of children a mastery of the language that adults now do not have.

Kipling's classics—*The Jungle Books, Just So Stories, Stalky & Company*—were neither sappy nor condescending, and taught an easy fluency of reading and a love of good prose. The only recent work of the same stature is Tolkien's trilogy with its quietly elegant English and fine story. It is a good read for a fourteen-year-old; and also for a reader of fifty who can appreciate the unerring weave of Carolingian myth, the northern sagas, Arthurian legend, and English rural life, all wrapped in a complexly ordered philological backdrop that delights the literate.

The illustrations accompanying many of the old books were not the grinning pabulum of Hollywood, but as good as the writing. The illustrators, if they were commercial artists in that they earned money by their drawing, were also fine talents who cared about their work and evoked worlds that those who read them never forget: Tenniel, Rackham, Shepard. To read *The Jungle Books*, to savor Shepard's illustrations in Pooh, and then to see what the cultural cockroaches of Disney have done to them, is to yearn for a horsewhip.

We pay a price for enstupidation. There floats around the Internet what purports to be, and probably is, an eight-grade exam from a school in Kansas in 1895. Most graduates of today's universities could not pass it. One of the questions requires the giving of the principal parts of the verbs "lie" and "lay." I can do it instantly: lie, lay, lain; lay, laid, laid. I know what both mean and when to use them. I don't have to think about them.

I can do these things not because of any particular acuity, but because I went to Robert E. Lee Elementary in Virginia long ago, and then to the junior high of Athens, Alabama in 1957. We were expected to know what principal parts were, to memorize vast numbers of them, and to diagram (I was sure at the time) every sentence ever written.

Diagramming is now equated with deadening mindlessness. No. I learned how my language worked, what a subjunctive was, the difference between a direct object, an indirect object, and a predicate nominative. One reason why Americans in Mexico have such a terrible time learning Spanish is that they know none of these things.

The effect of learning how a thing ought to be done is that it becomes painful to see it done badly. The misusage one hears today is awful: "I was laying down." "For he and I." "There's six on the table." The abominable and increasing, "Me and him was talking." "If someone comes into the ladies' room, tell them to fix their hair themself." The appalling confusion of "its" and "it's," "your" and "you're." Once is a typo. Five times in a few paragraphs is semiliteracy.

Grammar is not the only decedent. Words that meant different things no longer do. "Sensuous" does not, or should not, mean "sensual," or historic, historical, or militate, mitigate, or tragedy, disaster; or stoic, stoical; or oversight, supervision. The result is that writers have to use circumlocutions if they want to be sure that younger readers grasp their meaning.

Those who cannot read cannot write. A common complaint of professors old enough to be fully literate is that their students aren't. They cannot spell, or organize a coherent paragraph; they think that a verb agrees with the object of the nearest preposition, and lack a gerbil's grasp of the simplest principles of composition.

They don't know, and don't know that they don't know. Here is the nut of the matter: once a generation loses all cultivation, no one remains who remembers what it was, and there is no one either to teach it or remember why it was a good idea. We are there.

The promiscuous reading that once was common among intelligent children provided an unordered but broad schooling that the schools couldn't, and were not expected to. Much of it was of no lasting value, as for example the literally dozens and dozens of Hardy Boys, the old and new Tom Swifts, the Nancy Drews, the Plastic Man and Wonder Woman and Classics Illustrated comics that we inhaled by sheaves in drug stores. They taught speed and fluency.

Yet much of it in its sheer un-thought-out profligacy did teach things of value. At perhaps age seven I went on a fairytale kick, reading Grimms, Edith Hamilton (I regarded myths as fairy tales), Andersen, Bulfinch, *The Tanglewood Tales*, the *Jatakas*, and a book of Hawaiian mythology in which I encountered

Pele, the goddess of volcanoes. (I understand that she later played soccer for Brazil.) It was worth doing.

A peasantrified population is, among other things, politically malleable. A bright child of seven who reads turns into a kid of eighteen who thinks, at least during moments of hormonal respite; who graduates to serious history and literature and, when lied to, will go to the library and check out a book. Those who live for television will believe what they are told, having no inkling that they are being bamboozled. Is this intended, or just incidental to the larger aims of our cultural vandals? I don't know.

CHAPTER 6

Madison Avenue and Radioactive Garden Slugs

I'm going to breed giant radioactive garden-slugs that drip cobra venom, and latch onto their prey like ticks on a cow, and turn them into formless gunch, and absorb them. I figure we'll feed them advertising executives. I just put a bunch of slugs in a cigar box, with a radium watch thrown in so they'll mutate. I'm not sure how to get them to have a hunting instinct. Maybe I'll let them watch late-night TV about sharks and Nazis.

I'll leave them at night on Madison Avenue. Come morning, some wretched ad goober, who probably specializes in singing toilet paper, will get into the elevator. He won't notice an eighty-pound carnivorous slug stuck to the roof like a sticky sleeping bag. When the door closes it will drop, scloop....

"Aaaaaaaaaaaaaaaeeeeeeeeeeeaaeeeeeeeeeeeeeeeeaaggggggghh!"

Glurp.

Hehhehheh.

You can't get away from advertising any more. It's the only reason they keep us around. Ads keep sneaking deeper into our lives. I had to unplug my fax because all the paper got used by ads from people selling me toner. Five times a day some parasite calls to sell me aluminum siding or dance lessons. Pizza operations festoon my doorknob with ads for artery cement. Pounds of ads come with my Visa bill. Three quarters of my mail is junk, my spam filters overflow, and now they have pop-up ads for nekkid pictures of underage girls or for dimwitted digital cameras.

I can't stand it.

You know those weird plastic isolation bubbles they keep people in who don't have immune systems, so bacteria won't eat them? I'm going to get one, and live in it. It's because I'm sick of looking at footage of snow storms, and hearing about how some dismal deodorant will fill me with the purity of nature. Or how if I drink Pepsi I'll turn into a grinning New Age wimp with a waxed chest, and hot babes will chase me like ants after a sandwich.

I'm in retreat, but it's getting hard to know where to run. First I quit listening to radio. I didn't want to hear witless voice-majors shrieking about Home Depot every five minutes and how I could get a wonderful battery-operated drill I didn't want, free, if I bought carpeting I didn't want either.

Next I began wearing ear plugs when I went to Safeway. I'd be contentedly looking for bachelor food. From the PA system would come a woman's voice like pancake syrup with too much butter in it, saying, "Shoppers! Today we have *oooooooh*! a special...*yes!*...on some marginally edible glop you would never think of eating on your own...." She always has a contrived yodeling lilt in her voice, as if gargling a frog, and sounds as if she wants to lick the microphone.

Shoppers. That's all we are. Sales objects.

Television went next. After seeing the same preternaturally stupid ad for "the new!....Toyota!...Erotic Sludge" fifteen times in an hour, I decided I'd never drive again and canceled cable. Yes, I know it wasn't just any old Sludge. It was the New Improved one with more headroom, more trunk room, and more power. It has had more room every year, till I figure you could put the Yucatan Peninsula it, along with lots of battery-powered drills and inedible glop.

A car ad used to tell you something about the car—horsepower, valves, cubic inches. Now it shows the thing swooping powerfully along a desert road. This is to make you think that, if you buy it, you'll be wild and free and at one with cosmic something-or-other instead of being a cubicle dweeb with a huge mortgage, bad knees, and three delinquent kids.

Ads aren't about products. They're about how we'll feel about ourselves if we pop for them. Products are pretty much identical, so ads compete as cures for boredom and inner emptiness. Often they create, and then assuage, anxiety. "Everybody thinks you smell like a hog-rendering plant. Wash with Dial and they'll stop whispering behind your back...."

What happened was, three hundred years ago nobody had anything, except goiter and tuberculosis, because the economy wasn't invented, and so every-body wanted a washer-dryer and refrigerator. You didn't have to advertise. People knew they wanted things. They just couldn't figure out how to get them. There was more demand than supply.

Then inventors figured out how to make more of everything anybody wanted, and more of things it was almost impossible to want, than anybody in his right mind would buy. (That may have been a sentence. If it isn't it's because it had a bad childhood. Maybe its mother got too close to the radium watch with the slugs on it.) So useless junk started piling up and threatening to crush things. Home Depot lost a factory they couldn't find under a mound of battery-pow-ered drills.

Supply had exceeded demand. The situation was desperate. The trick was for admen to make people buy things that would embarrass a junkyard.

They did. That's why you have to have home theater. You probably lived most of your life without it. After all, movies are terrible. Watching them on home theater is like using a magnifying glass to look at warts. The better you can see them, the more you wish you hadn't.

Then ad weasels learned to make people get competitive about useless non-sense. Today men want the latest in home theater because it makes them feel potent, like a swamp bird with funnier tail feathers than the others have. Ever notice that magazines devoted to gadgets—cameras, cars, stereo—appeal almost exclusively to men? Women want better addresses, stranger clothes that are hard to take care of, and jewelry that attracts barracudas if they swim with it. (I wouldn't wear earrings that looked like wounded fish, but maybe that's just me.)

Then the admen discovered that poaching on competitors was easier than inventing something new and different that people would be better off without. That's why you see an average of 1600 ads per hour for indistinguishable kinds of aspirin to treat headaches you probably wouldn't have if you didn't watch too much television. (How many aspirin would you take a year, left to yourself?)

Advertising is like a presidential election. It doesn't change anything, but just decides who gets the spoils.

What if people suddenly thought: "I'm paying forty green ones a month for cable, so I can watch demented perverts squeezing toilet paper and grinning? Have I lost whatever residual mind I may have had?" The economy would come to a calamitous halt and we'd all suffocate beneath mountains of uneaten aspirin.

Slugs, I tell you. Great squalid ones. With radioactive cobra venom.

CHAPTER 7

Why We Fight, Why We Don't, and How We Lie About It

Permit me a few thoughts on things military, roused by hype about our recent access of patriotism for the War on Terrorism, and maybe by one too many war documentaries on late-night television.

(1) Men seldom enlist from patriotism. They enlist in time of peace because they are bored, need jobs, dream of travel, don't know what else to do with themselves, want to prove their manhood, or have heard lurid tales about the women in Hong Kong. Patriotism is at best an afterthought.

In time of war, reasons again vary. Some enlist to get the service least likely to see combat. During Viet Nam, the National Guard was popular for just this reason. Gutsier men will join because they want to see combat. They simply like the action. Some of these later become correspondents, and go from war to war. A few men, the ones who adhere to the elite commando outfits, carry with them an intense and angry aggressiveness for which they seek an acceptable outlet. They want to kill people.

None of this is patriotism. Nor is it a desire to save the world from communism, National Socialism, slavery, or the misbehavior of the Japanese. The truth is that people do not care greatly about unpleasant political systems in places they have never seen. Truth, virtue, and morality are add-ons convenient for explaining things done for less noble reasons.

(2) Most men actively do not want to fight for their country, and will go to great lengths to avoid doing so. That is why in serious wars we need a draft. After the war, draftees may find it socially useful to discover that they were inspired by patriotism.

(3) Soldiers often have not the slightest idea why they are fighting. Oddly, they don't seem to care.

I doubt that one enlisted man in fifty could have found Viet Nam on a map. Nor could have much of the public on whose behalf they were said to be fighting. Few soldiers knew what communism was, other than a darkly threatening Very Bad Thing. Few could spell it, nor did they care. Books were available. They didn't read them. Nor, usually, did the public. Soldiers didn't care in the least whether the Vietnamese, whom they generally hated, lived under communism.

(4) Draftees go to war not because they are brave, but because they are not brave enough. It takes courage to volunteer for war. It takes courage, or at least decisiveness, to hide in Mexico. It does not take courage to be drafted. This is why the draft works. It relies on the principle that at each step, from reporting for training to getting irrevocably on the troop ship, it is easier to cooperate than to resist. A draftee may fight bravely. Yet he wouldn't have gone unless compelled.

(5) Much of America does not like its soldiers, or its military. The upper classes hold servicemen in contempt. The Ivy Leagues for example provide almost no volunteers. Parents near bases often forbid their daughters to date servicemen. Our grade schools expel boys for drawing soldiers. At the end of a successful war a maimed GI may get a week of drinks bought for him, but after that he just makes people uncomfortable. Veterans of Korea were ignored. Those from Vietnam were often despised.

(6) In democracies, prosecution of war depends on hiding the nature of war. On the History Channel we endlessly see the bombers of WWII flying over Europe, to stirring music, amid clouds pocked with flak, turrets blazing at

incoming Messerschmitts. Bombs fall, flash-flash-flash, across the remote city below. It's an adrenal rush, exciting, and calls to something deep in the audience.

You don't see little Hans, far below and four years old, screaming because something wet and messy is oozing from Mommy's head and her eyes are funny and the fire is getting closer and why doesn't someone help him? Nor do you see the turret gunner with his intestines hanging out like greasy rope and blood pooling in low spots.

The anger such observations arouse in many military men is a dead giveaway of their discomfort. Governments know that if people saw much of this, they might not fight.

(7) American wars often begin, through unpreparedness and simple stupidity, with the pointless sacrifice of countless troops, which is usually explained as springing from the perfidy of the enemy. In WWI, WWII, and Korea we were utterly unready. Pearl Harbor occurred because we didn't bother to track the Japanese fleet.

Having bled our soldiers profusely because of inattention, we congratulate ourselves on winning in the long run. Stirring music again accompanies the congratulation.

(8) Officers, characterized by physical rather than moral courage, usually seem more interested in protecting their careers than the lives of their men. They will assault a beach, but won't open their mouths. The higher the rank, the more they behave like cheap politicians. I saw this many times when I covered the military.

For example, a pilot once wrote me saying that certain social policies were gravely damaging the capacity of his service to fight, and would lead, in a serious war, to substantial military incapacity and loss of life. He then said for God's sake not to use his name or identify his unit. CYA. The same pilot flew many missions over Baghdad.

(9) After a war, veterans often dislike their own country more intensely than they do the enemy. A soldier goes to war, perhaps encouraged by martial bands

and splendid uniforms, to fight someone he is told is the enemy. He returns missing a leg, wearing a colostomy bag, or remembering things that it is better not to remember.

He then finds that people at home have been partying and living the good life while he was bleeding, that they don't really care about him, that some laugh at him for having been stupid enough to go. He no longer has anything in common with them. An impassable gulf separates him from the country.

Year by year as the war recedes, its apparent importance diminishes. The enemy, like as not, suddenly becomes an ally. Yet the soldier still has the colostomy bag, still sits in the wheelchair. He feels used by the happy people who stayed at home, decides that he was had, that somebody, he's not sure just who, maybe the whole country, played him for a sucker.

And he hates them for it.

CHAPTER 8

Birthing the Ogpu

It's going fast now. Not just the searches and growing federalization of law enforcement, but the military as secret police. It's getting dark out there. I'm going to burrow into Tahiti with a brown maiden, change my name to Oogawaga, and hope they overlook me.

In Chicago on the flight to Guadalajara I was as usual detail-searched by domestic aboriginals. They say searches are random, but they are lying. They would be random if mediated by a random-number generator, which they aren't. Somebody chooses who to harass. If you have a beard and a cowboy hat, or wear a Harley shirt, they'll randomly select you at least once per trip. I promise.

Which has nothing to do with security. They are searching people of whose appearance they disapprove. Priss cops.

I had my scuba gear in a shoulder bag. Our highly trained security mechanics pawed at it like monkeys who had found a fruit basket. Great. Kink the hose near a connection and I suddenly don't have air at 130 feet. One of these frauds pulled out my dive computer. He looked as if he wasn't sure whether to inspect it or peel it.

"What is this?" he asked.

"A coconut," I didn't say, or I would still be in jail. I did say, "A dive computer."

He looked at it without comprehension, then asked me again what it was. Presumably he suspected that it might have turned into something else in the intervening two seconds. It's how dive computers are. One minute a computer, the next minute a rainbow-colored unicorn.

Brainless thoroughness complemented thorough brainlessness. They pulled everything out, knowing what none of it was, and stuffed it back in, having accomplished nothing. The exercise was pointless. I had two dive lights containing twelve C-cells. They could have been carefully sealed Semtex. The dive computer could have been full of C4.

And the airlines wonder why people fly less.

Tell you what. I'm going to call Homeland Security in an Arabic accent and say, "We sending suicide bomber, he haff explosive prostate. Heeheehee!" Then I'll buy railroad stocks.

Anyway, to continue the grisly chronicles of unwanted security:

Having reached Guad, I was chowing down on really great ribs at Bruno's when a buddy handed me a printout from the *Washington Times*. First sentence: "Language tucked inside the Homeland Security bill will allow the federal government to track the email, internet use, travel, credit-card purchases, phone and bank records of foreigners and U.S. citizens in its hunt for terrorists."

Bingo. I told you it would happen, but I thought it would be slower—a gradual linking of DMV records state to state, police records becoming electronically available, and so on. Nope. We're going for the whole totalitarian enchilada at once. Yes indeedy. The Mommy State is going to watch us very carefully. For our own good.

Better yet, the Defense Department is going to run the Total Information Awareness program. (I didn't make that name up. I couldn't. TIA in Spanish means "aunt," which fits. Aunty will keep an eye on us.) Yep. The military is going to be another federal police force. You want to be watched, don't you? It's so we won't be terrorists.

Says the *Times* "Computers and analysts are supposed to use all this available information to determine patterns of people's behavior to detect and identify terrorists...."

Patterns of behavior. Data mining. If you have lunch three times at Kabab Bazaar, and charge ammunition at the shooting range where you take your daughter plinking, and read a book on torpedo design because you like military history—the computers will kick your name out, and the feds will show up to ransack your life.

I'd rather have the terrorists.

Note the attempt to sneak this cybernetic Stalinism surreptitiously into law. Legalizing unlimited surveillance of everybody is not trivial. If a worse law has been passed, I am unaware of it. You don't try to make massive changes in the tenor of society without mentioning it to the society. The White House knows this.

But that is exactly the scam being worked. It is underhanded, deliberately deceptive, far more dangerous to the country than Moslem terrorists. It is the product of minds that have no idea of how America is supposed to work.

If you think TIA is going to be used only to fail to catch terrorists, you are kidding yourself. Knowledge is power. It gets used. I'm from Washington. I know. For example, the congressman who decides not to run again because his political enemies have discovered his taste for little boys. It happens.

Who of us doesn't have some skeleton moldering in the crawlway? Do you want your wife to know about the time at the Watermelon Growers convention when you ended up in the sack with that gal who, though married, wasn't married to you? You probably aren't going to make waves, are you?

Once the barrier is breached between governmental and private records, surveillance will grow like kudzu—so that we will be safe. If the government can have access to all existing records to protect us, it will shortly want to create new ones to protect us. At Fort Meade in Maryland broods the National Security Agency, which is not supposed to, and may not, spy domestically. It has phenomenal capacity for intercepting, decrypting, collating, storing. Just the thing for prospecting for terrorists, don't you think? You can bet the Homeland Security people have thought.

Fear not, though. These same Homeland Security people have said that, why no, they would never, ever, do anything wrong, and they even have a Privacy Officer to make sure. What could be more reassuring? Building a system to spy on Americans, the government assures us that it won't use it to spy on Americans, and to protect us against the possibility, the government will provide a Privacy Officer who works…for the government.

I never thought I could possibly want Clinton back. The man was a detestable, lying, libidinous arguable psychopath who did chunky interns, looted the White House, and sold pardons like an escapee from Chaucer—but he begins to look like a mere amiable clown. Bush means business.

If you are ever in Papeete, ask for Oogawaga.

CHAPTER 9

Watering Jane

It was my last night in Arlington, chilly, portending rain, traffic heavy on Wilson Boulevard. I was doing ribs at Red, Hot, and Blue on the theory that a coronary occlusion was better than saving myself for the tumor. A benefit of life is that you have choices.

RH&B claims to have the "best barbecue you'll ever eat in a building that hasn't already been condemned." That sounds about right. I like condemned buildings. On the lobotomy box a psychologist, expounding on the mental state of a sniper then popular with the press, babbled about self-actualization. I could tell because the closed-captioning said so. Captioning is supposed to be for the deaf, but really it's for bars.

He was the squishily pretty kind of psychologist with the bikini-line beard and the condescension that comes of infinite understanding. I decided that priss spigots and barbecue don't go well together. His gestures carried a whiff of closeted heterosexuality. I know: You can't say that any longer. Heterosexuality, the last taboo. I wanted to brain him, but it appeared likely that someone already had.

I walked up Wilson toward Little Saigon and, beyond, the American Legion post where Honky-Tonk Confidential was playing. Lower Arlington is a ferment of dives, beer chutes, and changing restaurants that pop up every time we lose a war. It's good juju. Washington is the left ventricle of the heart of darkness, but there are regions with a lively urban feel.

As the years have passed the city's night life has become more and more a circular swirl around the Beltway. Long ago, people from the suburbs went into the city for music, dancing, drinking. As crime worsened, traffic gummed up, hostile city governments made parking tickets a revenue source, and taxation drove businesses into Virginia and Maryland, night life shriveled downtown. In Rosslyn, Virginia, where Key Bridge crosses the Potomac from Georgetown, you see huge high-rise office buildings. They are Washington's tax base. It went away.

Life follows money. In the safer outlying states, the amenities of urban life sprang up in enclaves around the Beltway: Arlington, Alexandria, Bethesda. Restaurants, shops, bars, and music of all sorts flourished. High-tech businesses plopped themselves down in exurban parks instead of going downtown. Soon a generation arose who never went to the city. Anything they wanted could be found around the Beltway.

When a city makes itself unlivable, people stop living in it. Now there's a concept.

In a conurbation that amounts to office parks scattered around a slum, with fern bars speckled about, you have to hunt for night spots that have any life to them. There are some: Whitey's in Arlington, a former biker bar; Cowboy Café South, the Zoo Bar on Connecticut Avenue across the street from the entrance to the Zoo. The latter is narrow, dark, and smoky, and has bands consisting of three blacks you've never heard of who play good blues. It could be in a real city, maybe Manhattan or Chicago.

The Legion is a little place, a converted house, on a side street. The décor is 1954 institutional cafeteria, unpretentious as an all-night diner. I like it because people aren't trying to impress you. The crowd is mostly aging. There, and at the VFW, you run into old guys on the way out who remember the Pacific War, far-off days of sun and blood on turret armor and Hellcats screaming off wooden decks. My father was there. There is an honor in these of the leaving that means nothing to conniving lawyers and nominal men with ear rings.

The band was setting up. HTC is a deeply Washington band derived from the major ecosystems of the city—media trash, computer wieners, and Civil Serpents. DC is an odd city. Excepting the underclass, it consists of pols, who live by lying and stealing; bureaucrats who molder pointlessly in offices painted federal-wall green; support troops in the computer trades, and the press, who misreport the others. Washington is a city without a soul. There is no blue-collar presence, and few ethnic neighborhoods except black and Latino.

Yet it is the nation's most educated city, heavy on brains, expertise, and hidden desperation. Sometimes raw talent breaks out for good purposes, usually in the dark of night, like Superman from Lex Luther's kryptonite jail. HTC is such an eruption, a truly fine country band in the least country city on earth. You can imagine country in New York or LA, but the music of DC is the hum of a paper shredder destroying incriminating documents.

I've known them for a decade at least. Diana Quinn, Mike Woods, Geff King. With three lead singers each of whom could carry a band himself, or in Diana's case, herself. They write their own distinctive stuff. ("Down in Washington/ You can't have a gun/The bad guys all got one…") They will never make it on MTV because they can sing with their legs together.

At break I went to the whizzenzimmer. In each of the urinals a portrait was pasted, obviously designed for the purpose and impervious to expired beer. It was Jane Fonda. She remains perhaps the most hated human in a country that has never heard of Vidkun Quisling. Lock and load, I thought. I gave her credit for persistence. Three decades after crewing the North Vietnamese antiaircraft site, Hanoi Jane was once again making a splash.

I don't understand the rich and famous. The woman at the next table was quoting Zsa Zsa Gabor, perhaps correctly, as saying, "All I want is a diamond on my finger and a mink on my back." As a guy I'm happy to have a mink on her back, though I'd look funny in diamonds. Washington goes in more for semi-rich but powerful, skip the garishness. These people have $750,000 mortgages in remote McLean on ugly piles set next to each other like those square warts on a waffle iron and called Oglethorpe Mews. I guess Grotesque Box Cluster wouldn't catch the desired flavor.

They spend their whole lives rising slowly at Housing and Urban Development, like bubbles in pancake syrup, so they can be GS-15s and regarded with awe by other federal termites who don't do anything worthwhile either. If they had the brains the good Lord gave a claw hammer, they would buy hang-gliders, eat ribs, and listen to bar bands.

But they don't. It keeps them out of my way.

The Legion had really good Budweiser. I got another because I wanted to pay my respects to Jane again. My mother brought me up to be a gentleman. Diana lit into "I Ain't No Texas Gal," and I reflected that an advantage of Washington is that, sometimes, you can almost believe you aren't there.

CHAPTER 10

Steve Hatfill, Anthrax, and Bushwah

This isn't going to be a cute column. It may be a bit long. Some things need saying, so I'm going to say them.

Recently stories have appeared in the press implying that Steve Hatfill, among other things a former ebola researcher at the Army's biological-warfare research center at Fort Detrick, Md, sent the notorious anthrax-bearing letters to people around the country. The implication is that he is a murderer.

I know Hatfill socially, though we are not intimate. We met years back in Washington at a party held by a common friend. We have the occasional beer, bump into each other every year or so at parties, and infrequently participate in minor pub-crawls.

Hatfill interested me because, aside from being good company, he was smart and knew a great deal about things technical, as for example ebola. I regard him as a friend, and will continue to do so until it is established that he has been killing people, which I think unlikely.

My involvement: In August of 1997, I published in the *Washington Times* a column I wrote with Steve's help on the vulnerability of the US to biological terrorism. At the time I was writing a weekly police column. Terrorism fit. The column re-emerged in connection with the Hatfill-as-murderer stories.

Since then, though now living in Mexico, I have gotten email from countless media outlets asking for interviews about him: The *New York Post, Nightline*, the *New York Times*, and such. In most cases I begged off. I know what television is, and know better than to subject myself to its directed editing. However, I have followed the stories. Overall the coverage has been contemptible, being half stampede and half lynch mob.

When the professional crosses into the personal, writing gets difficult. Personally, I'd trust Steve with my life. Journalistically, I can't tell you he didn't do it. How could I know? I don't think he did, but that is a judgement, not a fact. Jeff Dahmer seemed to be a nice fellow until you learned of his grazing habits. Neither can I prove that you didn't send the anthrax, or that Steve isn't a robotic space-alien disguised as an ebola researcher.

I can tell you, however, that the stories have embodied every trait that makes people detest the press. They have been mostly innuendo. They rely almost totally on unnamed sources, and largely fail to make sense. Many have been of the sort that run, "Sources say that Smith was seen walking past the parking lot. The next day a body was found there." The reader is invited to make the connection.

It makes me want to wash.

As one example chosen from many, Nicholas Kristof of the *New York Times*, one of those who emailed me about Hatfill, wrote in a column about "Mr. Z," recognizably Hatfill.

Asks Kristof, "Have you [the FBI] examined whether Mr. Z has connections to the biggest anthrax outbreak among humans ever recorded, the one that sickened more than 10,000 black farmers in Zimbabwe in 1978-79?"

Hatfill is now promoted to mass murderer. No evidence, no facts, just the leading question. The implication is one of guilt by geography. Hatfill went to medical school in Zimbabwe. Kristof doesn't have the guts to make an accusation, or the honesty to admit that he has nothing to go on—so he relies on innuendo. Welcome to journalism.

Personally, before I implied that anyone had endeavored to kill many thousands of people, I'd want a tad better evidence.

I am not familiar with the incident in Zimbabwe. However, anthrax comes in three varieties: intestinal, cutaneous, and "inhalation." The inhalation variety, the only one useful in warfare, doesn't sicken people. It kills them. If ten thousand people die of inhalation anthrax, there is no doubt that it has been done deliberately. Did they? Kristof doesn't say.

If it wasn't the inhalation variety, what was it? Kristof doesn't say. How you give 10,000 farmers intestinal anthrax isn't obvious. How clear is it that the incident, if it even happened, was in fact deliberate? What did Hatfill have to do with it? The reporting is so bad as to be meaningless.

Laura Rozen, in *The American Prospect*, June 27, writes that genetic "analysis of the letter-anthrax suggested that it was indistinguishable from a strain developed by USAMRIID [i.e., the US Army.]" Unstated implication: Hatfill had access to the bug, so he must be guilty. Is this plausible? Hatfill would of course know that the bacillus would be DNA-sequenced and immediately traced to military sources. Why would he use a traceable variety? Conceivably he is secretly a space-alien psychotic android killer-bot. Stupid he isn't.

"*Suggested* that it was indistinguishable...."? That is careful reportorial weasel-wording. Was it indistinguishable, or was it not? Was the strain available elsewhere also? Anthrax has been the subject of all manner of research by civilian scientists. They get specimens from somewhere, probably ordinary biological supply houses (though I don't know).

Kristof also says, "FBI profilers are convinced that the real anthrax attacks last year were conducted by an American scientist trying to pin the blame on Arabs." I see. Then it really makes sense to use a variety identifiably developed by the US military, doesn't it? Exactly what Arabs would have.

By the way, Nick, which profilers? Name one.

Oh.

Virtually all of the sources given in these stories are anonymous. "FBI profilers," "some of Hatfill's colleagues," etc. Now, I'm in the journalism racket. I know about anonymous sources. There's a saying, "You can bullshit the fans, but you can't bullshit the players." When anonymous sources exist, and they don't always, they have agendas, which the reader doesn't know about, and they play stupid reporters like cheap pianos.

Reporters, characteristically, are writing about things they don't understand. I'd give heavy odds not one in 500 knows purines from pyrimidines, PCR from RFLP, electrophoresis from a performing bear. Such things are the baby talk of genetics.

Aside from the shoddy reporting, a tremendous naiveté runs through this stuff. Kristof berates the FBI for not having an expert compare the handwriting on the letters with Hatfill's. This implies that Hatfill wouldn't know that handwriting is distinctive. Likely, don't you think?

Another story reported that one of the letters had been mailed from near Hatfill's residence. A child of ten knows about postmarks. Kristof wants the stamps DNA tested to identify whoever licked them. Does he think that Hatfill, a first-rate bio-research guy, doesn't know about DNA sequencing? This is smear by unsubstantiated implication.

Speaking as a sometimes reporter, the stories stink. If there is solid evidence that Hatfill is guilty, then publish it. But lame journalism craftedly skirting the libel laws doesn't cut it.

CHAPTER 11

Poor Widdle Fings: The Killer Instinct in the Air Force

I discover, through a story by Rowan Scarborough in the *Washington Times*, that military catastrophe has overtaken the US Air Force in Afghanistan, and is being concealed from the American public. Complaints of inhuman conditions from troops at the air base at Bagram are frightening. Insiders at the Pentagon speak quietly of imminent withdrawal, perhaps even mutiny.

It's because the Air Force has damp laundry.

Yes. Not really soggy but, well, humid. Morale is plummeting. This and other hardships are chronicled in a series of photographs from Afghanistan obtained by Scarborough.

The *Times* quotes an airman regarding the laundromat, "Unfortunately, they recycle their water too many times, and they do not ensure your clothes are completely dry. Therefore, when your wadded-up, bagged clothes are placed back in the bin, they sit there."

Grim. One thinks of the siege of Stalingrad, of Napoleon's retreat from Russia when men dropped, spent, in the snow to die, or the Death March of Bataan. Yet those were not as terrible as things faced daily at Bagram. None of those men had to endure damp laundry.

Of course, one might wonder what bagged clothes are expected to do when placed in a bin, other than sit there. Clothes by their nature are not very active, sharing the world view of tree sloths. Suppose they had gotten up and wandered off. The airmen would have had to spend time catching them. Would this have been better for the war effort?

There is worse. "Troops sleep in crowded tents, work out in inadequate fitness centers and volleyball courts, and squeeze into small bathrooms. Lines are long at the base exchange and the chow hall."

The country never learns. The Marines storming ashore at Iwo Jima also had inadequate volleyball courts. Do you have any idea how hard it is to get a serve over the net in the sand of a tropical island? It's all very easy for us at home to get by without adequate volleyball courts. We can endure long lines at the sushi bar, since we are not subject to the stress of war. It's different in a combat zone. Airpersons need the best in sports equipment.

A worrisome question: How much time do these fellows spend squeezing into small bathrooms? (Actually, since the photo was of the inside of the women's bathroom, where a man would be unlikely to go, the odds are that the complaints came not from Airmen but from Airpersons.)

The Air Force unit at Bagram was not identified, but sounds like the 22nd Tutu Repair Battalion. The story mentioned runways. The airmen in question may be runway models. This will not surprise Marines, who have long suspected as much.

I do not doubt that our airmen, damp though they be, strike fear into the hearts of the Afghans, twelfth-century peasants who can live for months in deep snow with minimal clothing, eating half-decayed meat, and sodomizing young boys slow enough to be caught.

Reports Scarborough, "Air Force troops have grown accustomed to some of the best amenities when they deploy to far-off lands. They often are bedded down in air-conditioned tents, enjoy televisions and modern fitness centers, and eat the best chow."

And now they don't. The shock to their delicate systems must be deplorable. It must be almost like being in the military.

Actually there was some doubt in journalistic circles as to whether these killers wanted air-conditioners or hair conditioners, and perhaps skin lotions. No one denies, however, that conditions are gruesome. Combat zones are like that. A photo obtained by the *Times* shows a woman brushing her teeth in a small bathroom. The caption says, "One sink and three showers for all the women in the AF village." One gathers that when an airperson hears that war is hell, she thinks it means being out of range of a flush toilet.

Some of the accounts are gut-wrenching. (I've always wondered what a gut wrench might be.) A devastating hardship in Bagram, the kind that wears a man down until he loses the will to live, and lies down, and expires on the spot, is long lines for breakfast. Our warriors complain, "You wait through the line even if you just want to grab cereal, milk and fruit."

It's more than flesh can bear. Think of it. Even if you don't want eggs, you still have to wait. You get up in the morning, looking forward to a bowl of Tootsie Wootsie Pops, and I'll bet all they have is corn flakes. But you still have to stand there. I'd be *tho* mad!

Other perils stalk the unwary fly-person. "The dust is about two inches thick on the road, the consistency of talcum powder. Doesn't brush off. Just sticks to you. Gets up your nose, in your eyes and mouth. You cannot get away from it."

Marines I knew in Viet Nam came close to tears over dust. I remember one hardened veteran sobbing quietly to himself, "I can't stand it. It just ruins my nails. I can't do anything with them. Dust."

It isn't right. If we can't put our devil dogs and doggesses in a hotel with decent room service, we shouldn't send them to strange places where there might be fighting.

We owe them better. The answer might be Mall Simulation Companies to give our lethal emissaries the surroundings they are used to. Maybe an inflatable Gap store, a video arcade (but no games with violent themes), and a hangout with really comfy seats—just like in Patton's army.

Little things mean so much to troops dealing with dust that doesn't brush off. We could add diapers to their MREs and maybe a security blanket and a rattle. Perhaps a squad of Combat Damp-Laundry Grief Counselors would help the afflicted understand that they are still Good Persons, and that it's OK to have feelings about that yucky damp feel. A suicide hotline is imperative.

I remember a paragraph from *The Sharp End*, a book about the daily life, and death, of soldiers in WW II, as for example the disadvantages of being trapped in a tank:

"A tank that is mortally hit belches forth long searing tongues of orange flame from every hatch. As ammunition explodes in the interior, the hull is racked by violent convulsions and sparks erupt from the spout of the barrel like the fire-balls of a Roman candle. Silver rivulets of molten aluminum pour from the engine like tears…When the inferno subsides, gallons of lubricating oil in the power train and hundreds of pounds of rubber in the tracks and bogey wheels continue to burn, spewing dense clouds of black smoke over the funeral pyre." I wonder whether the 22nd Tutu Repair are quite ready for this.

CHAPTER 12

Condescending to Blacks

An obvious truth that one dare not utter: White America, and in particular the media, academia, and government, hold blacks in utter contempt. This becomes clear the moment one looks at behavior instead of asseveration. It is especially true of those people who imagine themselves to be liberal.

Let me back up.

Decades ago, I decided that blacks should be judged on their individual merits, just as everyone else should be, without regard to race, creed, color, or national origin. For this I was called a liberal and sometimes a commy.

Since then, my views have evolved. Today I think that blacks should be judged on their individual merits, as everyone else should be, without regard to race, creed, color, or national origin. I am fascinated to find that in the intervening years I have become a racist and a Nazi.

It's wonderful. A racist is one who believes that people should be judged without regard to race.

This is not a lunge at rhetorical cleverness, but literally true. Suppose I suggested (as I do suggest) that admission to college should depend entirely on scholastic qualifications. Suppose that, to ensure racial impartiality, I further suggested that an applicant's race be concealed from the admissions committees until after it had made its decision. I would assuredly be denounced as a racist.

Why?

Because the universities believe that blacks cannot compete intellectually with whites—that is, that blacks are either stupid, lazy, or disinclined to study. They must therefore be given what others are expected to earn. The implied contempt is clear enough.

"Affirmative action," the evasive phrase for this disguised scorn, presupposes inferiority. To state it clearly, if you are good enough, you don't need it. If you need it, you aren't good enough.

It's that simple. Yet affirmative action pervades racial policy. It *is* racial policy.

Note that I'm not describing my attitude (which is that people should be judged without regard to race) but the self-evident attitude of nearly every institution in the country.

The theory behind affirmative action originally was that blacks, handicapped by past etceteras, should be hired despite being slightly less qualified than others. The expectation was that they would work hard, catch up, and progress thereafter on their merits. This was governmentally perilous: It began the tribalization of America. It carried a risk that people once accustomed to unearned advancement would come to expect it. Yet if it had worked, it would now be regarded as wise and good.

It didn't work. It has turned into a permanent entitlement, in which badly unqualified blacks are advanced and advanced again, without ever being expected to compete equally. If you think this isn't true, name one instance in which a date has been set to end affirmative action. Only the permanently crippled need permanent crutches.

The deleterious effects of an oppressive apartheid were said to justify special help. Fair enough. If I had grown up in a sharecropper's family in the Mississippi Delta in 1945, I'd have done less well academically than I did as a mathematician's son.

However, if racially narcissistic whites really believed this, would they not press for rigorous schooling for blacks? Would they not reason that twelve years of genuine schooling would eliminate any need for affirmative action? Wouldn't they recommend for black children (as I do) more homework, more required reading, more-serious courses?

But they don't, do they? Try to remember the last time the media seriously urged that academic performance be demanded of black kids. The only possible reasons for this, er, oversight are (1) they don't care or (2) they don't believe blacks capable of a high-school education. Take your pick.

That's respect?

I have read that 47% of Detroit is functionally illiterate; subtracting residual whites, the figure for blacks must be well in excess of half. The figures are catastrophic, but not new. Yet the racially virtuous take them in stride. Why, if not because of unconcern or contempt?

The whole business is revoltingly patronizing. "There, there, we know you can't behave at a white standard. It's all just too hard, isn't it? Let Mommy Government hug you and feel good about herself." It would be more honest to wear shirts saying, "You Can Call Me Bwana."

It is hard not to conclude that a lot of racial policy is aimed less at helping blacks than at sating twisted inner needs of whites. Liberals in particular seem more concerned about feeling superior to conservatives, whom they hate, than about helping blacks, who don't interest them. The results often are disastrous for blacks.

Consider the cascade effect in universities. A black kid who would be among equals at Georgetown gets recruited by Yale, where he is badly outgunned and fails. A kid qualified for George Washington University gets recruited by Georgetown where, being outgunned, he fails. A university that cared about its studentry would accept only those applicants fully able to do the work, instead of desperately seeking to bag trophy blacks. I'm surprised they don't stuff them and put them over mantelpieces.

Institutional contempt breeds individual suspicion. For example, I will not take my children to a black doctor. The reason is not that I hate blacks. Rather it is affirmative action. I know that black students are not held to the same standards as white students—that they are admitted to university with lower qualifications than whites, given grades they didn't earn, passed because one doesn't fail blacks, admitted to medical school on grounds of pigmentation, and so on.

If I knew that black doctors were held to the same standards as whites, I wouldn't hesitate to go to them. I want competence, not color. Yes, there are competent black doctors. But how does one recognize them?

I wonder what being eternally patronized does to the psychic world of blacks. They cannot help but notice the low expectations, which must infuriate those who did the work and advanced on their merits. If you were raised in a country which by inescapable implication treated you as hopeless, while earnestly insisting that it was doing no such thing, how would you respond?

Two courses come to mind. First, you might think, "You sumbitches think I can't do it? Stick around." Then you would study like a demon to beat them at their own game. Second, you might think, "These suckers want to give me everything free. I'll just take it. Beats working." You especially might choose the second course if you had come to believe the low opinion held of you by the government, the media, and the schools.

CHAPTER 13

Night Train: A Tale of Playing With Extinction

August of maybe '66 was waning when Jimmy Auld and I decided to hop a freight train from Virginia to New York. The idea was a bad one. My best ideas always are. Good ideas, I have found, are overrated. We were nineteen, dumber than dead owls, and didn't know squat about trains or, for that matter, life. We hadn't been there yet.

We went to the Pot Yards—the Potomac Rail Yards in suburban Alexandria, Virginia, northern terminus for the old Richmond, Fredericksburg, and Potomac, now closed—and looked through a high chain-link fence. It was getting dark.

I was a skinny country kid with a crazy streak and a paranoid delusion that I was secretly Jack Kerouac. I may have been right. Jimmy was a head case. He had been valedictorian at King George High, where we had been rivals for Alpha Wise-Ass. He would kill himself eight years later by swimming into the Rappahannock River at midnight in January. Between, he had a few productive years of transcontinental hitchhiking, motorcycling across the Western deserts, indulging a gargantuan appetite for drugs, and discovering late in life that he was homosexual.

I know, I know. But the times were different then.

After dark we went over the fence. The Y of barbed wire at the top of fences was easy if you knew how. On the other side, box cars and gondolas loomed against the light pollution of nearby Washington. The yard smelled of creosote and insulation. We fell prey to an exhilarating sense of being where we weren't supposed to be.

We sat in a patch of shadow and wondered what to do next. It is one thing to want an adventure, another to know how to have it. Fog rolled in from somewhere and put halos around lights. The night cooled in the coming autumn. A yard mule howled and wheedle-wheedled in the drifting mist, big diesels surging as it moved cars around. The mass and raw power exalted us. All good, but how did you actually hop a train?

Cinders crunched. An old black man was walking along the tracks with a plastic jug of water. We chatted. I forget his story. He was down on his luck and living in an abandoned building, I think. He didn't know what trains were going north. Ask the yard crew, he said; they'd help us. And they did. People in the low demographics will give you a huss. They know the need.

He said goodbye and walked down the tracks.

Jimmy got up his nerve to ask a yard guy who approached with a flashlight. He pointed to a line of cars and said, "That one. She's going to New York City."

We chose a boxcar that for whatever reason had cardboard on the floor and a door open just enough to let us slip in. It was stupid. If someone had closed the door we could have died of thirst before anyone found us.

Then, nothing. The yard mule howled, dim figures moved in the night, but the train sat there. Half an hour later, still nothing. We lay on the cardboard to sleep. Finally the beast began to move. You could hear the couplings go tight along the line of cars, *bangbangbangBang!* then metallic creaking as she started laboriously to roll.

The rest of the night it moved and stopped, being a local, moved and stopped. We woke up briefly from time to time and went back to sleep. I don't know how long we drowzed after it stopped. It didn't matter. On the road you don't have to be anywhere. Come late morning, we hopped out, eager to finagle our way to Manhattan.

We were still in the Pot Yards. A yard engine had been pushing us up and down the yard all night, putting together a train.

Some adventures work better than others.

The next try we made it. This time we picked a gondola with a couple of huge pieces of machinery, generators I thought, chained down. I hoped the chains were healthy. A freight is a huge merciless machine that will squash you like a bug if you get in the wrong place. We realized this. We just didn't know where the wrong places were.

A crazy exaltation comes with rattling through the evening on a pounding, clattering monster as if it belonged to you. It was a big feeling. We hopped around the generators, whooped like wild Indians, and decided to climb from the gon onto the roof of the box car in front of us. It wasn't smart. We weren't either, so it seemed about right. Statistically it wasn't dangerous. The swaying ladder on the box was within reach. With both hands on a rung it would be hard to fall under the wheels. Well, fairly hard.

Don't try it at home. Some things are best left to idiots.

We were as gods—atop a shaking whanging steel python, hollering like maniacs in the wind blast. Outside the rules lies a freedom most people don't notice. The hurtling thunderbolt was pure muscle yet we had tamed it…we thought. We could smell the passing forest. Isolated houses flashed by and I felt the strings on my face.

Strings, distinct cords hanging from something we had passed under.

From some dim forgotten cranny of my mind there popped up one of those crucial datums you don't know you have. As a kid I'd read everything within reach, without judgment. Somewhere, maybe in some seven-year-old's Big Book of Trains, I learned that strings meant you were coming to a tunnel. They were a night warning to train crew.

I shrieked at Jimmy and tackled him. A moment later we indeed went through a tunnel. We'd have hit the concrete at fifty and dripped in globs onto local newspapers.

Now, I may get email from a dozen train crew saying, Fred, you're full of it, there ain't no such strings and there's no tunnel between DC and New York. I never verified my string memory. Jimmy and I hopped some other trains and it is barely possible the tunnel adventure happened on another run. But there were strings, and there was a tunnel.

Tell your kids to read more.

Some day I'll tell you what happened in the Village and the Waverly yards and sailing back on a flat car through Philadelphia in the Cagle Cape and how you could tell the passing factories by their smell—tires, chocolate-chip cookies, something based on petroleum. Meanwhile it's a pretty good rule in life: When you feel strings, duck.

CHAPTER 14

The Joys of Grocery-Rack Literature

Nine-thirty a.m., hunched over the computer in a friend's bachelor pit in Washington. Surrounded by dirty clothes like nesting material for a Norway rat. Cup of coffee you could degrease an engine block with. Stack of grocery-store tabloids: The *National Enquirer, The Star, The World Weekly News.* I'm preparing to mine the nether regions of the American zeitgeist as soon as I have a pulse.

I know. You thought this column got written on a sprawling wooded campus in the Catskills, with marble libraries, research assistants with nice shapes and plaid skirts and big brains. No. Sometimes I write it from a Dempster Dumpster in lower Manhattan. Laptops are wonderful for that. Anyway, on the screen wait twelve Viagra ads and a plug for breast enlargements. Maybe I'll get a breast enlargement. Or better, a codpiece. If it has a zippered compartment so I can keep my keys in it.

Some of this stuff is mysterious. "Fred Reed! Do you want a larger penis?" Whose, I wonder. How much is shipping and handling? Is there a display case?

And how do they know what "larger" is? There's probably a federal data base.

In front of me is a copy of the *National Enquirer*, the mother of grocery-rack eddas that chronicle the pervasive decline. It used to be good for keeping up with decapitations, space aliens, and manifestations of Elvis. It carried stories nobody else did: "Woman Gives Birth to Trilobite." "Giant Carrot with Face of Dalai Lama." "Dwarves, Evicted From Posh Hotel, Honeymoon in Cardboard Box."

Now it is about movie stars. Or parts of movie stars: "Amazing Photos: Stars with Cellulite." Does that not make the heart sing? A lot of people must have too much time on their hands. The cellulite in question belongs to "Demi, Goldie, Nicole Kidman, J.Lo, and more," none of whom do I know who is. They're probably important, like Aristotle. The photo shows what I took to be the back side of the moon, actually the back side of either Demi, Goldie....

I worry about movie stars. A website somewhere shows photos of presumed hot tickets in make-up, and then in candid shots in the street. They run from ordinary to ugly. Some have the allure of golf bags, especially the ones trying to look thirty years younger with what seem to be injection-molded cosmetics.

What's the social undercurrent here? Strap in: We're about to probe a dark rivulet of the collective unconscious. In the groc-tabs, it's not "Miss Jennifer Lopez" or "Mr. Scott Peterson." It's J.Lo and Scott, with the easy familiarity of a high-school sleep-over. The product here is artificial entré. If you're forty pounds overweight, lonely or wishing you were, and stuck in some boring low-level job at the post office where you can't even shoot people any longer—why, the *Enquirer* will put you on a first-name basis with glamorous over-promoted nonentities. For only $2.99, you can do a line of coke with Sylvester, or share a Cellulite Experience with Demi.

Television. That's what does it. It makes people in trailer parks, which for practical purposes is most of us, think life ought to amount to more than feeding the mortgage monster and bailing ungrateful kids out of whatever disaster they've most recently managed to create. In 1900, before television, nobody expected life to be fulfilling. And it wasn't. You could depend on it. Unless of course you thought it was fulfilling to lead a decent life and raise your kids happily in a small town in Missouri.

You didn't have any knowledge of the rich and useless. You knew they were out there, like malaria and the *chupacabras*, but you didn't have to look at them.

Now the lobotomy box rubs the aggregate face in the rompings of the California glitz kennel, where every guy is a hunk and every gal a babe, by definition golden and happy and smiling, and off to Paris by private jet to interminable gratification.

So people without jets ponder their lives and think, "Is this all there is?" Yep.

I don't understand supermodels either. But the tabs love them. Face it: They're a mess. They've got no breasts, no hips, and no fannies, and walk as if they had something wrong with their feet. You've heard of crossed eyes? They've got crossed ankles. Imagine that a mad Japanese scientist tried to design a human robot and came reasonably close. Or think of women designed by homosexuals.

The poor creatures prance down the runways wearing funny-looking clothes that no real woman would let her dog sleep on, looking pouty and sullen like spoiled adolescents—and they become celebrities. Yes. Everywhere women stop eating: They too want to look like broom handles. I don't get it.

Super-modeldom is probably treatable. Force-feed them Big Macs with lots of Secret Sauce, give them estrogen supplements, and tell them to drop the snotty expression or you'll drown them.

The *Weekly World News* is what really worries me. They should put something in the ink that sterilizes anyone who reads it. May 13: "Viking Frozen in Block of Ice," plus, "Eight-Year-Old Pianist Has 14 Fingers." Probably from West Virginia. "Ancient Egyptians Invented Baseball." I picture Tutankhamen sliding into home, spikes high, while an intermittently swooning Nefertete chomps hotdogs in the stands.

Who reads this stuff? I don't want names. A phylum will do.

I can understand, barely, reading about the cellulite of some talentless twit who may have been cute twenty years go, but probably wasn't. Given a choice, I'd rather pound my thumb with a claw-hammer, but I'm a curmudgeon. Yet movie stars actually exist to an extent. You might want to know something about them. Scientists study those weird funguses on the damp sides of trees that get all orange and purple and goopy. Demi's cellulite can't be much worse.

But..."Gal Keeps Hubby's Corpse in the House"? You can hear the far-off mournful tolling of the bell curve.

I mean, do people actually believe this stuff? "Satan and Saddam Were Partners—and This Picture Proved It!" A Photo-Shopped picture of a cloud over Baghdad with a diabolic visage, in need of braces, peering from it. Sure, an obvious plant by the Bush administration, probably straight from Ari Fleischer, the White House ventriloquist. If you can't have anthrax, go with a demon, I say.

But...but...do even, I mean...do even *Weakly World News* readers reckon the Devil His Own Self is now a weapon of Mass whatever? That scientists are going to revive a nonexistent frozen Viking? (How would they know when they had?)

If there's any hope, I tell you, it lies with bugs and plankton.

CHAPTER 15

Evening the Score in the Evening of Society

The creeping lunacy creeps on, creepishly. It gives life a constancy comforting in an uncertain world. For this we should be grateful.

In the *GreeleyTribune* of northern Colorado I see that Mitch Muller, a boy of thirteen, has been expelled from school for a year. Yep. Gone.

You might surmise that he committed some grave crime, that he assaulted a teacher perhaps or was discovered to be selling bulk-lot cocaine. No. He played with a small laser pointer—the sort that projects a red dot onto maps during lectures. It was, said the depressing drones who run the school, a "gun facsimile."

This is fascinating, like a rare and aggressive tumor. Let us think about it.

To begin, there is no substance to the charge. A laser pointer does not look like a gun, no more so than a ball-point pen or a lipstick tube. It isn't a weapon, doesn't look like a weapon, and is not intimidating, being less dangerous than, say, a fist.

Further, note that we are not confronted by a somewhat overzealous application of a reasonable rule. If young Muller had disrupted class and gotten tossed for a week, that would have excessive but not absurd. (Excessive because unnecessary: When you have a male principal who has not been administratively neutered, he says, "Bobby, stop that. Now." That's all he says.)

The child was suspended for a year, not for misbehavior but for possession of a legal and harmless object that was determined ex post facto to be gunlike. You see. Crimes carry harsh penalties, but you cannot tell what things are crimes until after you have committed them. That is, the authorities can find you guilty at will, whenever they wish to punish you.

This isn't discipline. It's sadism—sexless, boring, mean-spirited bureaucratic sadism. The school's officials are seeking to hurt the child because they enjoy doing it.

This Stalinism of the inadequate isn't a fluke. Across the country, time and again, little boys (always boys) are suspended for pointing chicken fingers and saying "bang," for drawing soldiers or the Trade Centers in flames. The schools are in the hands of sodden prisses, intellectual offal, who don't like male children. Mediocrity loves revenge, revenge on others for one's own mediocrity.

"Passive aggression," if memory serves, means an attempt to hurt others while pretending that one's aim is pious. Passive aggression, and its cousin misdirected aggression, dominate American culture. Again and again, bullying is packaged as high principle.

Consider the persecution of smokers—which is what it is. Yes, reasonable restrictions on smoking are, well, reasonable. To have a smoking section in a restaurant is an exercise in consideration, given that having a stream of smoke in one's eyes is unpleasant.

By contrast, putting signs in a subway saying that "second-hand smoke" shortens the lives of children, which it doesn't, with a picture of a piteous, helpless, wide-eyed child, is sheer hostility. So are laws banning smoking within fifteen feet or whatever of governmental buildings. The intention is not to provide for the common comfort, but to make smokers as miserable as possible.

The giveaway of a mean-spirited law is that it doesn't do what it pretends to do, yet makes people unhappy. Consider the agitations of the rabble opposed to guns. These vessels of rightness transparently are not concerned to prevent crime with firearms. You hear nothing from them favoring mandatory heavy sentences for using a gun in a crime. Nor do they criticize the drug dealer in the ghetto who kills his enemies. Their efforts are aimed at law-abiding men who own guns.

It is personal hostility disguised as concern with crime.

Similar spuriousness underlies the degrading searches at airports. The government's policy isn't rational. If we armed pilots, watched Moslems, and conducted searches, I might believe that security was the motive. But we don't. Taking nail clippers is ridiculous, like suspending a kid for having a laser pointer. The searches seem designed to humiliate. I have been searched by, among others, Israelis and Japanese. Neither had people undressing in public, and neither was staffed by hostile minorities getting even.

There is in all of this, in so very much of American life today, a vindictive meanness enwrapped in moral pose—in hate-crime laws, in careers deliberately destroyed over imaginary sexual harassment, in people destroyed over any trace of racial incorrectness, in fathers prevented from seeing their children by vengeful exes and worse courts. Why?

I'll guess that the cause is a confluence of two social currents. First, the United States is an angry, divided, unhappy country, twisted by unresolved conflicts that it refuses to face. Racial tension is ugly, powerful, and a forbidden topic. Women are grindingly angry at men. Men, angry at the divorce laws, avoid marriage. Universal divorce causes deep strains that we don't talk about. Children raised as half-abandoned mall rats turn into angry young adults.

The recently acquired American habit of distributing emoluments by race and sex rather than merit rubs people raw. The decay of the schools into centers of indoctrination angers many. The inability to escape the filth that flows from Hollyork grates. Perhaps more so does the inability in a mass, centrally run, not particularly free society to influence one's surroundings, raise one's children in one's values, or escape ever-deepening regulation.

Repressed anger seeks outlets.

Further, I think that the United States is a frightened country, or at least an insecure one. People are afraid of terrorists and crime but more importantly vaguely afraid of a life that isn't satisfactory, yet seems uncontrollable by them. There is a widespread sense that the country is sliding fast toward something undesirable yet hidden in the murk. Insecurity breeds both meanness and a desire for control.

The feminization of society plays its part. On average, men prefer freedom to security; women, security to freedom. Women, having climbed into a male world in which they don't seem comfortable, seek laws, laws, laws to control every cause of angst. Men, hemmed in, feel trapped. Much of the tightening control seeks security—helmet laws for kids on bicycles, fear of smoke, seat-belt laws, ever-falling definitions of drunk driving, warning labels stating the universally known, the neurotic fear of laser pointers, the hostility of a female-run school system to competition and rough games beloved of boys.

The astonishing thing in the latter is that women, thought to be nurturing of children, will destroy, will permit the destruction, of boy children by an angry sisterhood in the schools. The instinct of motherhood is perhaps overstated.

The answer? I suggest Cebu, Mexico, or Thailand.

CHAPTER 16

Fiesta in Ajijic: A Partisan View of Mexico

At six in the morning, for two weeks, the skyrockets have started, *whoosh, fzzzzzt, blam*! Kerblooey! by the hundreds. They're big suckers, like the ones we had as kids in America before the mommy state got them. It was hard to hear the kerblams, though, over the marching band, which also started at six, with most of the world's brass instruments. The effect was much like Herb Alpert in a gun fight. It's fun. If you want silence, find another country.

Come night, things revved up. Ajijic is like every good Mexican town—narrow streets stoned not paved, with a central plaza loaded with plants and benches and a monster gazebo for bands. Street stalls sold tacos and explosive concoctions made with tequila and, to judge by the effect, Army-surplus rocket fuel.

Mexico celebrates the way America makes microprocessors: profligately, with abandon, expertise, and intensity. The country's entire population was there—I swear it: all of them—except the two-thirds who are in Texas. Lights blazed, smells of enchiladas and roasting meat drifted from stalls, the band played jazzy Latin numbers through two vast sets of speakers that if, focused, could down airplanes, and several million people walked in two concentric counterrotating circles—girls, boys, couples, dads carrying tots on shoulders, mothers holding slightly larger ones by the hands.

Kids are part of Mexico, not just poker chips in the divorce proceedings, not afterthoughts in the race to make partner at some carnivorous law firm. ("Dear, did we, well, forget something at Day Care?") Mexicans like their children, who actually recognize their parents. It's because they see them.

If you ask a Mexican mother where her child is, she says, "Over there." An American mother tells you to check with Missing Persons. It's a scientific fact. I think CalPoly did a study on it.

OSHA would go into a priss hemorrhage here. A Ferris wheel rose garishly from the narrow street, which it completely blocked, in front of Italo's hotel, where I once lived for two months. It probably didn't have a permit. Italo, an easygoing transplanted Italian with a practical view of life, didn't care. The cops didn't care. Nobody cared. Everything has to be somewhere, including Ferris wheels. Italo's just happened to be where this one was.

Kids swirled skyward in a vertical circle, shrieking happily. You could hear the music with your lungs. Rockets whizzed into the sky, kerblam, which would be seven felonies in the US. What else would you expect rockets to do? It's how they are.

I considered diving under a bush, gibbering weirdly, and trying to get money from the Veterans Administration for PTSD. Nah. Too much paperwork.

You've heard of flashing-eyed senoritas? They've got them here. They flash. You could use them for turn signals. They're actual women: no shoulder pads and little blue blazers from Brooks Sisters. It's a revolutionary concept.

I ooched through the crowd past Italo's and hung a right toward Tom's Bar, the cultural and intellectual center of Ajijic. Tom's is on a semi-dark street and looks like you want a road house in Texas in 1945 to look. Tommy himself is a highly casual former American with a complex past who came to Ajijic, married, and became permanent.

His daughter, a cute tad who came up maybe to my knee, ran over and looked expectantly up at me. She wanted to see the Reed Fish Face, which has been handed down in my family for generations. It makes me look like a dyspeptic camel. She thinks dyspeptic camels are wonderful. She giggled and I figured my existence was justified for the day. She will probably one day be as beautiful as her mother, which is impossible. If big girls responded as well to the Fish Face, I'd be happy as a hog in swill. But life is a rigged game.

Chango the bar cat leaped into my lap. A bar maid found him crawling as an abandoned kitten outside, adopted him, got him fixed (I wonder whether he thought he was broken), and named him Chango, which means monkey. Maybe zoology wasn't her best subject.

Later, the plaza was hopping. I got close to the gazebo to see the band. They had two drummers, who took turns playing. I guess it was obvious I liked the music. The off-duty guy motioned me to come up on the gazebo. I did. We talked, to the extent possible in the middle of a large brass band in full eruption into gigawatt speakers, and he hauled out a bottle of tequila. Would I like a shot? I guess he thought he had to ask. I do after all come from the country that invented Prohibition, a concept that still has most of the world scratching its head.

Chaos sluiced over everything. Lights flashed, rockets blammed, horns blatted, smells smelled, and kids watched it all with bright eyes. There wasn't any room, but people danced anyway. Latins can dance. They have hips. Presbyterians don't have hips. Maybe Calvin was a mutant.

The drummer had been at the tequila for a while, but it didn't hurt his playing. He wanted to try to speak English so I went through my standard routine of telling him I didn't speak English because I'm really Chinese. Half of Ajijic now calls me El Chino. If I wanted to speak English I'd go to England, where they still have it in remote valleys and desolate unvisited moors, but infrequently in the newspapers.

I can't imagine a bedroom city in Washington having a fiesta. We have to worry about maniacs poisoning our children on Halloween and, face it, honkies are stiff as dead cats. Maybe you can't be organized and enjoy yourself at the same time. Bill Gates is rich as Croesus, but I bet he never danced on a bar. These days, American society seems insecure, as if psychically devoted to the missionary position, worried about date rape and harassment, soaked in priggish correctness. We're kind of squashed.

Finally I threaded my way home through a mob undiminished well after midnight. From time to time I found myself looking into a two-year-old face at eye level: kid riding on dad. Past David's Restaurant, my breakfast joint, the crowd thinned. The occasional horse stood, parked. When I got to my street a flurry of rockets streaked into the sky to blow up like flashbulbs. So help me, another band was playing thunderously at the Pimienta Negra, the restaurant on my corner.

When you get down to it, Mexico is Mexico. Maybe I'm crazy, but I like the place.

CHAPTER 17

New Year ('Bout Like the Old Year)

Among journalists, the New Year's column is a reflex, like belching, and provides an opportunity to wallow in gratuitous sagacity. It also provides a way of filling space during a slow news season. It's a minor vice, and probably a better way to spend time than playing in traffic. Patience.

Thoughts on the internet-column racket:

This column has now run for 175 weeks. I find myself wondering why I write it, and where it fits into the journalistic universe, if it does. What is the place of internet columns in the scheme of things? Do they amount to anything beyond self-indulgence? Does anyone care? Does anyone read them?

I don't know. I don't know how many there are, or where, or what their circulations might be. There is (I think) no central entity to track them. Outfits like the National Society of Newspaper Columnists largely ignore them.

This column has some 12,000 subscribers, a number which has changed hardly at all in a long time. When I check WebTrends, the number of weekly visitors to the site is usually somewhere around 15,000, though it fluctuates greatly depending on the column. In one sense these are solid numbers: People who subscribe or visit the site actually read it. By contrast, a column in the business pages of a paper with 600,000 circulation does not remotely have 600,000 readers. Most people don't read the business pages, and may not care for the columnist.

And of course on the net pass-along is a huge, but immeasurable, component of circulation. People forward, and forward forwards, and some read the forwards, and some delete them unread. So I don't know. I think it's fair to say that actual readership of FOE is at least as great as it would be in a large metropolitan newspaper. Which is interesting.

It is interesting partly because it is circulation completely off the radar screen of mainstream print journalism. A column in any newspaper of reasonable size is noticed in the trade and taken seriously. For example, I write a technology column for the *Washington* (DC) *Times*. I get a steady stream of press releases by email from tech companies wanting to be written about, and any PR department in the country will return my calls. The *Times*, circulation roughly 100,000, is published on newsprint, and is therefore real.

A web column is not. Although FOE has a documentably higher circ in terms of actual readers than does my tech column in the paper edition of the *Times*, and perhaps than of the Internet version too, I have never gotten a press release addressed to the web column. With one exception (because I knew the editor), it has never been reprinted in a newspaper.

By contrast, radio has given it fairly heavy play. The column has been read, sometimes repeatedly, by serious talk-radio people: Ron Smith at WBAL in Baltimore, Barry Farber out west, Neal Boortz in Atlanta, and Gordon Liddy. I get email from readers saying that they just heard it on local stations in Montgomery, Alabama, or Fort Myers, Florida. Why? One reason is that talk-show hosts need something to talk about. Another is that they are far less grindingly politically correct and frightened than newspapers.

It is curious, is it not? Newspapers themselves collectively prevent discussion of the political matters they purportedly exist to discuss. And they do it with an iron hand.

Of mild interest is that a fair number of syndicated columnists read FOE. I know because they email me saying, "I wish I could say that, but you know how it is." Yep. Sure do.

Why write it at all? More and more I wonder. The column began as a spasm of annoyance against the strictly controlled world of newspapers. I had been a columnist of sorts for most of my working life and could feel the screws tightening. Some time before, I had been ejected from the pages of *Army/Navy/Air Force Times* for not being adequately progressive. I was sick of it, and wondered whether I could make a go of it on the net, then very new.

And I have geek genes. The net was fascinating and learning the ropes looked interesting.

I also had some hope that it might be possible, as part of the aggregate voice of the net, to make a difference. Not much hope: I'd been in the racket too long. But as I watched the precipitous collapse of culture, the decline of the schools, the growing blight descending over the media, the death of civility, and now the sudden shadow of our police state, I thought, quixotically as it turns out, that denouncing the culprits might help. It didn't. The forces of decay are too powerful. Oh well.

The crucial fact about web journalism is that there is no money in it. This inhibits the influx of independent talent.

Running a web site, and writing a substantial column every week, is work, lots of work. Ask anyone who has done it. Once in a long while you can go on vacation ("Fred is suffering from terminal brain cancer and will be out for a week."). The deadline is always with you, like a nagging incurable hernia.

Effort spent on a web column is effort not spent in making a living. A piece of similar length in a magazine brings in roughly $400-$1000. Worse, as a columnist of my acquaintance once said, "We only have so much bullshit in us." I can come up with one decent political rant a week, in addition to meeting other calls of the keyboard. I can't easily come up with two.

Nor can most writers. Further, most people who can write already do, for a living. The upshot is that people who could write a good column on the web aren't going to.

The other night I rode horseback under a full moon along the shore of Lake Chapala to a friend's restaurant, off toward Jocotopec. The night was cool, the air still. To the north the mountains rose dark against the stars. A couple of Mexican girls of maybe twelve chattered in front of me, riding as if they had been born on horses.

I found myself thinking, what the hell do I care about the northern demise? The end of a civilization is above my pay grade. Things are as they are because people want them that way, or don't care enough to change them. Who am I to squeak and gibber? It wasn't charitable, but I could see David's in the distance, and he has really good steaks.

CHAPTER 18

Faking Democracy

While the United States is freer and more democratic than many countries, it is not, I think, either as free or as democratic as we are expected to believe, and becomes rapidly less so. Indeed we seem to be specialists in maintaining the appearance without having the substance. Regarding the techniques of which, a few thoughts:

(1) Free speech does not exist in America. We all know what we can't say, and about whom we can't say it.

(2) A democracy run by two barely distinguishable parties is not in fact a democracy.

A parliamentary democracy allows expression of a range of points of view: An ecological candidate may be elected, along with a communist, a racial-separatist, and a libertarian. These will make sure their ideas are at least heard. By contrast, the two-party system prevents expression of any ideas the two parties agree to suppress. How much open discussion do you hear during presidential elections of, for example, race, immigration, abortion, gun control, and the continuing abolition of Christianity? These are the issues most important to most people, yet are quashed.

The elections do however allow the public a sense of participation while having the political importance of the Superbowl.

(3) Large jurisdictions discourage democracy. If, say, educational policy were set in small jurisdictions, such as towns or counties, you could buttonhole the mayor and have a reasonable prospect of influencing your children's schools. If policy is set at the level of the state, then to change it you have to quit your job, marshal a vast campaign costing a fortune, and organize committees in dozens of towns. It isn't practical. In America, local jurisdictions set taxes on real estate and determine parking policy. Everything of importance is decided remotely.

(4) Huge unresponsive bureaucracies somewhere else serve as political fly-wheels, insulating elected officials from the whims of the populace. Try calling the federal Department of Education from Wyoming. Its employees are anonymous, salaried, unaccountable, can't be fired, and don't care about you. Many more of them than you might believe are affirmative-action hires and probably can't spell Wyoming. You cannot influence them in the slightest. Yet they influence you.

(5) For our increasingly centralized and arbitrary government, the elimination of potentially competitive centers of power has been, and is, crucial. This is one reason for the aforementioned defanging of the churches: The faithful recognize a power above that of the state, which they might choose to obey instead of Washington. The Catholic Church in particular, with its inherent organization, was once powerful. It has been brought to heel.

Similarly the elimination of states' rights, now practically complete, put paid to another potential source of opposition. Industry, in the days of J. P. Morgan politically potent, has been tamed by regulation and federal contracts. The military in the United States has never been politically active. The government becomes the only game available.

And is determined to remain so. Any attempt to weaken the central power will arouse powerful hostility. For example, the persecution of those engaged in home-schooling has nothing to with concern for the young. The public schools have little interest in education and for the most part seem to have little idea of what it is. The hostility to home-schooling is simply the response of those with a monopoly of power to the specter of superior competition.

The elections do however allow the public a sense of democratic participation while having virtually no political import. That is, elections serve chiefly to keep the people from noticing the absence of democracy. This is a remarkable concept, of great governmental utility.

(6) Paradoxically, increasing the power of groups who cannot threaten the government strengthens the government: They serve as counterbalances to those who might challenge the central authority. For example, the white and male-dominated culture of the United States, while not embodied in an identifiable organization, for some time remained strong. The encouragement of dissension by empowerment of blacks, feminists, and homosexuals, and the importing of inassimilable minorities, weakens what was once the cultural mainstream.

(7) The apparent government isn't the real government. The real power in America resides in what George Will once called the "permanent political class," of which the formal government is a subset. It consists of the professoriate, journalists, politicians, revolving appointees, high-level bureaucrats, the extremely rich, and so on who slosh in and out of formal power. Most are unelected, believe the same things, and share a lack of respect for views other than their own.

It is they, to continue the example of education, who write the textbooks your children use, determine how history will be rewritten, and set academic standards—all without the least regard for you. You can do nothing about it.

(8) The US government consists of five branches which are, in rough order of importance, the Supreme Court, the media, the presidency, the bureaucracy, and Congress.

The function of the Supreme Court, which is both unanswerable and unaccountable, is to impose things that the Congress fears to touch. That is, it establishes programs desired by the ruling political class which could not possibly be democratically enacted. While formally a judicial organ, the Court is in reality our Ministry of Culture and Morals. It determines policy regarding racial integration, abortion, pornography, immigration, the practice of religion, which groups receive special privilege, and what forms of speech shall be punished.

(9) The media have two governmental purposes. The first is to prevent discussion and, to the extent possible, knowledge of taboo subjects. The second is to inculcate by endless indirection the values and beliefs of the permanent political class. Thus for example racial atrocities committed by whites against blacks are widely reported, while those committed by blacks against whites are concealed. Most people know this at least dimly. Few know the degree of management of information.

(10) Control of television conveys control of the society. It is magic. This is such a truism that we do not always see how true it is. The box is ubiquitous and inescapable. It babbles at us in bars and restaurants, in living rooms and on long flights. It is the national babysitter. For hours a day most Americans watch it.

Perhaps the key to cultural control is that people can't not watch a screen. It is probably true that stupid people would not watch intelligent television, but it is certainly true that intelligent people will watch stupid television. Any television, it seems, is preferable to no television. As people read less, the lobotomy box acquires semi-exclusive rights to their minds.

Television doesn't tell people what to do. It shows them. People can resist admonition. But if they see something happening over and over, month after month, if they see the same values approvingly portrayed, they will adopt both behavior and values. It takes years, but it works. To be sure it works, we put our children in front of the screen from infancy.

(11) Finally, people do not want freedom. They want comfort, two hundred channels on the cable, sex, drugs, rock-and-roll, an easy job and an SUV. No country with really elaborate home-theater has ever risen in revolt. An awful lot of people secretly like being told what to do. We would probably be happier with a king.

CHAPTER 19

With All Due Respect. I.e., Not Much

As the culture dies, the schools fail, the cities teem with functional illiterates and our children turn into tattooed primitives cosseted by a civilization whose origins they barely know, I watch them with…I will say it plainly…contempt. It is a mild contempt, yet it is contempt. Sadness also, for they have lost much, but yes, a contempt I do not want to feel but cannot escape.

So, to judge by my correspondence, do many people old enough to read fluently. None use the word "contempt." The taboos are too ingrained, the penalties too harsh, the unspoken laws protecting everyone's self-esteem too punitively policed. Again, it is not a contempt that people want to feel: All would prefer that things not be as they are. Yet contempt is unmistakably what peers through their letters.

Contempt is the proper reaction to the contemptible.

I sometimes think the country is dividing itself into two cultures. The first, and much the smaller, will be of those who read widely and know much, who are cultured and live in a wider world than the present. The second will be of those who received high grades without understanding that they were being cheated by their elders. An abyss will separate the two.

The chain of cultivation, once broken, is not easily rejoined. We are doing everything we can to break it. It is a shame. People deserve more. We are doing this, as nearly as I can tell, so that the dull and uninterested will feel good about themselves. We are doing it to conceal that some of us are better than others.

Yes, "better." That word.

In the past it was recognized that certain qualities were superior to others, and that people who cultivated those superior qualities were superior to those who didn't. The honest were thought superior to the thieving, the kind to the cruel, the provident to the shiftless, the wise to the foolish, the learned to the ignorant. Today one must not hold these views. They constitute the crime of elitism, which is the recognition that the better is preferable to the worse.

One must never, ever notice that some people are better than others.

Not to notice the inescapable requires stupidity, pretense, or moral blindness. Since few people are very stupid, we have chosen the road of blindness or pretense. We feign stupidity for reasons of politics.

It takes some serious feigning. If I said that Mother Theresa was no better than the Hillside Strangler—"she wasn't better, just different"—people would laugh. If I said that Albert Schweitzer was of greater worth than an illiterate drug-dealing parasite in what is called the inner city, I would be called a racist. If I said that a white suburban kid who couldn't do long division amounted to a medieval peasant without the excuses, I would be called, spare me, an elitist.

Which I am.

What, pray, should one feel toward intelligent people who cannot read without squinting laboriously, who know less of their language than a fourth-grader in 1954, have a shaky grasp of the multiplication tables, cannot write a coherent paragraph, and seldom read a book? Respect comes to people who merit respect. It isn't an entitlement. Contempt also comes to those who merit it.

I do not scorn, say, savages from Papua-New Guinea who wear penis gourds, eat huge grubs from within logs, and peer at distant airliners as those vouchsafed a glimpse of divinity. It is unreasonable to blame them for not having profited from opportunities they didn't have. I watch them with wonder, but not contempt.

But the lazy, shiftless, deliberately half-lettered, the feckless and socially worthless—yes, worthless: that, and "shiftless," are words that could well be resurrected—those who have had every opportunity to better themselves but couldn't summon the effort…for them I cannot help feeling pity. And contempt.

And what should one think of the bloated welfare mother with a second-grade education, with a litter of five she can't feed and won't school, by twenty-five fathers she can't remember, who spends her limited time between couplings in watching Oprah and feeling abused? The best I can come up with is revulsion. And pity, yes. Being a public uterus cannot be pleasant. Yet I will not pretend that it is admirable.

And what of the mall children of the suburbs, who leave high school with less arithmetical fluency than I had in the sixth grade in 1957 in the schools of Alabama? I didn't know arithmetic because I was particularly meritorious. I was a barefoot southern kid with a BB gun in one hand and a fielder's glove in the other. I knew arithmetic, we all knew arithmetic, because the society, the schools, and our parents made it plain that we ought to know it, and in fact were going to know it, at which point the conversation was over.

This brings us to a greater question: What should one feel other than contempt for a society that, enjoying virtually unlimited resources, deliberately enstupidates its children? We don't have to do it. We choose to. We are ruining our society on purpose.

Today I see mall rats who go through high school with the red puffy eyes born of dope, and literally count on their fingers to do multiplication. On graduation they take one course at the community college, play video games, and hang out pointlessly with their friends. I've got more respect for dirt. You can grow plants in it.

I once wrote a column on the almost comic state of regained subhumanity. A friend of mine responded:

"Johnny can't add coz (a) his grade school teachers are moron socialists, (b) his parents are mouth-breathing, TV watching losers, and (c) he's majoring in sociology so he can get a gov't job like everyone else."

I can't see much wrong with that analysis.

The desire to disguise differences in merit by ideological cleansing, and the atmosphere of pre-human irredentism now earnestly promoted in what were for a time the schools, will promote precisely the elitism they pretend to vanquish. Those who achieve will always look down on those who didn't bother. This is certainly true in regard to schooling. As the gap increases between the few who know their history and literature, and those who gurble ungrammatically about their favorite situation comedies, the contempt will become sharper. Two cultures.

Maybe self-esteem comes too high. Besides, who will have greater respect for themselves, the puzzled and half-literate, or those who read confidently and know that they have been well educated? If you want to respect your self, do something worthy of respect. Now there's a concept.

CHAPTER 20

The Ascension of Wunxputl

The remarkable rise of the Tloxiproctyl to academic prominence began at UC Berkeley, where the creeping fascism of George Bush gnawed at the professoriate. Worse, no one was paying attention to them, always distressing to the narcissistically irrelevant.

They desperately wanted to jumpstart the faltering engines of progressivism. (The metaphor doesn't quite make sense. Of course, neither did the progressivism.) To do this, they needed an irritating Cause.

This proved to be a problem. Every imaginable loony idea seemed to have been worked to exhaustion: promoting buggery of Boy Scouts by homosexuals, outlawing English, compulsory issuance of condoms to the unborn. Anxiety followed. In rooms filled with pot smoke and defective grammar, they pondered mightily.

Then, not foreseeing the consequences, they chose to revitalize affirmative action, which is the proposition that jobs should be given to people who can't do them.

It was an odd choice. Affirmative action was a hallowed principle of progressivism, but only one of several, and anyway it had been done.

There was also welfare, which held that money should be given to those who haven't earned it. Others were multiculturalism, which is the view that societal comity is best achieved by dividing the country into groups that hate each other; and bilingualism, the belief that countries work best when people can't talk to each other.

But the professors added a zinger: Incompetence was good, yes; no one debated this. But—did it not then follow that greater incompetence was better? Brilliant!

Conservatives, ever churlish, said that progressives really just wanted to annoy society, which they had confused with their parents. This was grossly unfair, though accurate.

Under pressure from the faculty, Berkeley lowered its affirmative-action standards. Theretofore, the school had accepted blacks, and others regarded by universities as inferior, with SATs 200 points below the white average. It was an easy policy, because those were about all they could find.

Now, so as to promote social justice, they were going to reject blacks with a 200 point deficit as being excessively qualified, and therefore inauthentic. Henceforth, only applicants with a 300-point deficit would be accepted.

The benefits for social justice were obvious. Minorities who had no business at Berkeley by 200 points, and therefore almost always flunked out, were replaced by those with a disqualification of 300 points, who failed without exception. Those with the 200-point deficit sued, claiming discrimination.

The ACLU was baffled. Its members knew they were against white Christian civilization. This, however, was a dispute between minorities. Who to support? After much soul-searching, they went with the principle that worse is better. But it was a close thing.

The more astonishing effect occurred back east when Cornell, striving for progressive leadership, began recruiting students 400 points below par.

Competitive incapacity had arrived. Soon schools were fighting each other to recruit the cerebrally understated.

A problem arose. The SATs did not go below 400, an arrangement intended to protect the self-esteem of furniture, cocker spaniels, and education majors. But now the universities needed ever lower levels of intelligence. The scale was dropped to allow lower scores and therefore greater ethnic authenticity.

It worked, at first anyway. Cornell reigned briefly as the Killer Kowalski of affirmative action. Its students displayed record levels of inability. The advance was not without problems. Many of the new students had trouble remembering where they lived. There was talk of equipping them with electronic homing devices.

Various luminosities of progressivism weighed in on the side of the new policy. Ted Kennedy, his voice trembling with emotion or, as some suggested, delirium tremens, introduced a bill requiring the federal government to give preference in hiring to the intellectually minimal. Republicans said he was cynically taking credit for a policy of long standing.

Everywhere advanced thinkers joined the vanguard. An ABC camera crew interviewed Hillary Clinton in the Bahamas, where she was sunning herself on a flat rock to keep her body temperature up.

"Cookies," she said, eyeing the cameras. "Children."

Pressed to elaborate, she said, "The hopelessly unintelligent are just as smart as the rest of us and just as valuable in the eyes of God, if there were one. Though of course there may be. We must work together to develop the wonderful abilities these people don't have. Cookies. Vast right-wing...."

One of the cameramen, an unreconstructed Southerner, muttered something about "crocodilian Betty Crockers," and vowed to write a book called "It Takes A Village To Raise An Idiot."

The race for academic nullity continued apace. Stanford ransacked the coma wards in the Bay Area, harvesting a rich crop for social justice. In Chicago it was rumored that the dead were applying.

Unfortunately there seemed to be a limit to witlessness. Soon the better schools had exhausted the neural tundra. The bus stations and prisons were picked clean. Desperation set in. Yale was caught registering a caribou, but said it was an honest mistake.

Things were getting a bit flaky, as even progressives privately admitted. At Harvard, Dr. Chuleta Marimacha-Mapache, who taught Central American Lesbianism, wrote a book called, "Patriarchy and the Oppression of Inanimate Objects." She argued compellingly that things had the same right to education people had. Some of the affirmative-action students seemed to be evidence of this. Bumper stickers appeared proclaiming, "Desks Are Students Too."

The culmination of the new progressive movement came, unexpectedly, from Wellesley. The anthropology department remembered an obscure tribe of naked savages, the Tloxiproctyl, who lived in the Amazon rain forest. Of uncertain genetic provenance, they drank rainwater, ate squalid grubs they found in rotting logs, and hadn't invented shoes. They spoke a language consisting of three words, none of which meant anything.

The Tloxyproctyl, Wellesley realized, were perfect for affirmative action. Mentally speaking, they barely existed. Because of inbreeding, they were actually evolving backward, and lived in danger of extinction because the grubs were too complicated for them.

Wunxputl, a thirty-seven year old Tloxiproctyl, was regarded as retarded (or, as Wellesley put it, "differently brained") even by his fellow primitives. It wasn't just that the grubs outsmarted him. He couldn't remember how to eat them. He sat wherever he was put, said, "Ooogh," and slowly lost weight.

Wellesley later refused official comment on just how the Tloxiproctyl got to the campus. Rumor had it that the tribesmen, seeing an air mattress, decided that it was the Mother of All Grubs, and thereafter worshiped the anthropology department. At any rate, they were soon enrolled in the School of Heartwarming Non-Western Cultures, each with an air mattress. The anthropologists, smug at having trumped Cornell, began grooming Wunxputl as department head. They figured he would get tenure in five years and last a long time, if fed intravenously.

CHAPTER 21

Race, Racer, Racist

From time to time I get mail informing me that blacks are being mistreated, as for example by not being sufficiently represented among the ranks of athletic coaches, and implying that I should oppose such inequity. Regarding which:

First, I do not oppose racial discrimination against blacks. In 1965, I did. My view then, as now, was that the law should be racially neutral. But inasmuch as racial discrimination against me, as a white, is today mandated by federal law, the government acting as agent for blacks, I am hardly going to worry about discrimination against them. I think it serves to level the playing field.

Second, if I were dedicated to improving the lot of blacks—which, the laws being what they are, I am not—what would I do? As an individual in Mexico of course I couldn't do anything. But suppose I were president, or even dictator. What could I do? What would blacks want me to do? They seem to be unhappy because whites are not doing the right thing. What is the right thing?

Many blacks are functionally illiterate. Most cannot compete academically on equal terms with whites. Clearly (to me, at any rate) people who cannot read well, who have at best a rudimentary education, cannot hope to succeed on their own in a modern country. If I were trying to do everything in my power to help blacks, an emphasis on schooling would seem to me vital. Am I wrong? Do blacks disagree?

But what could I do? Here I mean practical things that might actually produce results. If children are to learn, they have to do their homework. I can't make black children study, nor can I make their parents see that they do. It is not obvious how I, or any other whites, can get somebody else's children to read, study, and flourish.

It isn't that I don't want black children to do well. It's that I can't achieve that result.

Nor is it that I'm unwilling to spend tax dollars to school black children. I would happily do it—if I knew how to get results. I can't offhand think of anything more important domestically. But nothing has worked. The country tried Head Start. It was a reasonable idea, well-intentioned, and worth trying. It didn't work. We tried compulsory integration. It didn't work.

What would work? Being white, when I think of improving schools I think of raising standards, hiring better teachers, and adding advanced courses. Do blacks want this? The answer of course will be that some do and some don't. Most seem not to. With all the good intentions in the world, as dictator, president, or queen of the May, I couldn't make blacks want to study.

The illuminating question is: If blacks were entirely in charge of the schools, what would they do?

In many cities, as for example Washington, DC, blacks *are* in charge of the schools, which are terrible. Why? It isn't lack of money. Whites do not forbid blacks the purchase of textbooks, and do not insist that they hire poor teachers. The schools just don't work well.

I derive no pleasure from this stagnant disaster, but neither do I see what whites can do about it. If blacks complained about potholes in the street, I would know what to do: Fill the potholes. If black kids were contracting polio, I'd know what to do: Vaccinate them. I simply do not know what to do about the schools.

A question that I have never seen asked, much less answered, is What do blacks want their children to study in school? As a white father, I want my offspring to study English grammar and literature, mathematics, chiefly European history with considerable attention to other parts of the world, languages, and the sciences. This is what educated white people do. It's how we are.

If blacks want the same, no one will discourage them. But do they? I don't know. Blacks are not European and may have no interest in Europe, or mathematics, or French. I have only passing interest in Uganda, so blacks may have only passing interest in Germany. If my children were required to study Swahili and Shaka Zulu for twelve years, I would object. Perhaps blacks object to today's curriculum. Were I in their place, I might also.

The question then becomes: What, specifically, do blacks want their children to study? Different blacks will want different things, yes; but what are the main currents? And how could I, if I had any influence, effect their desires? If black parents want a curriculum greatly different from that desired by whites (and I don't know that they do), I see no way to provide it other than separate classes or separate schools.

For that matter, do blacks parents want their children to go to school with whites? Do black children? I don't know.

Going beyond schooling, what could I do about conditions in the sprawling socially isolated slums of the cities? Curiously, I've probably seen more of the blasted urban heath than many blacks. Working as a police reporter has, if not its advantages, at least its revelations. The slums are ugly. Illiteracy is very high, unemployment the rule, crime a way of life, and existence without obvious point. I wish it on nobody.

But what am I supposed to do about it? From a black point of view, what is the answer? Here I'm talking about specific, concrete answers conducing to results as distinct from votes. What exactly could I, or any white, or all whites, do to turn huge largely illiterate populations into productive and happy members of society?

I just don't know.

It may be that there are some problems people have to solve for themselves, because no one else can. I'm not sure that picketing about the Confederate flag is the solution. It may also be, though I'm not sure, that today's free lunch of special privilege, though in the short term profitable for blacks, will in the long run be less so. The price of dependency is more dependency.

Prices, like termites, are not always visible. Does President Bush, by his policy of racial favoritism, gain more votes from blacks than he loses in abstentions from whites? How would he know? Do blacks help themselves by deliberately antagonizing whites instead of requiring that their children study? How many whites are quietly sick of what has become not a quest for fairness but a racial spoils system?

I'm not sure. Nor, except as a freelance social pathologist, do I any longer care.

CHAPTER 22

Marx in Disguise

On the principle that ebola is more interesting if you understand why your fingers are turning to soup, permit me a few thoughts on Karl Marx, his dismal theories, and our descent into a Disney version of them.

Marxism is a stupid and almost comically wrong hotchpotch of nonsense by a man who had little grasp of humanity, politics, or economics. He is an economist whose theories invariably lead to impoverishment. As a claim to greatness, this seems less than compelling. He is a major figure for the same reason that Typhoid Mary is—for damage done rather than intelligence exercised.

(Bear with me. This is not boilerplate denunciation of all things leftist. There is actually a point coming.)

Further, the errors of Marx were not of detail. They were fundamental. For example, he expected workingmen to unite. Instead, WWI showed that, with monotonous regularity (and perhaps questionable wisdom), their loyalty went to their countries. He thought that revolution would come first in industrialized nations with suitable proletariats. Instead it came first in creaky agricultural countries, and never did come where he expected it. He thought that European economies would never give rise to the liberal democracies that seem today to be what everyone wants. They did.

In short, he was a crackpot. He was, however, either a crackpot who had correctly calculated the manipulability of the congenitally angry, or just lucky. No one, ever, has been responsible for as much death and brutality as Karl Marx. It wasn't what he had in mind. But it is what he caused.

It is what Marxists always cause. With perfect predictability, Marxist states are police states. The chief trait of the workers' paradise is that the workers all want to leave, and must be kept in with machine guns and land mines. In divided countries like Korea, we have what approach being laboratory experiments. South Korea is a high-tech industrial power. In North Korea, they eat grass and, occasionally, each other. If Korea is a geographical example, China is a temporal one: As soon as it began to abandon Marxism, it began to progress.

Marxism is a proven disaster. And Marxists know it. Elementary history is not a secret.

All of this would be of academic interest only, if the same spirit, under other names, were not so very active in America today. We see it in a variety of disguises. When Russia practiced censorship, we called it "censorship." Here, we call it political correctness. You still have to look over your shoulder before saying the wrong things. The difference is…what? In Russia, Marxists preached class warfare. Here they preach multiculturalism. The difference is…what? The Russians, unable to speak openly, passed around samizdat. We have the Internet. The difference, other than efficiency, is…what?

Our domestic Marxians are journalists, academics, racial professionals, multiculturalists, bilingualists, radical feminists, and educationists. Most of them lack the intelligence and schooling to know what they are helping to do. (I think the phrase is "useful idiots.") The leaders, as for example in the universities, do know. They are less lethal than Lenin and Trotsky, but their direction is the same.

The key to understanding them is the recognition that Marxism is not a system but a mood: a grim, implacable, vengeful hostility toward the surrounding society. Its devotees are haters. This distinguishes it sharply from normal European democratic socialism. One may debate whether, say, Sweden is too socialist or not socialist enough. Yet Swedish socialism is not evil. Marxism is.

At its heart are (1) a desire for total control of everything, including of thought (2) a willingness to compel obedience by any means whatever, (3) an unconcern with economic reality and thus with material well-being, and (4) a contempt for humanity ("the masses"). It is simply resentment politicized, aimed not at helping the downtrodden, but at hurting the uptrodden.

Now, people who viscerally realize what is going on often want to debate with our Marxians. It is a mistake. Economics is not a mathematically verifiable subject. Politics also being imprecise, it is easy to argue for or against any position until the debate dissolves into murk. A case can easily be made for communism, or Nazism, or democracy, or Catholicism, or atheism, or paedophilia.

Instead, you have to remember who they are, what they are. They are people who want to bring down the ambient civilization.

This explains what might otherwise seem to be contradictions. For example, radical feminists, very Marxian in spirit, denounce imaginary discrimination against women in America, but say little about compulsory clitoridectomies in African and Moslem countries. This makes no sense if you believe that they want to benefit women. It makes perfect sense if their goal is to create division with an eye to destroying America (or, what is the same thing, remaking it according to their ideology.)

Or note that the hard left talks endlessly about mistreatment of blacks in America, but conspicuously does not urge things, such as better schooling, that might help blacks. Why? Because (1) they do not really care about blacks, except as political tools, and (2) if blacks prospered, they might join the middle class and cease being usefully divisive.

Similarly, for Latino children our Marxians advocate bilingual education, which has a proven record of hindering the learning of English. Why? Latinos who spoke fluent English would marry people named Ferguson and become Americans. So much for class warfare.

And this is why Marxists, everywhere denouncing oppression, invariably practice it. There is no contradiction. They have no objection to oppression. It is central to their purposes. (Name a Marxist country that isn't oppressive.) Denouncing it is just politically expedient.

The last thing they want is for backward countries to flourish and become liberal democracies.

Tactically, they are on solid ground in America. The United States always having been successful in assimilating groups, the Marxists needed to reverse the process so as to have class warfare. They couldn't use the usual proletariat because it had moved into the middle class. They consequently needed to promote or invent new divisions. They did. It worked.

Black against white was an obviously useful fault line that the hard left didn't invent but has carefully cultivated. Opening the southern border amounted to importing a divisive class. Setting women against men was remarkably successful. Fanning homosexuals into hostility provided yet another serviceable resentment. The emotional terrorism practiced against boys is school (cops-and-robbers is violence, Ritalin), hate-speech laws, the punishment of dissent (as for example by being fired) are all the Soviet Union writ small.

So far.

CHAPTER 23

War in Iraq: A West Virginian View

Yesterday I sat on the stump in the front yard and tried to figure out the War on Terrorism. It was hard going. It didn't seem like there was a war.

Of course, I've been wrong about the War before. When those camel molesters dropped the buildings in New York, I didn't think the funny little countries over there would let us fly over them so's we could bomb Afghanistan. Was I ever wrong. Maybe I can work at the State Department.

Those Bush folk can do some coalitions. I have to give'em that. I reckon if you left George I or W. on an uninhabited planet, a week later he'd have a seventeen-nation coalition. The family cat could probably get half a dozen. I notice we sure are getting to have a lot of presidents from that family. Maybe they'll start one of those dynasty things like that Egyptian guy Two-Ton Kamen did, or maybe didn't. Another Bush or two and we can start a Hedge.

Anyway, after New York, we had a huge uproar, like when the Baptists held their picnic on top of the yellow jackets' nest. Everybody was patriotic for a week and stuck little flags everywhere. They didn't join the army, though. I guess they forgot. They probably figured that when Afghanistan found out we all had little flags on our radio antennas, they'd give up. That's what usually happens.

So Mr. Bush said we were going to have a War on Terrorism, and catch Bin Laden, and smack the terrorists upside the head, which they must have expected because they were already wearing bandages. (One ol' boy from North Fork thought Bush said War on Tourism, and figured it meant he could shoot yuppies from Washington.) Anyway, America was on the war path. Look out A-rabs. Like somebody said, when your leaders are named Bush, Dick, and Colin, somebody's going to get screwed.

I can't figure out what happened to the war. Best I can tell, we didn't catch Bin Laden. Maybe we decided we didn't want him. I don't. Most likely he's water-skiing at Tahoe.

We dropped bombs on Al Qaeda, and probably on Mrs. Qaeda and all the little Qaedas, so Al just took them all to Pakistan to live until we went away and they could come back.

Then we were going to destroy the Axes of Evil. I puzzled on that. If I thought Evil had an ax, I'd get my deer gun and shoot him from a hundred yards, and keep the ax to cut firewood. But I'm simple.

We haven't done that either. All the axes look like they're still there. None of"em got religion, or took the pledge, or started beating the drum down at the Salvation Army. They look about as evil as they ever did.

It's a pretty funny war. It seems like nobody's fighting it, except a few Marines and some of those army guys with those green hats that look like melted water-melons. Nobody much knows about it. Mostly the war ain't even in the news-paper unless it's a slow day for football.

The other afternoon I went down to Red's Bar to talk about the war to try to understand it. Red used to be in the Marines so he knows lots.

It was dark inside. That big old purple-and-green jukebox was singing about divorce and train wrecks and the TV babbled like somebody's crazy relative that the state hospital wouldn't take. Red was polishing glasses. He's built like a beer truck, and has a tattoo that ways "USMC' with a picture of an eagle sitting on the world, like it was waiting to see if it would hatch.

"Red, how come we don't smack them Arabs?"

"Can't. Bud?"

"Yeah. How come?"

"Nothin' to smack'em with. Wanna glass?"

"I usually don't drink beer with a straw. Why can't we smack'em?"

"Can't. I saw it on the satellite last night. Eighty percent of the US of Army is unwed mothers and the rest is queers."

"Naw. Can't be."

"Would TV lie?"

He had a point.

"It was on 20-20, this special about some Armored Stroller Battalion and this daycare platoon didn't have enough pacifiers. Said it was national emergency."

"Red, you're lying again."

He looked embarrassed. "Yeah. Not by nearly enough, though."

Then he said, "See, we got a two-army system now. There's a little bitty good army, the Marines and the Airborne and Rangers and some others, and a great big pretend army, and some airplanes. So Bush has to figure out how to do everything with airplanes and a little bitty army. That's hard. You see those new bass lures Jake Scoggins got?"

"Yeah. I heard he caught a five-pounder down at Deep Creek Lake. Don't change the subject on me. Why don't we just put a bounty on ragheads? They look like Q-Tips."

"Can't. Seven-Eleven wouldn't last a week. 'Sides, we gotta suck up to'em or they won't let us bomb Afghanistan."

"That makes sense. Like mustard on valve springs. In WWII, I guess we sucked up to the Japs so we could bomb Tokyo."

"We probably just didn't think of it."

We talked for an hour until work let out at the sawmill and people started coming in.

Red's idea was that if you want to beat us in a war, all you gotta do is hide till we can't remember the war anymore, which he said is usually about three years. What he said was about half of Americans don't like America and they're the ones that run it. I don't know if it's true. Maybe it just looks like it.

I said well, at least we beat the Al Qaedas.

Red poured himself a beer. It's an advantage of owning a bar. Maybe I ought to get one.

"Well, think about it," he said. "They blew up a couple of our best buildings full of lawyers, killed several thousand people, made fools of the US to the whole world, and about crippled the airlines and hotels. Then they made us spend billions on Afghanistan and more billions on stupid security stuff for airports and you still can't get on an airplane without hopping around barefoot like a damn fool, and the FBI gets to spy on us three times as much as it used to. Now we're waiting for the A-bomb to go off somewhere and fry everybody's catfish. So we got mad and blew up some mud huts and never did catch anybody important."

He looked thoughtful.

"It's a good thing we won. Suppose we'd lost?"

CHAPTER 24

Em on the Rocks

I'm mostly useless, I grant, but I do great daughters. I guess I'm a sort of bio-logical idiot savant. A dozen years back, when my younger daughter Emily was maybe seven, she and I and a then girlfriend and the girlfriend's small boy, also about seven, were vacationing on North Carolina's Outer Banks. Call the kid Jake. Jake wasn't a bad kid, just too full of himself.

He has probably recovered from the shock. Or he may have become a serial killer. I don't know. He probably has post-dramatic stress disorder.

Anyway we were going to a try-your-luck-at-hang-gliding place. Jake was tell-ing Emily that he could do anything better than she could—not a good idea with Emily. You might have to back it up. I thought he was pushing it too hard. Maybe it was his age. Maybe he was insecure. He was aggressive, and she was getting tired of it.

We got to the hang-gliding school, which was in a sporting-goods store. Well, it turned out that the store had a climbing wall. That means a concrete cliff with little nubbins stuck out so scrawny muscular seventeen-year-old boys can scamper up it to impress their dates. It wasn't built for children. It wasn't dan-gerous for them either, because to climb it you had to get into a real rock har-ness and they used a top-rope belay so you couldn't fall. But it was for big kids.

When Emily saw that wall, she alerted like a bird dog that's discovered a partridge. She was going to go up it. There was no sign saying she couldn't. She didn't care who it was for. That wall could have been for space aliens or professional wrestlers or giant squids.

It's how she is. As they say in Alabama, she ain't got the sense God give a crabapple. It comes of being a Reed. I paid the five bucks and they somehow made the harness small enough to fit.

She started up the wall. She was small but wiry and made good progress at first. She was also cute so the guy belaying her started trying to help her by pulling on the rope. That isn't how she does things. She hollered, "No! Don't help me!" I guess she was determined to fail honestly. I knew she wasn't going to climb all of it.

He slacked off. She managed, I'm not sure just how, to get to the overhang.

Now, overhangs are tough, even for mature climbers with long arms. Em was just a brash kid with short arms. Everybody could see, at least everybody who had done any climbing, that it was too much for her. But nobody wanted to tell her.

She wouldn't have listened anyway. She has always been a creature of decided opinions. At the time I was dating Jake's mother, Sally let's say, and Emily didn't like her. It wasn't anything personal. She didn't like anybody to date me. It was nearly Halloween and Sally, trying to be conciliatory, asked Em what she was going to be. "Oh, a princess," said Em. Then, unwisely, Sally asked, "And what should I be?"

Whereupon Emily smiled her most pixyish smile and said, "You could shave your head, and go as a cancer patient."

She didn't mean it. She was a softhearted kid. It was just that she had a strong editorial voice.

Jake didn't say anything. I could tell he wasn't sure he wanted to try that wall. To be fair, he wasn't really a milquetoast. He played kid-hockey, and on the ice he was hard to intimidate. But he looked shaken by Em's progress. He had shot his mouth off a little too much. I think he knew it.

Anyway she had run up against the overhang. The awful truth was dawning on her. Or maybe it wasn't. However she hadn't fallen yet and rule said that you could try till you fell. She kept trying to find a path but couldn't. She tried this and she tried that. She was also getting tired. A few more people came over to watch the display of bullheadedness.

Jake wasn't saying anything. He just sat and looked at the ground.

Em had been on the rock for several minutes now and it showed. I got ready to give her an ovation and run over to console her because I knew she wanted to climb that thing and I knew she couldn't. The tireder you get, the less hope you have. If she could have done it, she would have done it early on.

More fumblings at handholds that weren't there, more slips that she just barely saved. She was getting weak and she was desperate.

Now, in rock climbing there's something called a "committed move." It means you can't change your mind in the middle. Suppose you are trying to jump twelve feet across a pit of ravening alligators. That's a committed move. You can't jump half way and then decide, heh, oops, that maybe you want to come back and think about it some more. Either it works or you're protein.

I'm not sure what idea came into her mind, or what she saw on the rock face, but she lunged wildly sideways, somehow got a handhold above the overhang, somehow got another one, muscled herself up, threw a knee—*and she was above the overhang*. I have no real idea how she did it. She scampered the remaining few feet up, rang the bell, and the store burst into applause.

And her daddy wasn't proud of her. Oh no. Who, me?

After that, Jake wouldn't even try. He just stared at the floor. It was sad. But maybe he had learned one of life's lessons: First do it, then brag about it. Getting it backwards is asking for trouble. There's always a faster gun. Besides, if you have to tell people that you are wonderful, you probably aren't.

Of course there's no reason to brag at all. It is better to convey your virtues by overwhelming inference. If people don't draw the inference, well, it probably wasn't there to draw. That has always been my approach. I haven't impressed many people, but I haven't made a fool of myself either. Well, not that way, anyhow.

In a sense Jake had ambushed himself. Em was tough. She just didn't look it. At age twelve she found out that legally she could get her scuba cert. She let me know that my life wouldn't be worth living unless I did the right thing. That summer we went diving together in the Keys.

Jake was very quiet the rest of the day. I felt bad for him. But there's the Chinese proverb, "*Dz dzwo, dz shou.*" Self do, self receive. I don't think he really became a serial killer. Probably

CHAPTER 25

Pulling the Plug: Thoughts on Expatriation

Yesterday, after two months in Mexico, I flew from Guadalajara International back to the sprawling gringo asylum above the Rio Grande. I wouldn't have, except I had to go back to Washington, the heart of all darkness, to rent my condo before relocating to Guad. I guess I was in a philosophical mood. Or maybe jalapenos are mildly hallucinogenic.

"How reasonable is this?" I thought, an hour into the flight. "I'm flying at six hundred miles an hour in an aluminum box, seven miles in the air. It weighs tons. Probably it doesn't belong here. It may not stay." My knees were up around my chin and my feet were in my pockets. Airline seats get smaller by the week. I think they make them of some material that shrinks.

A Brandenburg concerto was pouring out of my headset. Johann Bach, I happened to know, was dead. What is the world coming to? Dead men write music and nobody thinks it strange. If a dead cat chased mice, they probably make a movie about it.

Further, I was listening to musicians who weren't there. If I listened to little voices from the receiver the CIA put in my brain, they'd say I was crazy as three monkeys in a briefcase. When I listen to musicians who aren't there, through a wire coming from the furniture, I'm called a passenger.

Maybe, I thought, a schizophrenic is just someone who sees what is going on.

Outside, Mexico drifted slowly beneath us. They ought to tie it down, I thought.

Why am I moving to Mexico? Because it represents a more advanced form of civilization, or maybe a less advanced form of decay. (If I'd gotten more sleep, I could make this more plausible. You'll just have to deal with it.)

I was in Tom's Bar the other day when a horse stuck its head in the door. The owner knew Tom and wanted to talk to him. The horse apparently wondered what was inside, and stuck its head in to look. It seemed reasonable. It was how I would have done it.

If you even rode a horse in Washington, you'd need three permits, a parade license, turn signals, and a horse diaper. The paperwork alone would require help from an accounting firm. They'd x-ray the horse for explosives. It would probably mutate and turn into a huge gurgling cephalopod.

In Mexico, you get on a horse and point it where you want to go. Nobody gives a damn. It's a horse.

A lot of things work that way in Mexico. I was in a restaurant on the plaza when a woman came in with her dog. It curled up under the table and occasionally cadged bits of enchilada. It's what dogs do. It's OK. In the US, people keep dogs in their houses for years and nobody dies.

If the same dog came into a restaurant in Arlington, a SWAT team from Public Health would storm the place in funny-looking gas masks, confiscate the dog for analysis, and seal the premises for forty years. The United States can't tell a pup-dog from the Black Death.

Further, Mexicans like their kids. The reason may be familiarity. They spend enough time with them that they can generally recognize them. The concept is novel but bears investigation.

It's a good thing they like them. The place is awash with progeny. On a flight out of Mexico, the average age of passengers is about four and a half. It is not true that every seventeen-year-old girl in the country has a baby in her arms. Sometimes they put them down. Yet if fecundity is any indication, they evolved from kudzu. At birth they begin crawling northwards, like salmon, toward the frontier. A Mexican nursery has no doors on the north side. It's so they can keep them in.

I hate airplanes.

To support myself in Guad, I decided to write a series of novels about a female computer geek named Monitor Lewinski who could crack 128-bit encryption in her head. I thought a little more and decided not to. Aren't you glad?

Anyway, Mexico. These folk have no idea how to run an airport. For one thing, they're civil. Their security people are not surly urban aborigines one step removed from human sacrifice. Further, they aren't crazy. If a six-year-old boy were discovered to have a rubber pirate's dagger, they would not wrestle him to the ground and strip-search his grandmother. They would figure he was a kid with a rubber pirate's dagger.

It's frightening. I think of walking the plank from an MD-11, and shudder.

In the town I lived in, near Guadalajara, the main vortex for nutcake gringos is indeed Tom's Bar—it of the exploratory horse. I think technically it is called the San Andreas Bar. The clients are the usual overseas pot-poury of pilots, a couple of journalists, a mechanic refugee from the creeping Stalinism of Canada, and various curiosities who got sick of the lunacy elsewhere.

Anyway, Tommy's is best known for a wildly colored cow's skull on the wall, a wildly colored clientele, and the tendency to get strange late at night. Recently a Mexican barmaid, a pretty local gringa, and a Yanqui writer were seen dancing on the bar at two a.m. (I decline to answer. Talk to my lawyer.)

If you think I'm crazy, check this out: As we were taking off from Guad, the PA system said that by federal regulation we had to put our Bistro Bags under the seat for take-off.

Yeah. Federal regulation of sandwich bags.

A Bistro Bag is a sandwich that tastes like cardboard and a nickel's worth of potato chips. It meant the airline didn't want to feed us. It also meant they didn't want me to fly with them again. I guess they think that if they call it a Bistro Bag I'll think it was personally prepared for me by a homosexual French chef and flown in by satellite.

You want crazy? I lived in a country where the government tells me where I can keep a sandwich. You could take all the drugs at a Grateful Dead concert and not get that twisted. It's for my own good, of course. ("Man Emasculated by Carnivorous Tuna Sandwich in Lap.")

In Mexico, you take your chances with sandwiches. It's still the Wild West there. I'm going to take a shower and sleep for a week.

CHAPTER 26

Mourning as a Performing Art

September, 2002, just before the anniversary of 9/11—

We're going to do it, I know we are. We're going to celebrate Bin Laden's Victory Day. By all indications, it will be a media circus, like when Princess Di did—a grand battle in the ratings wars. We'll wallow in mawkishness, and whimper, and humiliate ourselves. Watch. There will be manufactured solemnity, factitious reverence, sorrow by Disney, and an unremitting ooze of therapy. Heaven help us, we'll probably get in touch with our feelings, and Heal. Maybe booths will sell cotton candy.

It's embarrassing.

I suppose I have a bad attitude about the upcoming festivities. On my office wall is a row of magazine covers I shot for *Soldier of Fortune* in a previous life as a freelance photojournalist. One of them (November, 1983, written as Rick Venable) shows Marines coming ashore in Beirut, the lead guy carrying an M-203. I spent a week or two with those guys, patrolling downtown and suchlike. Shortly afterward, the truck bomb arrived. Moslem terrorists. Two hundred forty-one dead.

America didn't do anything about those killings, then or later. There was no carnival of mourning on the anniversary. I guess the networks forgot. What do you suppose? As for dead Marines, who cared? After all, they didn't go to Princeton, and you never saw them in pricey booze chutes in Manhattan.

Judging by appearances, the forthcoming coverage will be appalling both in quantity and moral fraudulence. The ad agencies, I have read, are pondering what tone to use on September 11. It is a delicate question. The trick is to gull the rubes without disturbing their sensibilities. (Singing toilet paper may not be just the thing. Unless it sang a dignified dirge maybe. Mining the dead for ad revenue is harder that it might seem.)

The Moslem world is going to love every minute of it. In fact, I see in the *Washington Times* that they are going to have anti-American rallies in London to celebrate the great day. How convenient, they must think: The Americans are going to crawl for us. I'll give you odds Bin Laden is comfortable somewhere, probably in Saudi Arabia, laughing and laughing and laughing. I would be.

Maybe he's not really in Saudi. Maybe he's in Vail, waiting for good powder. But he ain't been caught. I tell you, he's one slick A-rab. I don't like the guy. I'd shoot him if I could, and poke holes in his towel. I have to respect the sucker, though. He changed the United States forever. We're going to be a scared security state for all time, with the cops reading our email. The home of the free, land of the brave.

I assume, subject to correction by events, that we'll have every television truck on earth at Ground Zero, and the rest at the Pentagon. There will be endless tributes to the Hallowed Dead, who will be treated as saints crossed with Joan of Arc. Actually of course they were just people who happened to be at work on the wrong day. Being hit by an airliner is no more heroic or tragic than being run over by a dump truck. This is the age of Oprah Consciousness, though. We'll have contrived tears from televised airheads who didn't know the dead and don't care about them.

People get mad if you say it, but, fact is, we got stomped. One raghead with a few subordinate loons took down the Trade Center, turned us into a docile police state, made us spend billions bombing peasants in Afghanistan without result, frightened us into letting our airlines go into bankruptcy, and now we have Homeland Security, which makes flying so unpleasant that most of us will take trains. The best we could do now is just to shut up. Naw. We're gonna wave it around on prime time. We'll let everybody watch it again.

Time was, this wouldn't have happened. When the Japanese bombed Pearl Harbor, we squashed them. When the Nazis attacked us, we invaded. But that was before Oprah Consciousness. Now the Moslems kill a few thousand people in New York, and the President immediately goes to a mosque. Don't you love it?

After Pearl Harbor, did Roosevelt go to a Shinto temple?

The whole thing is surreal. We can't even admit who did it.

Quiz: What people have been consistently kicking our teeth in for decades? Chippewas? Latvians? Tibetan monks? Or Moslems?

It was the Iroquois who took over our embassy in Tehran and make fools of us for months, until Jimmy Carter sent in that comic-opera rescue team and independently made fools of us. Isn't that what you remember? Iroquois?

The Norwegians blew up the Marine barracks in Beirut, right? Damn those Norwegians. The Cole? The Starke? Presbyterians did it. I'm sure of it.

Is there no limit to our absurdity? (No. The question was rhetorical.) We all know who the terrorists are, but we won't even search Moslems because that would be discrimination. We won't arm pilots because guns are, *Squeeeeak!* so *fwightening.* We take away fingernail clippers as deadly weapons. This is the country that stormed Iwo?

It gets sillier. We're going to wage an international crusade against terrorism, yet we throw little boys out of school for drawing pictures of soldiers, and we don't let them play dodge ball because it's so violent. The earth must be laughing.

A pretty good rule of diplomacy might be that you shouldn't huff and puff if you aren't going to back it up. It's undignified. It invites more trouble. The Towers went down, and we huffed. Grrr, woof. Bush said fiercely that we were going to make terrorists everywhere wish they had never been born. For at least two weeks everybody was solidarified and America was on the march and companies sold Instant Patriotism kits, with a little flag for the aerial and a bumper sticker. Bow-wow-wow. Wurf.

And then we fizzled. We bombed Afghanistan some, but I can't see that it did much. We sound as though we may do something unpleasant to Iraq. I guess that'll get rid of terrorism. We'll see. It's hard to know what we're going to do. These days wars are declared by the president, not congress.

I'll root for us, but bet on them. The Moslems have got our number. They have the momentum. They appear to rely on what is becoming an international formula for defeating the United States: Don't give the Yanks a point target, and draw the war out until they get bored. Do you reckon it's working?

CHAPTER 27

America. It Was an Interesting Experiment

How stable, one may wonder, is the United States?

The answer would seem to be, "Exceedingly." The country has had no coups, attempted coups, or revolutions. Our only civil war came over a century ago. Political stability has contributed mightily to American success. We have avoided the internal wars, shifting governments, and dictators that have plagued the political adolescents of Europe.

Yet we are not a happy country. Below the surface lie anger and hostility that seem to have no resolution. Strains exist that we do not, may not, talk about. We hide these problems, and hide from them, hoping they will go away. Perhaps they will. Perhaps they won't.

The odds, I suppose, are against an explosion. It is as hard to imagine violent change in the United States as it was, fifteen years ago, to imagine that the Soviet Union would spontaneously disassemble. (Part of Marxist theory was that the state would one day wither away. It did.) On the other hand, the country seems to me to be quietly, growingly—angry.

I wonder.

If, as a debating exercise, I were to argue for the possibility of cataclysmic upheaval, of race war, revolution, a coup, or widespread civil unrest, I would make my case as follows:

Our problems are grave. For example, we have a black minority of about thirteen percent that seethes with anger, and does not seem to be assimilating. Blacks quietly gain political control of more and more cities. While their standard of living rises, their degree of allegiance to the larger society does not.

We have an equally large and faster growing Latino minority. To what extent Latinos will assimilate is not clear. Their children do poorly in school, which does not bode well. If they turn into a self-aware group in opposition to white America, into brown blacks, we will face a quarter of the population, and rising, hostile to the mainstream (and in all likelihood hostile to each other).

Whites back passively away, frightened in their own country, moving deeper into the suburbs, acceding to every demand. The others advance, knowing that the advantage is theirs. But it may be that this just raises the stakes should conflict come.

The racial divide is by itself every bit enough to cause disaster.

Profound division, and profound anger, permeate white America itself. Some of it follows the fault lines of partisan politics, but partakes of something deeper. It is not politics as usual. The antagonism is between the traditionally American and what for brevity may be called the politically correct. It verges on hatred.

The dispute among whites is not about details, not about the fine tuning of this or that policy. At stake are crucial, emotionally explosive matters such as the de-Christianization of the country, the ever-tightening governmental control of behavior, social decay, the replacement of merit by racial and sexual patronage, the forced mixing of racial and ethnic minorities that don't want to mix, a Latino invasion resented intensely by a majority of whites, and the relentless imposition of values abominated by the traditional America.

And there is the curious hostility between men and women. It won't erupt, but it aggravates tension. When instincts are thwarted, the limbic temperature rises. Generalized anger has a way, sooner or later, of focusing itself.

Historically, America's elastic democracy has prevented revolt by yielding to pressure. If women decided they wanted to major in chemical engineering, the country said, fine, sign here. Assimilation has been a chief instrument. If the Irish were held in disregard in one generation, in the next they moved up, blended, became generic Americans, and ceased being resentful or resented.

But are today's resentments thus eradicable? What happens when groups don't assimilate, when nonnegotiable values of one group are inherently incompatible with those of another group?

Mechanisms of change appear to be lacking. We have two essentially identical political parties that refuse to address the aforementioned crucial questions: immigration, race, etc. Instead of looking for solutions, we hold the lid on by compulsion and censorship. It could prove dangerous. Think of Yugoslavia.

By stifling dissent, are we, as many think, giving our problems time to disappear? Or are we coiling a spring?

Further, we have cornered ourselves. The increasing centralization of government, and the increasing scope of its jurisdiction, make retreat impossible. In 1900 a town in Montana could run its schools as it liked. Washington and New York had neither the manpower, the communications, nor the interest to intervene. True, Montanans then probably had even less influence over Washington than they do now. Crucially, Washington had less over them.

Today remote bureaucracies monitor small towns and their schools, their textbooks, the racial and sexual ratios and failure rates in Algebra II, prescribe what they may and may not teach, what morality must be instilled, whether people can say "One nation under God," and send federal marshals should transgression occur.

Just as Tito held the lid down on Yugoslavia, the metagovernment prevents explosion (metagovernment being the curious amalgam of the media, academia, and their allies of which the federal government is the instrument). But Tito is never immortal. Then what?

Such are our domestic circumstances. Abroad, we face further stresses that we equally fail to resolve.

We find ourselves in a partial, half-noticed war with, depending on your degree of realism, terrorism or Islam or countries that have oil. The country suffered a devastating attack in New York. So far, we have done essentially nothing about it. We now live in anxious expectation of further devastation. The government, flaccid abroad, reacts chiefly against Americans. Surveillance of the population grows, police powers advance, and governmental accountability diminishes.

The importance of the conflict with Islam is not easily calculated nor its consequences predicted. Will there be further attacks a la New York? A government unable to protect the country, widely detested at home, and respected nowhere is not a recipe for fealty. We are getting there. Institutions fall when they cease to work, or when people believe that they have ceased to work.

What could provoke—what? A coup? Revolution? I cannot imagine it. The control of communications is too great, the passivity of the white population near absolute. People have enough to eat and five hundred cable channels. The military is safely emasculated.

The likelihood, I think, is that we will muddle on, dissatisfied but not too dissatisfied, turning into whatever we are turning into, learning obedience. Yet the tension is there. Remember the LA riots. Nothing lasts forever, not even America. A fascinating question is when and how it will stop lasting.

CHAPTER 28

Commies, Conservatism, and Trash on the Trail

I'm trying to figure out environmentalism and why everyone hollers about it. I'm having a hard time.

My own environmental prejudices: I like back-country camping. I don't see the advantage in having a trail covered with beer cans and styrofoam. Maybe there is a benefit, and I'm just slow, and don't understand. But I don't want to look at the stuff. Nor do I want a four-lane highway through the Grand Canyon, five malls, and a gooberish theme park. I'm sorry. I'm just primitive that way.

Scuba diving is a hobby of mine. Maybe I'm selfish. I don't want the fish coated with industrial waste, or the mangroves, where things breed, turned into yuppie boxes by some real-estate developer who wants another Cadillac. We have enough yuppies. I say poison them to make room for mangroves.

I grew up on the Potomac River, where people crabbed for a living until sewage from Washington killed the crabs. Environmentalists pushed through a treatment plant and it got better. I'm trying hard to see why this was unpatriotic. I figure that if conservatives want to swim in Washington's sewage, they're stranger than I thought, but it's their business. They can put it in their swimming pools. If they live upstream and want to make me swim in it, I need to talk to them with a ball bat.

So I guess I'm a radical green, and worse than Bin Laden.

Actually, the whole debate is rife with fraud. To begin with, everyone thinks that the dispute is an ideological war between liberalism and conservatism. Why? In Russia, it was the communists who fouled their country. Apparently about half of Russia is radioactive now, and the rest poisonous. In America, it's the capitalists who act like communists.

Both camps occupy the moral sump. The moral difference between Left and Right is zero. Capitalism is far more economically efficient, but just as willing to run sweatshops, pollute the rivers, make the air noxious, and profess the highest ideals while doing it.

Ideologies are of course just systematic ways of misunderstanding the world. They are the province of herd thinkers, people who have the answer before they've heard the question, and they always have the same answer. The more ardently liberal or conservative they are, the worse they are. Serious ones get bitter and start lying without even knowing it, mostly to themselves.

Environmentally, both Left and Right believe in virtue, but only when it suits them. If I suggest that maybe we don't really need to clearcut the redwoods to make decks for liberal yups that conservatives hate anyway, the conservatives tell me that people need jobs. But isn't that an argument for expanding the federal bureaucracy? People need jobs?

Like communists, capitalists express concern for the working class—when it is convenient. For example, when it comes to replacing workers with automation, then, what do you know, suddenly efficiency is more important than jobs. Principle and profit always coincide. Isn't it remarkable?

Why do conservatives want to turn the country into an industrial desert? They don't, of course. By no means all conservatives favor irresponsible exploitation, any more than all liberals want to make us into robots. The problem is that the worst of both camps are noisiest and most angry, and therefore shape policy.

Here you have to understand one of the (few) fundamental differences between the far Left and far Right. The Left wants to maximize governmental power so that it can misbehave, usually by imposing some form of tyrannous conformity that everyone hates but can't do anything about.

The Right wants to minimize governmental power so as to avoid restraint on its misbehavior, which usually involves any profitable abuse of anything. Both want to behave badly. They just go at it differently. The Left likes group misbehavior. The Right prefers to free-lance.

A highly explanatory element of angry anti-environmentalism is, I think, a lack of aesthetic sensitivity. There are people who simply cannot tell that the Grand Canyon is a lovely thing that should not be made into a landfill. They may say that it's beautiful ("Huh? Oh yeah. Real nice.") because they know this to be the expected response.

But they have no more real appreciation than a congenitally deaf man does for music. They honestly don't understand why anyone is upset. I'll bet that if you went to their homes, you would not find one decent picture on their walls that they chose themselves.

These people are just louts. Neither Left nor Right has a monopoly on loutishness.

Finally, there is sheer embittered combativeness. The politically excited often do not greatly care about the things they say they care about. They just want to fight.

For example, during the Cold War conservatives didn't hate communists, who wore baggy pants and couldn't organize a sock hop. Instead they hated liberals, communism being little more than a pretext. Similarly liberals do not like blacks, whom they regard as shiftless mentally defective bushmen. If they did care about blacks, they would favor schooling, etc. They hate conservatives, and find blacks to be a useful mallet.

Often, politics isn't about anything. It's just politics. Putting it less cutely, the joy of embitterment outweighs desire for content. In the 1930s Hitler discovered that it was much easier to convert a communalist to Nazism than a contented burger. Catholics have likewise found that atheists make easier and more enthusiastic converts that do agnostics. Zealots want enemies, allies, and simple answers. They don't care which enemies, allies, etc.

Thus many conservatives on examination turn out to have little interest in the environment. Instead, they hate environmentalists. Hating environmentalists is easy. Often the greens are tiresome zealots with a preening immature snottiness that recommends strangling.

In environmental politics as elsewhere, Left and Right need each other. Conservatives create much of the support for environmentalism by their hard-eyed rapacity. Loon environmentalists create much of the hostility to their cause by their unreasoning extremism. Neither sees or wants to see a middle ground.

For example it is perfectly possible to drill for oil without trashing the surroundings, build a pipeline that has no ill effects, and tear it all down when the field is exhausted. Both sides will fight to the death to avoid any such commonsensical solution.

It's depressing. Sometimes conservatives seem as amoral as liberals seem immoral. The Left wants to degrade education, reward incompetence, and eliminate personal freedom. The Right would have us live in a mall-ridden, strip-mined wasteland. How, oh how, can I express my gratitude?

CHAPTER 29

Flogging the Kaboom

The fault really lay with Ian Braxley, a computer major from NYU who interned that summer with the data-processing department of the *New York Times*. By the time anyone figured it out, American military policy had been changed forever.

Braxley had an IQ of 193, a sense of humor, and access to the operating system. The combination proved fateful. One night he inserted in the print queue an imaginary Reuters story about problems in the Army's new tank, the M-28 Kaboom, which didn't exist.

It ran in the back pages. Nobody at the paper noticed. Braxley and his girl-friend had a giggle and forgot about it.

The *Washington Post* noticed, however. The *Post* had just hired a new defense reporter, Dieter Frieding-Finzi, a German-Italian Swiss. His credentials as a military writer were impeccable. His grandmother had marched with the Spartacists. His grandfather was an African-American from a labor battalion in WWI. He was the embodiment of diversity, and he ate quiche.

He called the Pentagon, which he had learned was in nearby Virginia.

What were the flaws in the tank, he demanded, and was it true that they were irremediable? Why was the Army hiding them?

Major William Grunderling, the Public Affairs Officer on the Army desk, was baffled. He was used to stupid reporters, had in fact regarded brainlessness as a job qualification. This took witlessness to a new plane of existence.

The Kaboom didn't exist, he explained. It was hard to say whether the flaws in a nonexistent tank were irremediable.

"Well," demanded Frieding-Finzi, "Can you think of a way to fix them?"

"No," responded Grunderling logically.

"Army Denies Flaws Fatal," ran the headline on page three, the subhead being "Pentagon Waffles."

The story might have stopped there. But things were slow in the news racket. Television, which gets its stories from the *Post* and the *Times*, fell on the tank like a sock full of chicken tenders. A reporter for CBS called an exasperated Major Grunderling who said, "Look, we don't have an M-28 Kaboom. There isn't one. Zero. We are a Kaboomless Army."

That night, anchorwoman Babbette Willowly reported the story. She was well qualified to cover tanks, having long silky lashes and an adorable stutter.

"Is the Army secretly developing a questionable new supertank without informing Congress? Sources question the legality of this black program…."

The story went national. Liberal senators trampled each other to reach the nearest microphone. "Clearly this is an unconstitutional program since we haven't been informed of it," they intoned. "The military is out of control."

Conservatives responded that the program was vital to national security, and said that liberals were soft on communism. Someone objected that there wasn't any communism except in North Korea and the Harvard faculty lounge.

"That just shows the unrealism of Democratic policy, being soft on it when they haven't got any," responded Republicans. Liberals said they were merely being foresighted. Communism might come back.

Across the country, editors of little papers read the *Times*, which is where they get their news, and wrote blistering editorials about the unconscionable waste of money on a flawed tank. Thereafter when any reporter did an internet search on the Kaboom, he found hundreds of corroborative stories. The weight of evidence overcame doubt. Even papers in Peoria knew that the tank was a dog.

The *New York Times* was stunned. The paper vaguely felt that it had broken the story, though it wasn't sure how. Yet other outlets were beating it. Try as it might, the paper couldn't get any firm information on the tank. The Army, always right-wing, continued to stonewall: There was no such tank.

Finally a break came. Nicholas Kristof, a columnist for the paper, was in a local bar in the Village. He had gotten his favorite seat, convenient to the men's room yet allowing a view of babes who came in. New York being New York, he found himself next to a delusional para-schiz with a snootful.

"It's a radioactive death tank from the CIA," said the schizophrenic, twitching slightly. "It squirts anthrax and smallpox. The receivers in my fillings told me."

Kristof wrote, "A well-placed source with connections to the CIA says the Kaboom shoots germs. Is it possible that the Army was responsible for the Black Plague?"

Someone pointed out that the Black Death occurred in 1348. In a follow-up column, Kristof said this showed the inefficiency of the Army's development programs. It made no sense. No one noticed.

The House Armed Services Committee began an investigation on the lagging progress of the tank. Many of the members knew the Kaboom didn't exist, but it was an election year and they wanted to look busy.

Then feminists complained that the M-28 had been designed without consideration for the needs of women. This put the Army on the spot. Since the Kaboom hadn't been designed at all, it hadn't been designed for women. The Pentagon was stung by the resulting headlines. ("Army Admits Neglecting Half of Human Race.")

Panic ensued among the Joint Chiefs. Funds were diverted from the enlisted housing budget to develop the M-29 Mobile Battlefield Familial Unit. It was a modified armored personnel carrier with porta-potties, makeup mirror, a playpen for dependent children and, in case these wanted to see their fathers, a DNA-testing unit.

A free press eventually finds the truth. The tank began to acquire focus.

In journalism, a fact is defined as idle speculation that has appeared in three major newspapers. Facts proliferated as reporters worked their sources. The Kaboom had rocket engines and rotors, weighed 700 tons, and carried nuclear weapons. Yet questions remained. Did the mystery tank have a rifled main gun, or a trendy smoothbore?

Dan Rather became the authority on the Kaboom. He knew nothing of rifled guns, or arguably of anything else, but was familiar with smooth bores, having been to cocktail parties in Georgetown. He concluded that the tank fired poisoned darts.

Things were getting out of hand. The Army's damage-control apparatus swung into action. In a tense meeting on the Pentagon's E-ring the service decided that it had to build the tank.

It didn't want a new tank. Especially it didn't want a 700-ton radioactive tank that squirted germs and had rotors. Yet if the service didn't produce the damned thing, they decided, the press would never stop. Besides, the Mobile Battlefield Familial Unit was coming along. It couldn't go into battle without a matching tank.

Then a small story appeared in the back pages of the *New York Times*, mentioning problems with the secret Air Force base on Mars. Nobody noticed. Except Dieter Frieding-Finzi....

CHAPTER 30

Fred Endorses Hillary

At some point you have to take the manly course, stop equivocating, and set the helm of your country in wise directions. I'm going to do it. I am for Hillary. I don't do this casually. I know that throwing the full weight of this column behind a candidate will alter the majestic currents of crime and moral pusillanimity that give direction to government everywhere. The fixed stars may deviate slightly in their paths through the sensorium of God. But someone has to do it.

I know: I have said bad things about Hillary, as for example that she looks rumpled as a teenager's room, that she probably belongs to some hitherto undiscovered arachnid phylum, that she is a cynical, calculating cold-blooded tax-and-spend virago with the personality of a walk-in refrigerator.

These days that sounds pretty good.

Strange times call for strange measures.

At least she is not embarrassing. While she may be a walk-in refrigerator, she is an intelligent walk-in refrigerator. I say that if you are going to be ruled by an appliance, get a bright one. She speaks English, whereas the encumberment [Bush II] only hints around at it. (I don't think a president should be permitted to make war on anything he can't pronounce. But I'm a traditionalist.)

There is every indication that Hillary finished high school. She is strong as distinct from fixated.

And she suckered New York. What chance do you think the UN would have?

Think about it. Hillary would be cheaper than Bush. All she wants is national health insurance, which would turn into a bloating financial disaster, a dead fiscal whale swelling rancidly on the beaches of government and attracting crooked doctors like blowflies. It would not, however, kill anyone. Not deliberately anyway. Note that Bush, continuing the Republican penchant for pricey entitlements, wants free pharmaceuticals, and wants me to pay for his wars. Does he pay for my hobbies?

By the time he finishes conquering any country his keepers tell him about, Hillary's bills are going to look like a breakfast tip in a rural diner. I note in passing that Hill has never killed a GI.

Hillary is the clear choice for conservatives, and the only choice for the intelligent, given that the Democrats chose not to field a candidate this year. I asked an ardent conservative friend what conservatives want. "Smaller government, lower taxes, avoiding foreign entanglements, and liberty," he said. So much for the archliberal Bush. He spends in the manner of a tour bus of Boise matrons who just got to Cancun, tangles the country everywhere like kite string in a ceiling fan, apparently has never heard of the Bill of Rights, and we're going to pay for his games with inflation. Which is just taxation without representation.

Everything points to Hillary as a conservative's candidate. At one point during the Clintons' sway in Washington, a minor scandal erupted because, according to sources in the great double-wide on Pennsylvania Avenue, Hillary had chased Bill around shrieking "Dickhead!" and throwing lamps at him. Now, given that conservatives hated Bill, should this not endear her to them? *They* never threw lamps at Bill. Again, she gets credit for forthrightness.

Further, Hillary has a better military record than the other candidates. During Viet Nam, Bush used pull to get drunk in Texas while those who couldn't escape that useful war died, and Kerry apparently used the three-strikes-and-you're-out rule and some phony wounds to get out of combat.

Nothing wrong with that. Most of the country wanted to do it. All the draftees of the time would have ducked if they could have. The difference between Bush and most of the draftees is that Bush had better connections. If you want to see how much the troops want to serve their country, in any war, give them the opportunity to come home without penalty.

But Hillary didn't dodge the draft, didn't besot herself in the Guard, and has nothing whatever to lie about in her military record. Her time in combat equals that of most of Bush's administration plus that of the entire staff of *National Review*. She must be up there with Audie Murphy. Notice that this supports the view of feminists that women can fight as well as most men. Or at least most politicians and editors.

I'm hoping she will make Bill her secretary of defense. It's a character issue. While Bush was pounding down shooters and waltzing Porcelain Mary in the Guard, Bill was forthrightly protesting the war in England. Like Eisenhower, he was against war, and had the courage to say so. Like George Washington, he didn't want to gum the United States up in remote regions with bad plumbing. It's true that he had a taste for chunky interns. I will give him the benefit of the doubt, and trust that as SecDef he would get sleeker ones.

Another advantage of Hill is that she seems to be a religious agnostic. Now, if Christianity means what CS Lewis did, I'm for it. But I worry about snake handlers, speakers in tongues, and those who regard themselves as the principal conduit between God and his wayward creation. When someone tells me that "the Almighty told me to do this," I want to see the transcript.

The rub is that if you figure God is sending you instructions, then you do whatever the little voices tell you without the least regard for common sense, observable fact, or human decency. Any stray thought that flickers through your mind becomes cosmic email from On High. It is a splendid way of avoiding responsibility for your actions. "I was only following orders." It is what makes Moslem loons dangerous.

Hillary may be an arachnid, but she isn't a delusional arachnid. I do not worry that one morning she will wake up and think, "I think we need a land war with China. And yeah, I guess that's what God wants to, or I wouldn't have thought of it. I'll nuke them."

I grant you that Hillary seems to have a taste for running real-estate scams. This is nothing more than enlightened self-interest. Better that she should make her own money (or perhaps someone else's) than go on welfare. She probably did it to save the government the cost of supporting her. It shows entrepreneurial spirit and self-reliance. I see a close kinship with Daniel Boone and Davy Crockett.

Write her in. It is, astonishingly, the road of patriotism, or at least of lesser humiliation.

CHAPTER 31

Yes, Mommy: A Well-Regulated State

We tell ourselves that in America we are the Free People. I wonder whether we might not better be called the Obedient People, the Passive People, or the Admonished People. I doubt that any country, anywhere, has been so regulated, controlled, and directed as we are. We are bred to obey. And obey we do.

It begins with the sheer volume of law, rules, and administrative duties. Most of the regulation makes sense in isolation, or can be made plausible. Yet there is so much of it.

Used to be if you wanted a dog, you got a dog. It wasn't really the government's business. Today you need a dog license, a shot card for the dog, a collar and tags, proof that the poor beast has been neutered, and you have to keep it on a leash and walk it only in designated places. It's all so we don't get rabies.

Or consider cars. You have to have a title, insurance, and keep it up to date; tags, country sticker, inspection sticker, emissions test. Depending where you are, you can't have chips in the windshield, and you need a zoned parking permit. You have to wear a seatbelt. And of course there are unending traffic laws. You can get a ticket for virtually anything, usually without knowing that you were doing anything wrong.

Then there's paperwork. If you have a couple of daughters with college funds in the stock market, annually you have to fill out three sets of federal taxes, three sets of state, and file four state and four federal estimated tax forms, per person, for a total of twenty-four. This doesn't include personal property taxes for the country, business licenses, tangible business-assets forms, and so on.

Now, I'm not suggesting that all these laws are bad. Stupid, frequently, but evil, no. Stopping at traffic lights is probably a good idea, and certainly is if I'm crossing the street. But the laws never end. Bring a doughnut on the subway, and you get arrested. And don't replace your windows without permission in writing from the condo association. Nothing is too trivial to be regulated. Nothing is not some government's business.

I wonder whether the habit of constant obedience to infinitely numerous rules doesn't inculcate a tendency to obey any rule at all. By having every aspect of one's life regulated in detail, does one not become accustomed to detailed regulation? That is, detailed obedience?

For many it may be hard to remember freer times. Yet they existed. In 1964, when I graduated from high school in rural Virginia, there were speed limits, but nobody much enforced them, or much obeyed them. If you wanted to fish, you needed a pole, not a license. You fished where you wanted, not in designated fishing zones. If you wanted to carry your rifle to the bean field to shoot whistle pigs, you just did it. You didn't need a license and nobody got upset.

To buy a shotgun in the country store, you needed money, not a background check, waiting period, proof of age, certificate of training, and a registration form. If your tail light burned out, then you only had one tail light. If you wanted to park on a back road with your girl friend, the cops, all both of them, didn't care. If you wanted to swim in the creek, you didn't need a Coast Guard approved life jacket.

It felt different. You lived in the world as you found it, and behaved because you were supposed to, but you didn't feel as though you were in a white-collar prison. And if anybody had asked us, we would have said that the freedom was worth more to us than any slightly greater protection against rabies, thank you. Which nobody ever got anyway.

Today, the Mommy State never leaves off protecting us from things I'd just as soon not be protected from. We must wear a helmet on a motorcycle: Kevorkian can kill us, but we cannot kill ourselves. Why is it Mommy Government's business whether I wear a helmet? In fact I do wear one, but it should be my decision.

And so it goes from administrative minutiae (emissions inspections) to gooberish Mommyknowsbestism ("Wea-a-ar your lifejacket, Johnny!") to important moral decisions. Obey in small things, obey in large things.

You must hire the correct proportion of this and that ethnic group, watch your sex balance, and prove that you have the proper attitude toward homosexuals. You must let your children be politically indoctrinated in appropriate values, must let your daughter get an abortion without telling you, must accept affirmative action no matter how morally repugnant you find it.

And we do. We are the obedient people.

As the regulation of our behavior becomes more pervasive, so does the mechanism of enforcement grow more nearly omnipresent. In Washington, if you eat on the subway, they really will put you in handcuffs, as they recently did to a girl of twelve. In 1964 in King George County, the cop would have said, "Sally, stop that." Arresting a child for sucking on a sourball would never have entered a state trooper's mind.

Which brings us to an ominous observation. America is absolutely capable of totalitarianism. It won't be the jackbooted variety, perhaps, but rather a peculiarly mindless, bureaucratic insistence on conformity. What we call political correctness is an American approach to political control.

Our backdoor totalitarianism has the added charm of being crazy.

Think about it. Confiscating nail clippers at security gates, arresting the eating girl on the subway, the confiscation of his Congressional Medal of Honor from an aging general at the airport because it had points, the countless ejections from school of little boys for drawing soldiers or the Trade Centers in flames, for playing cowboys and Indians, for pointing a chicken finger and saying Bang.

This isn't intelligent authoritarianism aimed at purposeful if disagreeable ends. It is the behavior of petty and stupid people, of minor minds over-empowered, ignorant, but angry and charmed to find that they can push others around. It is the exercise of power by people who have no business having any.

And we obey. We are the obedient people.

CHAPTER 32

asm.org: A Site for Dyslexic Sex Maniacs

Actually, I just wanted to say that. The column is really about how I'm going stark raving mad trying to get out of the Yankee Capital and go live forever in fronded warm lands where you never have to listen to Connie Chung in bars.

I know. You really wanted to read about the cross-eyed sex maniacs. Hey, it's a recognized sales scam: Bait and switch. Tell the FTC.

Anyway, I'm about ready. Condo rented, phone killed, power switched, addresses changed, stuff I don't really want stored where I'll never look at it again but think I might. Later I'll pay an arsonist to burn it. I've got a 48-page passport, multivariate shot card, and as much of my life as possible transferred to the internet. I'm packed: Bag of scuba gear, laptop, two pairs of shorts, three tee-shirts, and a pair of sandals.

The trick to living well is getting your priorities straight.

Maybe I'll leave one of the tee shirts. I don't want to be encumbered.

Expatriating is apparently a hot fantasy nowadays. I get a lot of email about getting out of Dodge. The urge to flee probably says something tedious about America, though I'm not sure just what. Sure, my correspondents aren't interested in *me*: I'm just some news weasel who snapped, started bouncing off things, and shot out the southern exit. They like the idea of bailing.

Letters say approximately, "Gee, Fred, I've always wanted to go somewhere exotic on a beach with funny drinks involving rum and lissome brown maidens if only as geographic credentials so I'll know I'm in paradise and no pestilential intrusive do-good government to make me feel like I'm being engulfed by a giant garden slug. Just once I want to listen to the waves crash and look at one of those sprawling gaudy-ass molten sunsets I figure they really make with PhotoShop because nothing that gorgeous can be real.

"But I've got two kids and a vast looming mortgage on a house I don't like and three cars I'm bored with and my wife doesn't like bugs. Or lissome brown maidens. So much for this life. It's shot. At least tell me about somewhere else."

I feel bad for them but don't know what to say. OK. Give me a couple of weeks. Reports to follow. But I'll tell you something: A whole more people could get out than think they can.

I suspect that if folk looked around and asked, "How much of this dismal junk do I really need? Want? Do I really have to have a riding mower on my over-manicured quarter-acre plot in some hideous suburb? Do I really want to spend the rest of my life cleaning gutters? Being a cubicle wart for Housing and Urban Development?"—well, passport applications might rise.

You just gotta do it.

Extraneous thought: Last night I talked for a couple of hours with a buddy who lived in the Pacific islands for years and married a Filipina, which is a good choice since they are not lemon-sucking shrews with shoulder pads. Which may explain why I met the woman I will probably marry on a dive trip to St. Maarten. [Note to reader: This was a blow-up sex doll the crew found floating in the water and put in my bed.]

They came back, looked at what is going on in the States, and started pricing return tickets to the Pacific. Neither hates America. They just wonder where it went.

Anyway, ex-pats these days form a sort of global community. The internet helps. You go to the local hangout in wherever—Bangkok, Mexico, the Philippines, Phuket, or a thousand places nobody has heard of with garish flowers and lizards on the walls—and in two weeks you feel as if you lived there. If you want to go somewhere else for a while, someone likely knows someone there. Email occurs. You arrive and you know people. You do the same for the next guy.

Ex-pats form roughly three tribes. You've got the retirees who don't really want to be in, say, Mexico, but want a warm place with low prices and cheap maids. Then you've got the unhappy single guys who drink themselves to death. Finally you have the ones who have girlfriends and wives (I don't mean at the same time) (though sometimes) and learn the language or parts of it and burrow in for the long haul. (That may be a mixed metaphor. I'll deal with it later.) They're smart, savvy, good company, and have stories to tell.

Why do these engaging oddballs abandon the US? Several reasons predominate, only occasionally involving law enforcement back home. First and commonest, believe it or not, is weariness with American women. This is heartfelt, almost universal, and saddening. I'm not sure what the problem is between the sexes in America, but it's there. Yes, there are lots of nice women in the US, etc. But I'm telling you what ex-pats say.

Whenever I mention the preference of American men for Asian women, or Mexican women, or Albanian women, I get (1) lots of letters from men, almost without exception saying, "Amen!" and (2) angry letters from angry American women angrily saying that men are pigs and foreign women are just sexually easy.

Not exactly. Actually American women are easier than those in conservative Catholic countries like Mexico. If all a man wanted was sex, he would have no reason to leave the United States. The men I know in Mexico are not marrying prostitutes. Universally they say they like the local women because they don't have The Chip, the Attitude. They're feminine. They're not always coiled to strike. They are just plain pleasant. Which is how I remember American women, back when. Some still are.

The other common reason given for crawling through the escape hatch is diffuse, but powerfully felt: An amorphous political dissatisfaction, a weariness with the background anger, growing incivility, and compulsory politics in the United States. Yes, I know that in towns in Wyoming it isn't this way yet. Most people do not live in towns in Wyoming.

The…"tension" may be the word…is unmistakable when returning after an absence. Part of it is the loss of the easy courtesy of America in former times, part is the unresolved racial hostility that quietly pervades the country, part is a sense of over-regulation and the suffocating miasma of political correctness. It shows as aggression on the road, aggressive begging, aggressive jay-walking. It's there.

But I won't be, soon. Hooo-*ah*. I may buy a burro, or one of those big Technicolor parrots. I'll watch storms come in over the mountains, and listen to Bob Dylan and Carmina Burana and a lot of blues. And never, ever see network propaganda. Not ever.

CHAPTER 33

A Sniper and National Character. If Any

The trouble with terrorism is that it produces too many psychotherapists. I'm trying to figure out what to do with them. My first thought was to take them to the sewage treatment plant over at Blue Plains and plunk them in, but I figured it would contaminate the sewage. I am a radical environmentalist, and deeply concerned about the rights of coliform bacteria.

Nuke the shrinks, I say, and save the E. coli. Bacteria are people too.

Anyway, terrorism. We have a sniper lurking about Washington who has killed nine or so people. He has also started a moping industry. The media revel in moping. They like it even better than imaginary racism.

There's no escaping. In every bar in Washington the lobotomy box babbles and wrings its hands. At Gold's gym, the telescreens that dangle in front of people never stop emoting. If the sniper wanted attention, we are feeding him well.

The other day I saw a journalistic bimbo interviewing some vapid psychologist about the sniper. He (the psychologist) was the usual droning human hamster with the too-pretty salt-and-pepper beard and the vanity and soft edges that make you want to cross your legs.

Bimbo and Hamster made a matched set. I started thinking of them as E. Coli and She Coli, which shows how bored I was. She asked appallingly stupid questions, and he gave appallingly stupid answers. It's what physicists call conservation of symmetry.

The function of psychologists is to serve as secular priests for an irreligious age. They provide comfort for people who want reassurance provided by insipid hand-holders who smell slightly of some inner truth. They form a vacuous clergy relentlessly certifying the obvious. Talking to one of them is like being patted on the head and having your face wiped with a warm moist rag. It doesn't accomplish anything, but you feel attended to.

Hamster performed well. Asked to characterize the sniper, he said, "Well, I think we can say that these killings are the work of a disturbed individual…."

Oh.

I received this insight with gratitude. It was comforting to learn that serial snipers weren't normal. It is well that we have psychologists to study these truths.

The tube then cut to distraught mothers and daughters. The cameraman shot tight in hopes of catching a lip trembling. Television is about emotion. It's about ordinary people having feelings, and being validated. The producers presumably avoided asking little boys what they thought, as they might have said, "Wow! Let's get guns and go look for him!" It wouldn't have suited the tone of unfocused condescending reproof that was wanted.

More consultation about nothing followed between Bimbo and Hamster. He said that fear was normal but that if you couldn't sleep, and became obsessive, and couldn't go on with your life, you should seek counseling. ("Or maybe cyanide," I thought with more hope than expectation.)

Finally our pinnacle of journalism got an expression of dawning insight, such as a chimpanzee displays when it has understood a door hinge. Yes, she had had A Thought. She burbled (and this is verbatim, so help me):

"What I hear you saying is that it's ok to feel your feelings."

I thought: This is a society that is going to wage relentless international jihad against terrorism? People who have to ask a bearded parsnip before they feel their feelings, whatever that means?

I remember some years back when a local wit left a package near B'Nai Brith that had "Antrax" or some such misspelling scrawled on it. There was no anthrax. It was a gag.

The city shut down for a whole day. The usual media circus ensued, and all of the participants were solemn clowns. The entire story could have been condensed into a short graff: "It says anthrax, we're being careful, actually it wasn't anthrax, and we don't know who did it. Now go away."

No. Therapists, psychologists, alarm, updates. For a whole day.

Sure, a sniper is a bad and worrisome thing and nobody wants one, except reporters. Still, he has killed few people. And of course the media don't care about death unless they can make it into a therapeutic drama. If nine black drug dealers killed each other over a week or two, the papers would carry a two-inch story on page thirty, just after the truss ads. If a dozen people died in car wrecks, no one beyond their families would care.

This nonsense is now the normal American response to misfortune. The arresting thing is how utterly different it is from what would have been the response forty years ago. It used to be that trouble brought forth strength.

If we were attacked, for example at Pearl Harbor, the country rallied and fought back. When the Depression struck, people slogged through it. When life went sour, the expected response was chin up, keep a stiff upper lip, deal with it. You solved your problems, lived with them, or had the grace to shut up about them.

Today the country curls into a national fetal position and whimpers. No, not everyone does, and yes, lots of residual Americans regard the curlers with contempt. Yet the mainstream response is a passive, inward-looking, sniveling. We even have a vast apparatus of psychologists, therapists, and suchlike rabbitry to help us snivel better.

Preposterously, moaning is actually regarded as a sign of strength. If you don't whimper, it is because you are afraid to express your feelings, and therefore need professional help.

What happened?

I saw on the History Channel a while back an interview with a British woman, now ancient, who had gone through the bombing of London. How had she managed, the interviewer wanted to know.

"We had to do it," the woman said calmly. "So we did." She thought that covered it. So did I.

In those days, the British idea of a grief therapist was Winston Churchill. Brits still have some of their old iron in them. One does not easily imagine Margaret Thatcher blubbering to Oprah. She maintained her own and her country's dignity. We don't. The very idea of dignity seems to make us uncomfortable. Why?

Maybe we should again learn dignity. We face difficult times. Across the world the Moslems are blowing up people. A good guess is that we are going to be hit again, hard. I wonder how we are going to handle it when we have more pet-loss grief counselors than we do Marines. And I wonder what the Israelis think of us, or the Moslems.

Come to think of it, I don't wonder.

CHAPTER 34

Protecting Us. Couldn't We Just Be in Danger Instead?

When Rashid Ali Fata Bakh took out the Golden Gate Bridge by ramming it with an oil tanker, he did not regard himself as an agent of social change. He believed he was simply doing the will of God who, as Ali understood it, did not like infidels or suspension bridges.

The attack provoked America's accustomed response to terrorism. President Bush attended a mosque and announced his intention of converting. He did this to avoid giving the impression that Islamic terrorism bore any connection to Islam.

Morbid tolerance flourished. Across the nation the intellectually shiftless lunged into action. The National Education Association urged that school children be instructed in the evils of white patriarchy. Grade schools began knitting prayer rugs. Telebimbos rattled on for weeks, psychologists certified the obvious, and therapists validated feelings in ungrammatical English.

President Bush enunciated the philosophical foundation of this virility, saying, "A nation that is not confident in its bridges is not free to cross water. We will never yield to the Tankers of Terror. There is a price to pay for everything and whatever it is, Americans everywhere are united in unity."

Nobody knew what this meant, least of all Bush. A technical glitch had occurred at the studio. It was perhaps the first time that policy had been set by teleprompter failure. It didn't seem to matter.

Federal bridge-inspectors were hurriedly hired, largely from bus stations, and housed on all bridges. Most were surly urban aboriginals and functionally illiterate, but the president insisted that the bridge force look like America. TRW got a contract for 37,000 drive-thru film-safe non-mutagenic x-ray machines with explosives detectors.

Skeptics pointed out that only a few dozen bridges were in water navigable by tankers. No one listened. Meanwhile bridge traffic was searched by hand, resulting in the confiscation of several tons of nail clippers. There followed a seven percent drop in GNP as eighteen-wheelers backed up for weeks.

In West Virginia near Bluefield, Joe-Hog Tiller lived on a hard-scrabble farm consisting of twenty acres of vertical rock. He was called Joe-Hog because he'd get drunk and try to ride a massive boar-hog he kept in his back yard. Joe-Hog was a big man, so it was an even match, but it puzzled the boar greatly. Just beyond his front yard was a tiny rill crossed by an old stone bridge.

He sat on his front porch, sipping a glass of local liquor, and watched as federal construction crews put in barracks, an inspection booth, and a concrete pad for the non-mutagenic film-safe x-ray machine.

"Don't make no damn sense," said Joe-Hog "Creek ain't but three feet wide. Got no water 'cept when it rains."

FBI agents overheard this, noted his name, and began a background investigation of Joe-Hog. An official of the newly federalized bridge police told the press, "Our mandate is to protect bridges against the Tankers of Terror. Whether they are in danger is irrelevant. In law-enforcement, purpose is no substitute for thoroughness."

Thanks to Joe-Hog, Congress began hearings on a bill to broaden the Patriotic Waterways Act to include gullies. "The Tankers of Terror will strike where we least expect it," said the head of the new agency. "Where would you less expect a tanker than in a dry gulch in West Virginia?" The logic was irrefutable.

The President agreed, having just approved plans for the minaret being added to the White House. "We cannot leave America's waterways unprotected merely because there is no water in them. Dry rivers are rivers too." Everyone agreed that it was no end presidential, conveying undirected resolve without meaning anything.

Progress came on other fronts. Rashid Ali Fata Bakh was arrested in Paris with his brother Saladin. This caused confusion in the Southern United States, where Saladin Fata Bakh was mistaken for a menu item. The suggestion was made that with a little corn bread, it might be all right and, if not, you could sell it to Yankees. Both Fata Bakhs fought extradition on the grounds of freedom of religious expression. The State Department backed off and ordered several thousand copies of the Koran for Embassy libraries.

The United States, roused by the attack, struck back hard. The Pentagon assembled a force of aircraft carriers, heavy bombers, and cruise missiles, and sent them to destroy three mud huts spotted in the mountains of Yemen. "We are sending a message to the Axes of Evil and the Tankers of Terrorism," the President told the nation, apparently confusing the Navy with Western Union. 'We will destroy all terrorists in…you know. That place over there. Yemen. Whether there are any or not." On hearing this, the Chinese evacuated their embassy in Sanaa.

Meanwhile the FBI arrested Joe-Hog and interrogated him for thirty-seven hours. Asked why by the press, a spokesman for the bureau said, "He's a person of interest."

"What does that mean?"

"Nothing. It just has a nice rhythm to it."

The reporter muttered to himself that the spokesman had an IQ smaller than J. Edgar Hoover's dress size and stomped off.

Left-wing critics in the press pointed out that the Golden Gate had been destroyed by a tanker going under it, so why were the bridge police searching cars going over bridges? Had a Tanker of Terror, or any other kind, been spotted going over a bridge? A spokesman for the NTSB responded that since most bridges didn't have tankers going under them, it was impossible to inspect them. Cars however were available. "In real-life police work, you have to use what you have," he said.

Similarly, since the guilty terrorists were in Paris, supervising the new Islamic Studies program at the Embassy, law-enforcement had to make do with available suspects. On the afternoon of the following Wednesday, twenty-three federal agents descended on the trailer of Joe-Hog's girlfriend, Even-Dozen Throckmorton, usually called E.D. She got her name from having twelve toes, a consequence of the state's habit of festive inbreeding. When the agents left, her trailer was wrecked—contents of drawers on the floor, backs ripped of pictures. "It was awful," opined a neighbor. "It looked like a bachelor lived there."

E.D. filed an insurance claim, attributing the wreckage to tornado damage, and got a new trailer with the proceeds. Joe-Hog commented, "We oughta just send those feddle boys to search Iraq. Wouldn't be nothin' left." E.D. booked surgery to have her excess toes removed. It didn't pay, she said, to be an interesting person.

CHAPTER 35

Small Poxes: A Study of Left and Right

I am trying to understand Liberals and Conservatives. It isn't easy. I think I've about got it, though.

Conservatives believe in the wisdom of common Americans to manage their affairs and make decisions for themselves. Exceptions to this are the half of the public who regularly vote Democratic. These common Americans are unfit to run their affairs and make decisions for themselves. It is because they have been deluded by liberal propaganda.

Like conservatives, liberals believe in the inherent wisdom of common Americans, especially those who don't have any. They think that the mother lode of wisdom lies on the low side of the bell curve. They discern qualities in the stupid, ignorant, and shiftless that engender a capacity to govern a country they can't spell. Coincidentally, these people vote Democratic.

Liberals do not believe in the wisdom of the half of the country who vote Republican, as these are all CEOs of major corporations. The Left knows that CEOs, unlike welfare recipients, are motivated by economic interest.

Conservatives believe that it is not the business of government to legislate morality, and thus favor laws against abortion, pornography, sex education, and marijuana. Liberals don't want to legislate morality either. They want to eliminate it, along with learning, thought, civility, and other impediments to the undisturbed enjoyment of uniform mental darkness.

(A third point of view is held by Libertarians, but I'm not sure what it is. I have never been able to distinguish Libertarianism from a bull session in a sophomore dorm.)

The Right believes passionately in freedom, particularly economic freedom. The conservative therefore cherishes his right to strip-mine Appalachia. He does not, however, believe in your right to build a hog-rendering plant next to his house. That would violate zoning laws.

The Left believes in economic freedom too, specifically the unalienable right of the shiftless to be supported by someone else. Oddly, the someone else is usually a conservative businessman.

Now, confusion is essential to politics. Just as third-world countries regularly mistake incompetence for socialism, liberals mistake peasantry for equality. Thus they promote the decline of civilization with the enthusiasm of Crusaders sacking Jerusalem, making us into dim comfortable serfs ungrammatically grunting.

Conservatives also are subject to confusion. They regard unrestricted rapacity as a virile expression of freedom, like being in George Washington's army, and so favor reproductive incontinence, overbuilding, and the making of anything slow enough to be caught into dog food.

In short, Left and Right both strain to make the world unlivable, with liberals degrading the human world and conservatives, the natural. We can work together if only we try.

Economically, conservatives say that if it ain't broke, don't fix it. Liberals say that if it ain't broke, tax it till it is. The economic philosophy of conservatives is to take what they can get. The liberal philosophy is also to take what conservatives can get, and use it to buy votes. This is a form of trickle-down. Consequently liberals are seen to be Reaganites. The study of politics is endlessly enlightening.

Race is a major divide between Left and Right. Conservatives don't give a wan emaciated damn about blacks, whom they regard in electoral terms as the equivalent of a golf handicap. This distinguishes them from liberals, who don't give a damn about blacks, but find it useful to pretend. Blacks don't give a damn about blacks either, or they would cause their children to do their homework. In this tripartite agreement we may have the seeds of national accord.

Racially, the underlying difference between Left and Right is that the liberal policy is active, the conservative passive. Conservatives are content to do nothing and let blacks rot. So, usually, are blacks. Liberals make *sure* that blacks rot by promoting bastardy as a birthright and illiteracy as a credential of cultural authenticity. Otherwise blacks might make money and vote Republican.

However, liberals and conservatives agree on one thing. When their first child reaches school age, they head for the white suburbs. The difference is that while conservatives admit to each other that they are avoiding black schools, liberals say that they seek the wide open spaces or want their little boy to be near the hockey rink.

The Right opposes abortion as being murder when someone else's sixteen-year-old is pregnant by a tattooed drifter with a guitar and a vanishing IQ. This is why Roe-vs.-Wade will never be repealed: Conservatives also have daughters. Conservatives do think that abortion should be legal in cases of rape and incest, making it acceptable to murder children whose fathers behaved badly.

While conservatives see abortion as murder, liberals see murder as convenience. If a woman changes her mind twelve seconds before giving birth to a perfectly healthy baby, liberals want a doctor to kill it for her. Presumably it takes a curious sort of doctor, but that is another matter.

Left and Right differ in social consciousness. Liberals oppose elitism, and send their children to Harvard to avoid it. Conservatives support elitism, and send their children to Harvard to practice it. By elitism, the liberal elite mean that everyone but themselves should live in a uniform state of social and moral degradation. The conservative means by elitism the view that the better is preferable to the worse. He dislikes degradation, in part because it invariably produces Democrats.

Liberals like government because it enables them to misbehave. Conservatives believe that the best government is the least government. The perfect government is therefore no government. Thus conservatives are seen to be anarchists, like Bakunin.

Conservatives oppose the intrusion of government into private life, which explains why the Republican administration of Bush II is rapidly turning the United States into a surveillance state. Yet the leftist American Civil Liberties Union opposes the creeping advance of the unblinking eye. This might seem puzzling. Actually we are witnessing the formation of a hybrid system: The wretched political aims of communist regimes pursued by efficient capitalist means. No communist state could make computers good enough for the new watched hive. (I think of this convergence as Bimeddlism.)

Left and Right work together more often than you might think. Hollywood, the home of freewheeling unprincipled capitalism, is also the wellhead of the socially destructive social agendas of the left. The movie industry grows rich by promoting promiscuity, violence, and the use of drugs. Then its denizens appear on television to denounce the chaos they have engendered, blaming it on capitalism and conservatives.

OK. I've understood all the politics I can handle today. I need a drink, or maybe anesthesia. I know a bartender who has knockout drops.

CHAPTER 36

America Builds a Dream World.
And Moves into It

Today, news for people who are surprised by sunrise: The Associated Press reports that Marie G. Davis Middle School, of Charlotte, North Carolina, when given the chance to segregate itself racially, did. Some federal court, in a fit of intelligence, said that you couldn't force parents to bus children to schools politically acceptable to Washington. The school, 44% white the summer before the court made its decision, was that fall 5% white.

The whites went away. I'm all astonished, like I am when teenagers think about sex.

Of course the school resegregated. Any fool could have told you it would. Fact is, the races just don't want to be around each other. It's plain as a sore toe in tight shoes. If you watch what the races do, instead of listen to what the talking heads say they ought to do, you can see that both sides would rather live with hung-over alligators. But you get fired if you notice it, so we all look the other way and act like we're thinking about something else. ("Naw, I didn't see the sun rise. What sun?")

We talk about the American dream, but the country likes delusions better. We believe things are what we insist they are. If we think a pup-dog oughta be a backhoe, we figure all we gotta do is say he is, and act like we really *really* believe it, and lie, and make everybody pretend, and maybe put diesel oil in his dog bowl—and he'll sprout a scoop and start cutting underground telephone cables. It doesn't matter if everybody knows it's a lie, if you can make them pretend, and put them in jail if they don't. It's as American as tortillas.

Think about it. Where do black and white get together on purpose? I mean, without the police, national guard, federal marshals, judges, seven thousand laws, and the entire federal government, to make them? Answer: They don't. Give people the slightest say about who they want to be with, and they're gone. That's what happened in Charlotte, isn't it?

People like being with their own. Always have, always will. When you force them to be together instead of giving them the choice, then you get trouble. The less they have in common, the more trouble you get. Then you can holler about racism and squash folks together even more. It's like Prohibition, making people do what they don't want, because you think they ought to want it.

When black kids come into a white college, the first thing they do is want black dorms and black fraternities, and the white kids don't seem in much of a hurry to catch them and bring them back. It's how it always is. When I was a military reporter, the blacks on base wanted soul music at the club, and the whites wanted country and western. The blacks got the club because the commander was afraid of them. The whites went to town to listen to Merle Haggard. Which may or may not have been a reasonable choice, but it's what they did.

Go to a party of a hundred rich, white, unrelentingly good, racially correct people in Washington, and you will find three blacks to shuffle and look embarrassed and be credentials. The ninety-seven white people will make a point of talking awkwardly to them so everybody will know they are not prejudiced. Ask the whites in a loud voice where their kids go to school.

Do you see more whites at black parties? I don't know. I've never been to one. It's a segregated country.

How about at work? It's a snake pit, with the federal government making it hang together, barely. Best I can tell, blacks figure they're getting discriminated against, and oppressed, and enslaved. Whites—regularly, invariably, everywhere, every time—say most blacks don't work, have attitudes, advance entirely on pigmentation, and you have to do their work for them. You could argue about who is right, but that's just it: Neither side gets along well with the other, except when threatened.

Now, the AP story carefully avoided the crucial question about the escape from Charlotte: Why did the white parents instantly withdraw their kids from a black school when given a whiff of freedom? The writer implied that Charlotte, being in the South, was prejudiced, and that racism was behind the flight, snore. Reporters everywhere understand what they are paid to say, but I don't think his heart was in it.

Let me suggest another reason, which I have not verified. Should I be wrong, I will happily say so, and eat Jim Crow. But, knowing as I do the inveracity of the media, I will speculate.

I suggest that the black students at the school were academically far below the whites—that the white parents were trying to do something, anything, to keep their children at an intellectual level consistent with their notions of civilization. I suspect that the black students had no interest in European history, in mathematics, languages, chemistry. I don't say they should be interested, just that they pretty regularly aren't. If I am wrong, I will happily retract. Show me. I'd love to be wrong.

Maybe I am. It may be that academic performance of blacks at Marie G. Davis Middle School refutes the aggregate experience of centuries, of daily observation and common intuition. And Elvis may materialize in my room tonight and sing Heartbreak Hotel. I'd like that. Even stranger things could happen. The Redskins could win.

But I'm not betting the Vette.

Further, I will bet that the black kids ganged up and pushed the white kids around. It may not be universal, but an awful lot of white kids report it.

Now, maybe all this shouldn't ought to be true. And maybe pup-dogs ought to grow exhaust stacks and glow plugs. Thing is, sooner or later "shouldn't ought" runs into "is."

The reality is that if it weren't for unrelenting compulsion and intimidation, the races would separate like newly weds five years later. Without affirmative action and the EEO police, offices would barely be integrated. Schools, if parents were free, would do what Charlotte did. The whole lash-up is compulsory, artificial, contrived, and almost nobody wants it.

If you don't think so, drop the compulsion and wait five minutes.

No, I don't know what to do about it, except hide. My best guess is let people live how they want and hire people on merit. But that's not the American way.

Gotta run. Elvis just showed up.

CHAPTER 37

Monolith Over Harvard, Foundations of Civilization Shaken

I am informed by the Harvard *Crimson* that the boys among the studentry recently fashioned a large penis from snow on the grounds of the university. Grave consequences ensued. A great squealing arose, as if a Victorian spinster had found a man under her bed. There was righteousness enough to gag Jonathan Edwards. Feminists made solemn asses of themselves. It was a splendid show and a good time was had by all.

The—I will avoid all the obvious plays on words—construction of the offending organ was the sort of tasteless, crass, immature, natural, and entertaining thing that college boys are supposed to do. I wish I had thought of it. The reasonable response would have been for the administration to take it down and go about their business of mismanaging the school.

But no. The feminists among Hahvad's girl chillun promptly got their knickers in a bunch over the chill appendage. (The frigid attacking the frigid.) (Wait. No, I promised I wouldn't do that.) But then, perhaps the uproar represented progress. These basilisks being what they are, I'm surprised they recognized the thing.

As in all affairs involving feminism, language was the first casualty. One Amy Keel, class of '04, opined, "As a feminist, pornography is degrading to women and creates a violent atmosphere," which implies either that pornography is a feminist or that Amy wasn't paying a lot of attention in sixth-grade English. No, Amy, pornography does not create a violent atmosphere.

She then proceeded to pull rank by claiming to be a "rape survivor." This is a show-stopper for feminists, for whom it is a stock in trade. They cherish rape as a tobacconist does tobacco. The least of them, which is all of them, can quote statistics showing that seven out of every three women have been raped in the last minute and a half. To doubt the veracity of such a traumatized girl would be terribly insensitive and few men will essay it. Which is the reason for the claim.

Now, I know nothing of Amy, except that she speaks estrogenated Marxigunch. Yet I notice that an awful lot of feminettes parade themselves as rape veterans, and brandish their status as a political broadsword. Given that they tend to be phenomenal liars, in such cases it might be prudent to respond, "Yes. No doubt. You can show me the police report, I suppose. Otherwise the skeptical might think you had awarded yourself a Purple Heart. We wouldn't want that."

(Their response would be, "It was so destructive to my self-esteem that I didn't report it." Then, often, they tell newspapers about it. I can hardly think of a better way to keep a secret.)

Continuing her analysis of the snowy projection, Amy said, "Men think they have the right to force that on you. It's a logical extension." No doubt the sculpture was an extension of sorts, but...logical? The adjective would not have occurred to me.

Amy, with a roommate in support, assaulted the protuberance with the intention of deconstructing it. "A few people came out and crowded me with their bodies and one person shoved me away from the penis," she said. "It was gendered violence, because [their comments] were said in the context of our gender and accompanied by aggressive actions toward us."

As silly cant and boilerplate prudery, Amy's approximations of thoughts are amusing, but the undercurrent of prissy sexual fear depresses. When I was a college boy, the girls would have laughed, rolled their eyes and said, "Guys. What can you do with them?" and perhaps made invidious comparisons concerning their boyfriends. Then they would have wandered off and done something constructive. Study, even.

Understandably people get tired of "When I was a kid" wisdom. Yet there is a relevance. The girls of rural Virginia in 1962 were emotionally hardy, perfectly able to handle boys, seldom depressed, and couldn't have achieved neurosis with a bird dog and a buzz saw. As far as I know, the word "self-esteem" didn't exist. Anorexia and bulimia hadn't been invented, and would have found no market. Within the limits of the shocks the flesh is heir to, girls were happy and psychically sound. So were boys.

What happened? Those who devote their young lives to looking in closets and being perpetually angry when they have no reason for doing so, who seem devoured by pointless anxiety actively courted, cannot be happy.

Adolescence is not the exclusive province of the adolescent, though it loses its appeal in those beyond its proper ambit. Saith the *Crimson*, Harvard has a lecturer in Women's Studies called Diane Rosenfeld, who teaches Women, Violence and the Law. (Remember when Harvard was a university?) Said Diane, "The ice sculpture was erected in a public space, one that should be free from menacing reminders of women's sexual vulnerability…Women do not need to be reminded of the power of the symbol of the male genitalia. My guess is that they are constantly reminded of it in daily messages."

One imagines a long line of FedEx employees rushing up with the messages.

The solemnity of the incorrigibly absurd is perhaps its own punishment. I hope so. But whence the "sexual vulnerability"? The sorrow of my life in college was the lack of such vulnerability.

My guess is this. The sexual vulnerability of women springs not from rapists but from having been made by feminists into easy sexual game. When I was coming up, college girls could say "yes," and frequently did. But they didn't have to. They could choose whether, when, and with whom. The Pill existed, but society had not decayed to the point that a girl almost had to use it.

The rules changed, but women didn't. Under the old rules, a male had to stick around if he wanted sex. Since he was going to be around for a while, he chose someone he really liked. Sex was a wonderful idea, and always a possibility, but not the heart of things.

Under the new rules, the woman has to provide sex in advance to have any hope of anything else, because there is always someone else who will say yes. Among young males, the sex drive trumps everything if women let it. Today, waving the flag of liberation, they do. They still want respect, romance, commitment, and marriage. Yes, many will furiously deny it. Date them a few years later. But feminism and contraception have turned the tables not so much in favor of men, as in favor of sex over all else.

The effect has been to commoditize women, to make them into, yes, sex objects. One day they will come shrink-wrapped.

CHAPTER 38

Hooking with a Press Card: A Harlot's Progress

This is an annoyance column, perhaps of little interest. But I'm going to write it anyway. It's what columnists do.

In the *Washington Post* for November 28 I found this lead, by James Grimaldi, about the team of inspectors who will ransack Iraq: "The United Nations launched perhaps its most important weapons inspections ever yesterday with a team that includes a 53-year-old Virginia man with no specialized scientific degree and a leadership role in sadomasochistic sex clubs."

Jack McGeorge. The story, a hatchet job disguised as news, was picked up by television. The US is sending perverted amateurs to Iraq. Gosh.

I met Jack over fifteen years ago when I was writing a military column for Universal Press Syndicate. I then knew perhaps a dozen—"defense intellectuals" was the phrase. Some worked for beltway bandit outfits that did studies for the Pentagon. Some were independent consultants. They were exceedingly bright. I don't mean that they were valedictorians in high school or could have qualified for Mensa. Their baseline IQ was probably 160. They didn't socialize with reporters, whom they tended to regard as unprincipled fools. If they liked you, they were splendid sources and good company.

One such was Don Walsh, a friend of mine now in Bangkok. Don, a former research chemist, knew more about small arms than anyone else I had ever met, and had an encyclopedic grasp of a dozen subjects. I knew the names of various weaponized gases. Don could jot the syntheses on the back of an envelope.

I needed a quotable source on gas warfare. Don suggested Jack as very good. Don doesn't think many people are very good.

Jack turned out to be as smart as Don. He wasn't pretentious about it (it isn't easy to be pretentious when you look like the Pillsbury Doughboy), but it was there. His knowledge of the military, weaponry, demolitions, chemical and biological warfare was enormous. His company, Public Safety Group, specialized in counter-terrorism.

If you look at his CV, you will see that he was a Marine Corps demolitions technician, worked for the Secret Service at the White House level, and studied at nuclear-weapons school. You will then note years when he doesn't seem to have been doing much. If you were a reporter for the *Washington Post* and sufficiently stupid, which are associated conditions, you might assume he was unemployed. Grimaldi implies as much.

I wouldn't bet the college funds. When people work in fields that require security clearances, they usually have blank spots in their resumes. They don't talk about them. It doesn't mean they weren't working.

Now, why is the *Post* attacking him? Partly because Grimaldi isn't very good at what he does.

Reporters seldom know much about technical subjects. My military coverage coincided with Reagan's administration. I covered the same stories and went to the same bases and briefings as did the *Post*'s military reporters. With the occasional exception, they ran from incompetent to virtual idiots. Men in the Pentagon feared them, yet had to breast-feed them. They didn't know military history, tactics, weaponry, hadn't been in the military. Reporters enjoy power without responsibility. Think of a six-year-old with a large-caliber pistol.

I used to wonder why they were so bad, and speculated about pedestrian mentalities or narrow mental horizons. A friend of mine, a long-time writer, said, "Fred. They're stupid. That's all." It isn't literally true. It is close enough.

Grimaldi has neither the brains nor the knowledge to judge McGeorge's qualifications. (If he did, he would have.) Reporters who do not know their subjects become prisoners of their sources or, too often, source. He's writing what he was told by someone with an agenda.

As for the S&M business: It's true, though I'm not sure what sexual predilections have to do with inspecting weapons. Grimaldi is attempting character assassination by horrifying irrelevancy. He would not write, "Michael Baritone, a notorious homosexual, joined the Washington Ballet...." He wants do hurt Jack.

How much should we care about sexual behavior privately engaged in?

When I met Jack, I had heard of kinky sex, but had never encountered it. I said so. He invited me to a couple of parties and a bus trip to the old Vault in New York (where I once stood at a urinal next to Danny the Wonder Pony in full tack. Life is nothing if not interesting).

I expected the macabre and ghastly, stray organs lying wetly on tables, a collection of budding Jeffy Dahmers. No. This was suburban hobbyist S&M, games for otherwise ordinary bureaucrats and programmers who wanted to be paddled by their girlfriends, or vice versa. An S&M party looks like a Batman convention and smells like a storage room for saddles. The effect on me was like that of a Monster Truck Show: Interesting once, but then more of the same. I concluded that they were as dangerous as a bridge club.

In any big city, there's a sprawling sexual underground of people doing everything you've heard of and much you probably haven't. You've got gay bars, leather bars, lesbian dens, nudists, kinks, swingers, transvestites in both directions, surgically altered transsexuals, and men of thirty-five who like to wear diapers and frilly hats and drink from baby bottles. When I rode with the DC cops, around Ninth and M you found incredibly ugly guys who looked like running backs, wearing thong bikinis and size fifty high heels. There are sena-

tors quietly notorious for being whipped, important officials who wear linge-
rie.

Maybe I should care. But I don't.

Now, did the *Post* lead with the S&M angle from a principled aversion to per-
version?

No. Unless things have changed since last I looked, the paper's Style section, a
cutesy-sweetsie confection of middle-school puns and saccharine English, is
gay as an Easter bonnet. Gays are heavily into kinky sex, Lesbians being closer
to Jeffreyette Dahmers than the men. The paper usually covers up the more
grotesque aspects of gay marches on the Mall that would not play well with
respectable America. It definitely isn't opposed to twistedness. Grimaldi simply
recognized it as a character bludgeon.

But why the attack?

A friend's explanation: "Some candidate who didn't get selected for
UNMOVIC—apparently a former inspector—is pissed that he/she was passed
over in favor of Jack and is feeding this crap to the Post. Purely a rice bowl
issue."

Sounds about right. When reporters don't know much, don't really have
sources, don't have time or interest to find things out, they make easy marks
for leak artists and slant mechanics. Grimaldi, methinks, was a convenient
whore. He got used.

CHAPTER 39

Existence as Probable Cause

I'm trying to understand the Feddle Gummint. It's hard going, like driving a '53 Chevy through mud. Maybe it's because I grew up in the country, and wasn't very smart, and mostly studied my lunchbox. I never learned to understand things that didn't make sense.

Especially the Supreme Court.

Anyone who took civics in high school knows the Gummint is divided into five pieces: the media, the Supreme Court, Congress, the bureaucracy, and the president, pretty much in that order. And the Supreme Court is supposed to say whether the Constitution reckons a law is all right. That way no slick lawyer can slip in laws that make us into Comminist robots. At least, that's what this teacher lady told us.

I'm not sure it's working.

Somewhere I saw that there was a Supreme Court decision in 1896 called Plessey vs. Ferguson, about Negroes and white people, that said separate but equal was constitutional. They didn't say we had to do it. They just said it was fine with the Constitution.

Then in 1954 in Brown vs. the School Board, they said it wasn't constitutional.

Same Constitution.

I must be slow. I don't see how exactly the same Constitution can say exactly different things unless the court is just making them up as it goes along, and telling everyone the Constitution says so. That way we have to do whatever they say or the police get us. Like in Russia.

When the Court makes some decision that shows it hasn't got the judgment God gave a crabapple, which is usually, lawyers always talk about what the intent was of the Foundering Fathers. I guess that's reasonable. They wrote the Constitution, so if anybody knows what it means, it must be them. That's what those nine funny-looking apparitions in Washington are for: to figure out what the intent was.

Thing is, any fool can tell what the Fathers meant by looking at what they did.

Like the Second Amendment, that says, "A well regulated militia, being necessary to the security of a free state, the right of the people to keep and bear arms, shall not be infringed." They hadn't really figured out commas back then. Everybody argues like crazy about what "militia" meant, and did the Fathers really mean that everybody ought to be able to have guns, and it sounds all solemn and serious.

It ain't.

Back then, everyone and his Aunt Polly had guns, and all their pigs and chickens, and some tadpoles. The Foundling Fathers knew it. So did the Supreme Court. Nobody ever got upset about it. It never occurred to anyone that it was unconstitutional.

If the Fathers had intended something different, they'd have done something different.

It's the same with separation of church and state. Everybody knows that the Fathers didn't want the church to be the gummint, the way it usually was if somebody like Philip II was president. But did they mean that you couldn't have Christmas in school or sing Christmas carols on a public road? Of course not. In those days everybody put up mangers with Mary and Joseph in them and said prayers just about everywhere, especially if someone was looking, and nobody noticed it was unconstitutional. It only got that way recently.

What I think about the Court is, I'd rather be ruled by inbred possums.

Everybody knows why the Fathers stuffed freedom of speech into the Bill of Rights. It was because most of Europe was misruled by useless kings who whored around with courtesans and probably with the palace animals and were usually drunk and feebleminded and bought stupid jewels that looked like glass doorknobs with money they squeezed out of the peasants. And if anybody didn't like it and said so, he got burned at the stake.

So the Fathers wanted to protect *political* speech. That way when the president wanted to make people into robots they could say they didn't think so, not today. And they would have guns. Guns are a swell form of political expression.

Not now, though. The Court decided the First Amendment was about Expression, and dancing was expression, and nekkid dancing was even more expression, especially if it was on TV where children could watch it. So was all the outhouse language you hear in a low pool hall when everybody's drunk.

If the Fathers meant we had to watch Dottie Does Dallas, how come nobody noticed it, including them, until after 1950?

Ain't it something? Tom Jefferson was too dim to know what he meant his own self, and needs nine withered frauds to tell him. I guess that makes sense. Like rust cutter on doughnuts.

But if you work for the Feddle Gummint—well, this ain't a column about miracles but I mean if you get paid by the gummint—and you make a political statement about affirmative action and shiftlessness, and how you have to do your job and how come they don't, why, you get fired. That *is* political speech.

What it looks like is political speech is getting to be illegal but rutting like farm animals on TV at dinnertime is pretty near a constitutional duty. That's what Ben Franklin wanted, I guess.

Last I heard, the Fourth Amendment said, "The right of the people to be secure in their persons, houses, papers, and effects, against unreasonable searches and seizures, shall not be violated, and no warrants shall issue, but upon probable cause, supported by oath or affirmation, and particularly describing the place to be searched, and the persons or things to be seized."

The intent's as plain as warts on Marie Antoinette. But now the Pentagon is going to spy on everybody's email and bank accounts and credit cards because there might be a terrorist somewhere in the world, and if a ninety-six year old Christian woman in a wheel chair wants to fly on an airplane the feddle police will body search her and now they're going to open all our suitcases to check out our books and sex toys and whether our clothes are clean. That's reasonable?

When I was a kid my teacher always said I was special and she hoped I'd go a long way, though I think she'd have been satisfied with the next county. Well, I hope she meant I was special dumb, because if I understand the Supreme Court right, they're only riverboat card-sharpers in Zorro suits. Just about nothing the Court makes us do ever occurred to the Fathers. Mostly it's what they were trying to get away from.

Those grifters are making it up. That's all.

CHAPTER 40

War. Maybe We Could Go Bowling Instead

Wars are seductive as women in the night. Past midnight in February of 1967 we stood, the platoon and I, on the flight line at El Toro Marine Air Station, gateway to Asia. On the tarmac big jets howled and moaned. The smell of burned jet fuel blew in the Pacific breeze. We felt the exhilaration of being part of something huge moving in the darkness, of going to the action, of leaving the mundane. The attraction of war verges on the lascivious. It gets into your blood.

And so we went. Young men always go. Always there is another war. Always there are reasons. In the past these were straightforward: lust, booty, excitement, empire, a way to escape the family yurt, sheer joyous combativeness, the king was bored. Not much has changed.

Long hours later we landed in the sweltering sauna of Danang with its gun emplacements and fwop-fwopping helo traffic and sun-baked Marines with slung rifles; 105s boomed in the distance. It was, in the vulgar but irreplaceable expression of the times, a mind-fuck. We weren't back on the block combing our hair for Sally Sue and facing a career at the NAPA outlet. We were real soldiers, who couldn't find Vietnam on a map, fighting VC who couldn't find Vietnam on a map. We didn't reflect on this. Marines fought. Somebody else decided who they fought.

Perspectives change. Later, for veterans who no longer had legs or eyes, who had lost their guts or become paras and quads, the splendor dimmed. I came home in a packed Medevac 141 with a guy slung above me sprouting tubes that led into bags. He died en route. Those who survived soon realized that in six months no one would care what they had gone through, yet they would spend the rest of their lives in the wheel chair. A colostomy bag, they found, was not a great conversation piece in a singles bar. For them, the war never went away.

Spend a year on a casualty ward. When the girlfriend of seventeen from Chattanooga finds that her Mikey is blind and doesn't precisely have a face, her expression is something to see. Or not to see. You can become disposed to ask: Is this war for anything? Or is it just a war?

Mostly they are just wars. Vietnam was just a war. We lost, and nothing happened. You might be surprised how many in the Disabled American Veterans quietly hate those who sent them. Yes, I will get angry mail, from those fiercest of warriors, the 103rd Combat Virgins Division, *grrr, bow-wow, woof,* telling that that I am a commie and a coward and wear lace underwear. I'm impressed in advance.

Later, as a reporter, I spent a year between Saigon and Phnom Penh, leaving both cities with their evacuations. The Asia I saw in the complex warren off Truong Minh Ky was not the Asia of the GIs. It was complex, variegated, enduring. I liked the Vietnamese. I still do. I am glad that we killed only a million or three of them.

This you must never say. Wars are better if you don't look too closely. Never, ever, think about what is actually happening.

The Americans believed, or said they believed, that we were battling the evil of communism to save the Vietnamese, who wouldn't even help. To this day former GIs hate the Viets for not being enthusiastic about the war, which in fact they weren't. They wanted the war to go away so they could grow rice.

The Right thunders and the Left squeaks over the motives of the war, each bleeding cataracts of virtue. I remember the succinct analysis of a Vietnamese girlfriend I lived with: "At night, VC steal our rice. In morning, Marines kill us for give rice VC."

They were ambivalent about having a half million gringos running around their country and blowing things up, such as themselves. The GIs never understood. They didn't know that when an artillery round killed a villager's wife, all the young men picked up rifles.

After the GIs left Saigon I returned to Southeast Asia as a reporter for *Army Times*. For a while I lived in a rooftop apartment on Jawaharlal Nehru Street in Phnom Penh with Steve Hedder, a young stringer for *Time*, and his Khmer wife Devi. With us were the twins, pretty, playful girls of sixteen perhaps who spoke reasonable English. They were the people with soft hands that Pol Pot would kill.

At night the smell of charcoal and flower trees drifted from neighboring roofs and people murmured in Khmer. Reporters—mostly stringers—lay on the roofs in a fog of gin and Nembutal and listened to the rockets whistle in from the swamps. When the KR took over, Steve and Devi got out. The twins didn't. I don't know how they died.

I will be told I have a bad attitude. You bet I do.

Years later I went back on a magazine assignment, and saw Toul Sleng. Once a high school in Phnom Penh, it was used by the KR as a place of torture. It had become a museum. On the walls were photos of those who died there. I couldn't remember the lone Caucasian's name, but I had seen him around town. A friend of mine who went back found the picture of his girlfriend.

Another time I returned to Vietnam, again on assignment. In Saigon the Continental Shelf was glassed in and air-conditioned, not necessarily an improvement. For two weeks I worked my way upcountry from Saigon to Vung Tau, Nha Trang, Hue, to Danang, near where I had been stationed. Marble Mountain had become a pleasant tourist stop with shops selling stone carvings.

Further north, Hanoi bustled with shops and the insane but invisibly ordered traffic of Asia. My pretty little governmentally-supplied guide asked whether I wanted to see the Ho Chi Minh museum. I said I'd rather have my teeth pulled.

Oh, she said, apparently relieved, then let's just look at the city. We did. Nice place. I tried to remember what the war had been about.

As I say, it gets into your blood. For a couple of decades I worked as a military reporter. I liked the travel, the troops, the airplanes and ships. Eventually it wore thin. Over and over, in some place like remote Olancho province in Honduras, or Cuando Cubango in Angola, or this dusty clearing or that dusty clearing, the press would chopper out to be shown The Great Victory.

In the jungle would be three or four bedraggled bodies of teenagers fighting a shabby war for some dismal Marxist cause they couldn't spell, and a trove of captured weapons—couple of AKs, the stray M-16, maybe a FN/FAL or Galil. We were told it was progress. Some great cause was being served. Maybe it was. I got tired of seeing it.

Plus ca change, the more it doesn't.

CHAPTER 41

Worlds and Worlds

Last year I dove for a week on a live-aboard dive boat, the Caribbean Explorer. She's big and sleek, out of St. Maarten in the Netherlands Antilles, set up for luxurious diving with compressors, diving stations and a superb crew. She runs at night from dive site to dive site while the divers sleep. You eat, dive, off-gas on the sundeck, and dive again. Capitol Divers, my raffish semi-cowboy dive club out of Washington, had chartered the beast in her entirety. They're experienced, rowdy, bull-headed, addicted to outrageous practical jokes (but that's another story) and splendid company.

My motives were an assignment from *Soldier of Fortune*, for which I am the scuba editor, and a desire to spice up the column with far places and exotic climes. Maybe more the latter. Every time I go anywhere off the main roads of existence, readers want to know what's out there. Many seem quietly unhappy with their lives and looking for escape. Even in a rattle-trap web column. It's, if not quite sad, then poignant.

On my return I found myself talking about diving to a group of Washingtonians, nice people but sedentary by the nature of their jobs. I told them about the islands, where life is slow and hot and dominated by the ocean and people usually don't have a lot of money or much of a career, but don't seem to care.

A faraway look came into their eyes, not so much envy as longing. Gosh, they said, some of them, I've always wanted to do something like that, but…well, I got married, the kids came, responsibilities. They seemed to feel trapped, to suspect that a train had pulled out with them aboard that they didn't want, that life somehow had promised more than it was delivering. Some of this is to be expected. Some, I think, comes from a sense of the emptiness of the remote suburbs that dominate America now.

The particulars of the undesired train differ. Many had just followed the crowd. They got out of school, took a job thinking it was just for a while, moved into a huge mortgage they found they didn't much like, bought two cars that bored them, and got trapped by the retirement system. Others, less attractive, were ambitious, worked eighty hour weeks to make partner, dressing in K-Street fatigues from Brooks Brothers to claw their way onto a pinnacle that, when arrived at, seemed more a depression.

There are pinnacles and pinnacles. You have to decide which ones you want. There's a doozy in the waters somewhere off St. Maarten. I encountered it one morning near Statia, if memory serves. Everyone geared up and went overboard. The water was warm, endlessly blue, a delight. A giant stride off the dive deck, a profusion of bubbles, and you float like thistledown in another place entirely. I never get tired of it. I hung on the mooring line at fifteen feet and waited. The other divers exploded from above and we buddied up. We started down.

Near ninety feet, where light begins to fail and the sea becomes chalky blue in the distance, we found the top of The Finger (I called it), an enormous rock spire dropping way deep and having no discernible reason for existence. It was just there, encrusted in the twisted growths that look grey and brown in the dying color of beginning depth.

I stayed above 110 feet to save bottom time and just drifted around the thing. I wondered why I didn't live in the islands, do this whenever I wanted. A lot of people wonder, and some of them could. A few small sharks swam by, lithe creatures of a line more ancient than ours. They were curious about the bubbling hunchbacked apparitions with huge feet, but do not regard divers as being in their food chain. In the gangrenous tangle covering the spire, in cups of barrel sponges, wee crabs squatted, little mechanical monsters waving pincers.

It beats making partner.

The islands are as much an attitude as a place. The crew of the Caribbean Explorer were expats and about par for the time and place: A Canadian gal who served as hostess, dive guide, and chief underwater videoman, her French boyfriend, a South African if memory serves, and such like. They were good people—which is also par for the islands. Folk who work with their hands, who deal with the sea and with boats and with the things in the sea have something that people don't who spend their time lying, maneuvering, stroking, and backstabbing.

Back home, as Washington then was, I'd talk about the islanders and almost always get the same response: Americans could imagine themselves living on a boat, driving into the dawn with people assembling BCs and regulators on deck, salt spray chill in the air, hearing the diesels pound—something that had some flavor, that reminded them of spring in high school. Not all: Some were happy with their lives and liked what they were doing. But so many didn't. They were just waiting.

It is a mistake to think that boatmen are crude roustabouts. You don't drive a large boat with sixteen divers far from land without being very good with boats, very good at diving, and very good at keeping a boat running. It is not the nature of boats to run. They want to break. People who can fix them, who can manage night dives without losing anyone, repair gear or invent expedients, have a self-confidence that obviates the need to be disagreeable. The pettiness of minor bureaucrats springs I think from knowledge of their innecessity and a consequent desire to push people around in the only exercise of power they will ever know.

Those worlds are out there—dive boats in the islands, cabins at Prudhoe Bay, bars in Phuket. Many of those in these places had jobs they hated in the States, got fed up, bailed out, and winged it. A friend of mine, once a high-end bond dealer, pulled over his Lexus somewhere in Massachusetts and thought, "Why the *hell* am I doing *this*?" He couldn't find an answer. He has a dive shop in Manzanillo now.

Back at St. Maarten, we gravitated to an open-sided restaurant boisterous with laughter and tropical shirts and people tanned by the sun to the color of a baseman's glove. Waiters raced about with trays of beer and fish. The afternoon light slanted in over the water. Very few there knew who the Majority Whip was. Fewer would have known what he was good for, except maybe bait.

CHAPTER 42

A Literate American. Three Years Old

How is it possible to spend twelve years in school and not be able to read? How? It is beyond me. A sheet of dry wall would be reading in less time. Yet our purported schools are regularly achieving exactly that.

Start at the beginning. The alphabet consists of all of twenty-six letters, as mysterious as potatoes. Whoopee-do. How long can it take to learn two dozen little squiggles?

A story: When my elder daughter was barely two, my wife and I came back from a junket to Russia. We were on the sofa looking at a coffee-table book from Moscow when Macon waddled in and began hollering, "Bee! Bee!" Thinking that a wasp or some related monster had invaded our sacred domestic precincts, I went into protective-male mode and prepared to make war on the beast. No wasp. No bee. Perhaps the child was delusional, or a paranoid schizophrenic.

Well, no. She was looking at a balalaika on the front of the book which looked like a lower-case B. "Hmmm," I thought with my accustomed preternatural perceptiveness. The kid appears to be on to something. She was.

I got a set of those magnetic stick-em refrigerator plastic letters and began showing them to her for five minutes a day, about all the attention span she then had. Before reaching twenty-six months, she knew all of them, upper and lower case. It is true that her pronunciational mastery lagged her alphabetic grasp. You may not know of the letter "Bubble Dew." It exists.

At three, she was reading. Yes, it was, "Billy chased the cat up the tree," not "the eschatological significance of the kerygma." Still, it was reading. It was what millions of kids who have finished school cannot do, even at the cat-and-tree level. She thought it was splendid fun. It did not occur to her that any effort was involved. Of course Daddy was making an enormous fuss over her, which was not a discouragement. Daddy is that way about his girls.

How did I bring about this onset of literacy? The same way I later did with her sister, who also was reading well before kindergarten. I told her that c said "kuh," that a said "a" and t said "tuh." Kuh-a-tuh. Cat. And look here, Pumpkin, r says "err," and if you put it in front of "at" you get err-a-tuh, rat. Ain't that something?

She agreed that it was. Indeed she received all of this occult lore with attention and no visible puzzlement. It quickly dawned on her that you could string these letter things together to express interesting thoughts. Soon she could sound out words she didn't remotely understand and, when the multitudinous exceptions and peculiarities of English intruded, she simply learned them.

I don't know. About a month.

I didn't regard this as a miracle, because it wasn't one. Kids have been learning to read practically forever. They are absorptive creatures, awash in curiosity. A couple of dozen letters, associated sounds, retentive memories, and voila! There is nothing to it. It is *easy*.

And yet somehow, inconceivably, many children never learn to read. Now that's a miracle, like levitating a '54 Merc while sober. How can you keep children from learning for twelve years what a couple of small girls learned in a month?

Another question is how kids can be kept from wanting to read. Here too we have enacted a marvel that ranks with the fishes and loaves. When I was about seven, I was a literary omnivore, coming back from the library in Westover with armloads of indiscriminately chosen everything. The Orange Book of fairy tales, the Red Book, etc., Greek mythology, Kipling, WWII, battleships, what have you. I would happily attribute this to my unparalleled brilliance if I could find evidence. Unfortunately other kids were doing the same thing.

The drug store sold Hardy Boys books, Tom Swift, the Lone Ranger, long rows of them. Presumably they weren't there exclusively for me. I remember inventing what I called "sneak reading." When supposedly I was going to sleep, I held the plug of my reading lamp just far enough into the socket to turn it on, so that I could quietly turn it off by pulling it out slightly should I hear creaking floorboards. I was fooling my parents less than I thought I was, but this revelation came later. At various times I used flashlights and candles. (Book matches don't work. I know.)

I have since learned that all sorts of kids did the same thing. So much for my uniqueness in the universe.

How do you render witless these kids who by their nature want to know everything? In the early Fifties, when I was a wee tyke, toy stores sold chemistry sets. (Gilbert. One had fifty bottles.) You did actual sort of chemistry with them. They had the alcohol lamp, test tubes, NiChrome wire for jack-leg spectroscopy, as well as cobalt chloride, phenolpthalein, sodium silicate, sodium thiosulfate, and such like. There was a sphinthariscope so you could watch radium decaying and perhaps eat it and get bone cancer, and a booklet that explained atomic structure and the difference between atomic number and atomic weight.

In toy stores. For ordinary little boys. The same stores had Gilbert microscopes for ten bucks, though mine was a fifteen-dollar better model from Edmund Scientific. I knew about well slides, cover glasses, Canada balsam, Volvox, rotifers, every bug in the garden, paramecia, planaria. Michel Duquez and I slit our wrists ever so slightly so that we could look at blood. We were not gooberish socially defective nerds obsessed with science. We had baseball mitts and comic-book collections and explored storm sewers.

School? Much better then than now. At Robert E. Lee Elementary on Lee Highway we learned more fractions and English grammar than many college graduates today know. Smart women had not yet all become useless lawyers. Yet even then schools were tedious jails, robot factories. They refused to let kids learn what they were ready to learn.

In second grade my teacher decided that I was retarded. We were reading about a family of beavers, and Mrs. Beaver had three sticks and Little Bitty Beaver had four, and how many did they have together? I didn't really care. I wanted to read my astronomy book. I guess it showed.

So a psychologist lady came from the school board and every day for a week she tested me to put me in an asylum. Could I hear and see, she wanted to know? Yes, lady, actually, and now can I read my astronomy book? She had some dimwitted tests of logic and then of vocabulary, which I had lots of because I hadn't been paying attention in school. I had been reading things. In those days school wasn't quite a place intended to keep kids from learning, but it was getting there.

Now, it has arrived, God help us. And with what a thud.

CHAPTER 43

The Consequences of Feminization

In the United States women are, I think for the first time in history, gaining real power. Often nations have had queens, heiresses, and female aristocrats. These do not amount to much. Today women occupy positions of genuine authority in fields that matter, as for example publishing, journalism, and academia. They control education through high school. Politicians scramble for their votes. They control the divorce courts and usually get their way with things that matter to them.

If this is not unprecedented, I do not know of the precedent. What will be the consequences?

Men have controlled the world through most of history so we know what they do: build things, break things, invent things, compete with each other fiercely and often pointlessly, and fight endless wars that seem to them justifiable at the time but that, seen from afar, are just what males do. The unanswered question is what women would do, or will do. How will their increasing influence reshape the polity?

Women and men want very different things and therefore very different worlds. Men want sex, freedom, and adventure; women want security, pleasantness, and someone to care about (or for) them. Both like power. Men use it to conquer their neighbors whether in business or war, women to impose security and pleasantness.

I do not suggest that the instinctive behavior of women is necessarily bad, nor that of men necessarily good. I do suggest that that the effects of the coming change will be profound, probably irreversible, and not necessarily entirely to the liking of either sex. The question may be whether one fears most being conquered or being nicened to death.

Consider what is called the Nanny State by men, who feel smothered by it, but is accepted if not supported by women, who see it as protective and caring. (Yes, I know that there are exceptions and degrees in all of this, and no, I don't have polling data.) Note that women are much more concerned than are men about health and well-being. Women worry about second-hand smoke, outlawing guns, lowering the allowable blood-alcohol levels for drivers, making little boys wear helmets while riding bicycles, and outlawing such forms of violence as dodge ball or the use of plastic ray guns. Much of this is demonstrably irrational, but that is the nature of instincts. (Neither is the male tendency to form armed bands and attack anyone within reach a pinnacle of reason.)

The implications of female influence for freedom, at least as men understand the word, are not good. Women will accept restrictions on their behavior if in doing so they feel more secure. They have less need of freedom, which is not particularly important in living a secure, orderly, routine, and comfortable life. They tend not to see political correctness as irritating or as a disturbing restriction on the freedom of speech, but as keeping people from saying unpleasant things.

The growing feminizaton accounts for much of the decline in the schools. The hostility to competition of any sort is an expression of the female desire for pleasantness; competition is a mild form of combat, by which men are attracted and women repelled. The emphasis on how children feel about each other instead of on what they learn is profoundly female (as for that matter is the associated fascination with psychotherapy). The drugging of male schoolchildren into passivity is the imposition of pleasantness by chemical means. Little boys are not nice, but fidgety wild men writ small who, bored out of their skulls, tend to rowdiness. They are also hard for the average woman to control and, since male teachers are absent, gelded, or terrified of litigious parents, expulsion and resort to the police fill the void. The oft-repeated suspension of boys for drawing soldiers or playing space war is, methinks, a quietly hysterical attempt to assuage formless insecurity.

The change in marriage and the deterioration of the family are likewise the results of the growth of political power of women. Whether this is good or bad remains to be seen, but it is assuredly happening. Divorce became common because women wanted to get out of unsatisfactory marriages. In divorce women usually want the children, and have the clout to get them. But someone has to feed the young. Thus the vindictive pursuit of divorced fathers who won't or can't pay child support. And thus the rise of the government as de facto father to provide welfare, tax breaks, daycare, and otherwise behave as a virtual husband.

When women entered a male workplace, they found that they didn't much like it. Men told off-color jokes, looked at protuberant body parts, engaged in rough verbal sparring as a form of social interaction, and behaved in accord with rules that women didn't and don't understand. Women had the influence to change things, and did. Laws grew explosively to ban sexual harassment, whether real or imagined. Affirmative action, in addition to being a naked power grab, avoids competition and therefore making the losers feel bad. It degrades the performance of organizations, sometimes seriously, but performance is a preoccupation of males.

Men are capable of malignant government, whether authoritarian or totalitarian, as witness North Korea or the Russia of Stalin. I don't know whether women would behave as badly if they had the power. (I'd guess not.) But women have their own totalitarian tendencies. They will if allowed impose a seamless tyranny of suffocating safety, social control, and political propriety. Men are happy for men to be men and women to be women; women want us all to be women.

The United States becomes daily more a woman's world, comfortable, safe, with few outlets for a man's desire for risk. The America of wild empty country, of guns and fishing and hunting, of physical labor and hot rods and schoolyard fights, has turned gradually into a land of shopping malls and sensible cars and bureaucracy.

Risk is now mostly artificial and not very risky. There is skydiving and scuba and you can still find places to go fast on motorcycles, but it gets harder. Jobs increasingly require the feminine virtues of patience, accommodation to routine, and subordination of performance to civility. Just about everything that once defined masculinity is now denounced as "macho," a hostile word embodying the female incomprehension of men.

A case can be made that a feminized world would (or will) be preferable to a masculine. Perhaps. It is males who bomb cities and shoot people in Seven-Elevens. Yet the experiment has not been made. I suspect we will have the worst of both worlds: a nation in which men at the top engage in the usual wars and, a step below, women impose unutterable boredom.

CHAPTER 44

Mom, Drugs, and Apple Pie. Bobby Sox and Psilocybin

I wish someone would explain to me the War On Drugs, or at least why we think there is one. I grant that I'm just a country boy, and intellectually barefoot, and can't understand things that don't make sense. For that you have to go to Yale. Help me.

As the newspapers tell it, drugs are somebody else's fault. Mexico's, for example, which grows and ships drugs. Yep, our drug problem comes from them. Colombia makes us take drugs too. In Washington you often see Colombians with machetes to peoples' throats, making them use drugs. Sometimes they actually block traffic. The Afghans grow drugs for the American market, but it's not their fault, because they are our allies and love us and fight terrorism.

Does this make sense? Maybe it's because I'm slow, but it looks to me as if America has a drug problem because Americans want drugs. It isn't Colombia. You might as well blame Toyotas on Japan as blame cocaine on Colombia. If we didn't want Toyotas, we wouldn't buy them. Drugs, too.

Drugs are as American as barbecue sauce. Everybody here wants drugs. Kids want drugs. Country boys in pickups want drugs. Fancy consultants want drugs. All God's chillun want drugs. Throw in people who don't think they want their minds altered, but gobble Prozac like anteaters on a bug pile. They're drugged-up to the gills, but don't know it.

The War On Drugs has gone on for a good thirty-five years since the Sixties. It is as real as professional wrestling. Well, almost. What do we have to show for it? Nothing. *Nothing.* You can get any drug you have heard of, and some you haven't, from your daughter in high school. I don't mean that she uses them. I mean she knows where to get them, or could find out in fifteen minutes. Crystal, shrooms, ecstasy, acid, whatcha want?

Downtown, crack is common as corruption. Open-air drug markets are like Seven-Elevens—there's one every few blocks. Eight black guys hanging on a corner in the city? Good bet. The customers usually are blue-collar whites from the suburbs. The upper class does white powder. Kids do odd stuff. Nitrous, for example. Just Say NO2.

The schools actually promote drugs. When my daughter was in the third grade, she had never thought about narcotics. Then a nice cop with DARE came. He showed them what the drugs looked like and explained what they did. The kids were intrigued: Acid? You *see* things? Neat....

Who are we kidding? A lot of their parents do drugs. Yes, the Volvo People, shiny and prosperous. When the kids aren't around, the little bag comes out of the bottom drawer. (The kids toke when the parents aren't around.)

No, not everyone uses, or ever did. Not everyone drinks. But enough do it that it is acceptable, on the order of discreet adultery.

Drugs are a vital part of the national economy, like Boeing. The difference is that drugs have a future. We might as well try to outlaw gravity. Anyone caught stuck to the earth instead of floating in the air will be arrested.

People with too much time on their hands talk about legalization. Thing is, drugs *are* legal. It's a curious, tacit, off-the-books legality, a legality in bits and pieces, undeclared, but it's there, and has to be, because of the demographics. You can't arrest the half of the middle class, the upper class, the lower class, the high schools and the universities.

You sure aren't going to bust half the Gifted And Talented program at Central High, give them a narcotics record, and ruin their lives. So teachers just somehow…don't notice. Crime largely ignored is crime largely legalized.

When was the last time you heard of high-school or middle-school (don't kid yourself) students being busted at school on dope charges? Blacks only get arrested because they're visible, because drugs in the ghetto produce dead bodies, and because they are going to vote Democratic anyway.

The other part of de facto legalization is that penalties for the first arrest are meaningless—say, an appearance in court and some sort of stupid community service. For kids, it's a joke, an adventure, a badge of honor. Adults in the middle-class almost never get caught. They're discreet, and the cops don't really care. Besides, jailing the tax base doesn't fly.

For the middle class and up (and where is the power in the country?) drugs are illegal enough that no politician will risk taking heat for being in favor, but legal enough that people can still use them.

Why is this? Ah. Because too many folk fondly remember getting twisted in the dorm room years back, remember succumbing to the munchies and eating a whole loaf of stale bread or a ream of typing paper while Dylan honked and blew about the vandals got the handle.

Gimme break. For too many of us, doing drugs in college was fun, a rite of passage, like going to a speakeasy in the Twenties. It provided a sense of adventure, of shared disdain for laws seen as witless and meddlesome. We were chemical libertarians. And in any age the bright and adventurous are more likely to do drugs than are solemn drones.

This doesn't make drugs a good idea. It does make them unlikely to go away.

What do parents from the Sixties say when the budding tad asks, "Daddy, did you and mommy do drugs back then?" Heh, ah…urgh. Do you lie? "Oh *nooo-oo*, we never did *that*." Budding tads tend to know when they're being lied to. Or do you prevaricate greasily: "Well, I experimented, but it wasn't a good idea and I didn't inhale"?

I heard the story, perhaps apocryphal, of the father who told his daughter of eight years, "If you put your tooth under the pillow, the Tooth Fairy will give you a dime." "A dime of what?"

If the laws don't quash the use of drugs, what effect do they have?

They keep prices up for the drug cartels. Dealers enjoy a huge, federally guaranteed margin of profit.

Two groups most oppose legalization. First, the morality lobby consisting of hard-line conservatives, serious Christians, latent Puritans, and people who fear social devastation wrought by drugs. Second, the drug industry, which would expire yesterday if legalized. This includes folk with a few plants growing in a closet, Kentucky farm boys with a dozen rows hidden amongst the corn, judges and cops battening on bribes, the peddlers in the ghetto, and the cartels. All God's chillun.

When crime and morality are in league, precisely what war on drugs are we talking about?

CHAPTER 45

1953

Eight years after the end of WWII, 1953 sprang upon America like a tabby cat on a mouse. Children abounded in profusion. Thousands of virile men had returned from long years of such erotically depressing things as floating around the Pacific on a destroyer. They meant to make up for lost time. Boy did they. Thus, post demob, America brought forth moiling swarms of children exactly nine months and about thirty seconds old. The unsurprising surprised no one, except demographers.

Dukesy and I were sheaves among this bumper crop of human wheat. Dukesy (technically Michel Duquez) was a dark dashing kid of Frog extraction who assisted me in crime—for example, the great fraudulent Plastic Man for Polio crusade. He was quick-witted, good with his fists when he needed to be, and a wicked second-baseman. Later he joined the Foreign Legion and died gallantly, repelling a camel charge against Fort Digby by 12,000 hashish-crazed Bedouins waving poisoned scimitars.

Well, I expect he did.

Ours was a sunny world, hopeful and prosperous. We lived in new suburbs of pleasant brick boxes in Arlington, Virginia, each with one tree in the yard, laid out with as much imagination as the stringing on a tennis racket. We Americans had won the war. Evil had taken it in the shorts, at the end of an American boot. Now we were going to buy washing machines.

Everything made sense. We knew who we were, what we wanted, and how things should be. Our patch of Arlington had no diversity, (and therefore) no crime, no drugs, no illiteracy. In its exoticism, divorce was stranger than human sacrifice. Life was endlessly wholesome. Kids, itinerant herds of them, amused themselves with yoyos, glorious Gilbert chemistry sets with, yes, fifty bottles (Let's see, sodium thiosulphate, cobalt chloride, sodium silicate....) and of course baseball.

But I digress. I'm trying to tell you about Plastic Man and how he disguised himself as a Thanksgiving turkey to catch a malign force that was eating all the food in whatever city he lived in. (Maybe you didn't think you needed to know this. Well, you do. Read it.)

Now, Plastic Man—I know, this isn't obsessively organized—was an elastic hero in comic books, which we read along with anything else we could find. We *could* read: Feminism hadn't taken the intelligence out of the classrooms, producing a vacuum that sucked in the national dregs like a bored-and-stroked Hoovermatic that needed a better filter. The Waspish belief in work and study sat well upon the nation. You could have asked my friends Michel Duquez, John Kaminski, and Lynne Sverdlov.

On long summer afternoons when we couldn't find a pick-up ball game, and we wearied of climbing the willow in Bradley Furman's front yard and throwing spit-bombs at each other, we'd go to the drug store in Westover on Washington Boulevard and burrow into the comic racks. There were three of them, the kind that spun, close together so you could squeeze into the middle and hide. They enclosed a dim papery space like a fort, which appeals to all proper boys, and you could peer out between the comics and watch the customers. When we turned the racks from within to get new comics, they moved as by a ghostly presence.

Anyway, Plastic Man. (This is important. There may be a pop quiz.) He was a fixture with us, like Wonder Woman who had an invisible glass airplane and a magic lasso. He wore a red-and-yellow spandex suit (if memory serves) and blue sunglasses, so that he looked like a French bicycle racer. He stretched. If he wanted to see what was on top of a building, he just elongated his neck like a forty-foot soda-straw. He could make himself into any size and shape he wanted. He did this to fight crime. Dukesy and I hadn't reached puberty so this seemed the most profitable use for a protean talent.

Plastic Man hardly stood out in a crowd in 1953. Those were the days when Superman was always jumping out of windows amid much whooshing with the announcer intoning something about a Strange Visitor from another planet who fought for Truth, Justice, and the American Way, then thought to be coextensive.

I guess Ol' Plastic got all stretchy because his father, who was probably a scientific genius, accidentally spilled radioactive gunch on him. It's how things happened in 1953. Scientists often spilled stuff on a shrew or scorpion or something, and it would grow and grow into a terrible movie. Plastic had a vaguely Chinese sidekick called Woozy who was shaped like a wonton with legs.

Anyway, the bad guys would plot nefarious deeds and never notice a red-and-yellow umbrella in the umbrella stand. In one episode the Thanksgiving turkey was suspiciously red and yellow, but they didn't notice that either. Maybe they thought it was just moldy or something, till it turned into Plastic Man and wrapped around them like grinning rope till the cops came.

Polio, though. Dukesy and I came up with the idea of Plastic Man for Polio. At the time the disease did a land-office business and the March of Dimes was always collecting money to do something bad to it. We gathered our substantial supply of comic books and began going door to door in the neighborhood, telling all the mothers that we were selling them to eliminate iron lungs.

"Yes, Ma'am, we're selling used comic books. It's to help polio. Got some really good ones, see…" we'd say to the wife of a de-mobbed B-29 captain.

Of course no one believed us, but they didn't want to seem to be in favor of respiratory paralysis, so they smiled and gave us nickels and dimes. Soon we had several dollars, mostly in small coins that made it look like more. It suited us. Like Heraclitus, we believed in change. We'd count it and play with it in the manner of Scrooge McDuck. And then go spend it. I'd like to say that the enterprise taught us something lasting about commerce or the virtue of initiative, but mostly it let us go to Westover and buy more Plastic Man.

I'm not sure where this column is going. I had a feeling that Godzilla was about to come into it, trampling paragraphs while searching for something to eat—most likely Tokyo. He did that a lot at the Glebe Theater, while we hooted and threw popcorn boxes. I guess it's too late for the old lizard, and I don't have space to tell you about the Great Squash Wars on Soapstone Hill. Some other time.

CHAPTER 46

The Free Will of a Newtonian Particle

Wars, like the political eruptions of teenagers, groan under the weight of moral justification: We are fighting to protect ourselves, protect democracy, establish democracy, end atrocities, avenge former mistreatment, and dissuade dictators. We have to save something from something or for something. If we don't fight, this boogie or that boogie will take over the world.

When you notice that all teenagers do the same things at the same age, you suspect that what is involved is hormones. So with wars. Military adventures only seem to be about things. Really they are just military adventures. We fight for the same reasons fish school and peacocks strut—because it's how we are.

You don't think so? Step back, look at the world on a scale of centuries, and it is obvious. History is one long repetitive story of war. Start anywhere: The Old Testament, the Eddas, Homer. When the Greeks of classical antiquity were not fighting Persians, they fought each other. The Romans fought everyone they could find and often, when they needed a new emperor, each other. In the Middle Ages, knights fought as a hobby; when they couldn't find anyone to fight seriously, they held tournaments and fought for sport.

Wars pass by in their thousands, The War of Spanish Succession, of Jenkins's Ear, of the Roses, of this and that and practically everything. We're still doing it—everywhere, always, today, yesterday, tomorrow.

Why?

Because we are over-brained apes. Fighting is built into men (far less into women). Our instincts crave it. Watch young males in a movie theater when Star Wars is playing. They will be on the edge of their seats, leaning unconsciously with the maneuvering of the swirling space-fighters, adrenaline pumping, thinking "Get him, get him, *get him!*"

It's how we are. Videogames, football, boxing, jousting, paintball, NASCAR, gladiatorial games, drag racing, dueling, war, and bar fights are expressions of the same drive.

We fight as naturally, inevitably, and unthinkingly as dogs sorting out questions of territory. What is instinctive seems so perfectly reasonable that we seldom ask whether it makes sense. Perhaps army ants believe they are fighting for some forested virtue.

If you are male, and don't believe in instinct, find a big man with a pretty girlfriend, and put your hand on the wrong part of her topography. Without reflection, he will arrange for you to make several mortgage payments for your dentist. But why? You didn't harm her in the least. For that matter, how comfortable are you in a dark forest when you hear something...moving? Even if you know it has to be a deer or a house dog?

Instinct rules us. Little girls left to themselves play house and care for dolls. Little boys form hunting packs. As a kid of ten in a civilized suburb, I joined with my buddies to venture into farther suburbs unknown to us. We had a distinct sense of venturing into alien and possibly hostile territory. When we encountered other kids, there was a sizing up, a calculation of the odds, a question of whether to run, fight, or hang out. We were unconsciously practicing for adulthood, like tussling puppies.

If people have an inbred desire to fight, so do they have an inbred, if slight, moral sense. In the past a king could simply strip the peasants of their provisions and ride off to put cities to the sword. What people thought didn't matter. Today a modicum of support from the public is needed. In war, people do ghastly things that in time of peace they regard as hideous. Comfortable folk unafraid will not readily approve. Thus lying is essential to war. People must be frightened, enraged, or both.

It is easy to arrange. Half of the population is of below-average intelligence, four-fifths are not sure where the enemy nation is, and fully ninety percent do not know what countries border on it. Further, people do not handle abstractions well. Instead they personalize, confusing the enemy nation with its Evil Leader: Iraq is not twenty-five million rather ordinary people; rather it is Saddam Hussein. Cuba is not an island of eleven million agreeable people who sing and dance splendidly; it is Fidel Castro. Warring governments encourage this confusion.

Part of the boilerplate of war are the atrocity stories used to arouse hatred in the public. Armies commit atrocities—your army, my army, the other guy's army. Everyone agrees that everyone else does it. When no real atrocities are convenient to hand, governments manufacture them. Some are so conventional that there ought to be a rubber stamp: Babies are bayoneted, women's breasts are cut off, and pregnant women are disemboweled.

Curiously, a company commander who takes sniper rounds from a village of 250, and calls in an air strike, will say that he has never seen an atrocity. Nor were the carpet bombings of London and Hamburg atrocities; rather these were legitimate burnings alive of children, the unlucky, and the slow. If truth is the first casualty, reason is in the next ambulance.

It is useful in war that people do not respond emotionally to what they cannot actually see. A thousand abstract dead mean nothing, whether they died in a war or an earthquake. This explains the desire of the military to control the press. An inattentive democracy will tolerate a war provided that it is described as surgical and intended for high moral purposes; and that the footage shows videogame bombs falling precisely on distant targets. This also arouses pride in their gadgets.

If television showed a soldier, anybody's soldier, with his face shot away, interior of the mandibular joint glistening cartilaginous white, the man gurgling in agony with globs of yellow god-knows-what bubbling out of his throat, the war would suffer in the ratings.

Thus you will never, ever, ever see footage of the dead and wounded as they actually are if the government can prevent it. Not ever. This reticence is said to serve to protect the dignity of the injured. No it's not. It's to keep small-town Idaho from vomiting and saying, "Stop!"

Morality? Countries have none. They pretend for political effect. China objects to our brutalizing of Iraq, yet was perfectly happy to brutalize Tibet. France objects to our behavior in the Mid-East but behaved savagely in Algeria. Countries celebrate defensive wars to drive out invaders but, a few years later, are invading someone else's country. It's how we are. You might as well look for morality in a used-car lot.

CHAPTER 47

American Airlines. Like Sinus Drainage with Wings

You've heard of air rage? I've got it. I'm building an invisible plastic chain-saw with a six-hundred horse motor to cut the wings off every airplane owned by American Airlines, before chopping the flight crews into runny gruel.

Friday morning, August first 2003, San Francisco International. I showed up to catch a hop, AA 482, to Dallas-Fort Worth en route to Guadalajara. The line in front of the American ticketing was just flat huge. For an hour and twenty minutes by my watch people waited to check in. Yet between two-thirds and three-quarters of the check-in desks were closed. American, presumably wanting to save a nickel, preferred that we stand there like cattle. We did.

The flight left way late. Why? American couldn't find a vital stewardess. Yes. Just misplaced her. Maybe they left her behind a seat cushion. Who knows? In any event, a whole plane-load of people with things to do had to wait, and wait, and wait.

Incompetent management. Airlines know they need stewardesses. Thing is, the airlines also know that the public will accept any degree of inconsideration, stupidity, and humiliation. Which is why we get them. We're patsies.

Next, clonking down the jetway, we picked up our Bistro Bags. You know, nasty little sandwich, nickel bag of chips, thingy of peeled dwarf carrots. They call them Bistro Bags because somebody in marketing figured it would make us think we were having a European Dining Experience instead of a sorry bag-lunch. We boarded. No one actually said "Moo."

The cabin crew were par: Not quite surly, but not under any constraint to be agreeable. The major US airlines barely tolerate customers. One suspects that they would be happier without them.

Off we took, finally, after the usual claptrap read from a card at high speed about how to fasten our seat belts and how the stews are there for our safety. Actually they're just waitresses. Hoping to sleep, I slid into the vague unpleasant torpor that flying has become. Normally people put themselves to sleep by counting sheep. On these aerial Greyhound buses I pretend that I have leprosy and count my fingers falling off.

American squeezes you relentlessly. To deaden the ambience I asked for a dismal little bottle of bad white wine. Five bucks. Decent airlines, meaning foreign ones, don't try to milk you for everything from beer to headphones.

Predictably, the waitress didn't have change for a twenty. Why not? It's a common bill. Maybe she didn't know she was going to need change when selling drinks. How could she? After all, she had only done it four times a day for ten years. Maybe the association just hadn't quite flowered in her neural thickets: "*Urg…*Sell things…need change…*Ahhh!*" I pictured an evolutionarily advanced monkey learning how to poke at a coconut with a stick and shrieking with delight when it fell. She said she would come back. But didn't.

Over an hour later we were preparing to land, and still no change. The stew was forward, gabbling with her accomplices. Was she going to remember or wasn't she? The odds looked bad. I politely asked a near-by crewmember, a blonde kid with bad teeth who looked to be maybe twenty-four, if he would check on it.

He crossed the line from barely civil to deliberately snotty. "*Sirrrr!* We aren't going anywhere," followed by loud remarks, intended for me, to a passing stew: "He wants his change. Hey, the ATM's broken." Clever little wunx.

He knew he could get away with it. This is the operating principle of the domestic air-transport business: You can get away with it. Lousy food, late arrivals, missed connections, surliness, gouging. These engaging traits once characterized Aeroflot, but they've migrated.

The preponderance of power lies with the airlines, and they know it. Any remonstrance and they can make an air-rage beef out of it and you miss your next flight. They figure the public has no recourse.

Finally, DFW. I needed to make the connection because people were waiting for me in Guad. But with American, making a connection doesn't really help. My next flight, AA 1401, couldn't leave because they couldn't find the pilot. So help me. No pilot.

Why not? Was he hung over? Still drunk? Couldn't find the airport? Didn't feel like working? In a lineup at the local precinct? Who knows?

Perhaps American will think I'm being too demanding—another sorehead customer. Maybe they are right. Maybe it is unreasonable to expect airlines to provide certain things: ant farms, say, or the Bhagavad Gita in Swedish, or a Faberge egg, or a pilot. I mean, how could American predict that it might need a pilot?

We sat, and sweated, and sat. Finally they told us that they had found a pilot, but that he was on another airplane. Oh.

Either they can't staff their aircraft, or just don't care. It doesn't have to be this way. Used to be, flying United out of Dulles to the Far East, I always actually flew All Nippon Airways, which code-shared with United. ANA amounted to a major upgrade. Seats were larger, the food was great, the flight attendants hadn't recently graduated from prison-matron school, and they didn't try to gouge you for after-dinner cordials or a stray brew.

Now, I know that American has not the slightest interest in me or anything I might possibly do. (Of course, they don't know about the invisible plastic chain saw.) I fly only six or eight times a year, only two of those being long hauls to Asia. Business fliers are presumably American's money. I don't count. I know it. Still, what I did was call Claudia at my travel agency and tell her never, ever to book me on American, and always to choose a non-US airline when prices were close.

Nonetheless I note with delight that United Airlines went bankrupt (it's as bad as American, except that it usually has pilots), and American teeters on the edge. I hope it drops. Companies that peddle a sorry product with wretched service and abrasive personnel desperately need extinction. I'll celebrate with ribs and beer.

Would you go to a restaurant that couldn't find its cook and waiters, and got you your meal after leaving you in the parking lot for an hour and a half? Don't do it. Fly foreign carriers outside the US—they're better—and the econolines domestically when possible: JetBlue, AirTran, Southwest, Frontier. They're all good. If you subsidize lousy performance, you get more of it. If second-rate airlines go out of business, tough.

Splendid, in fact.

CHAPTER 48

Fred's Horrible Secret

Sometimes a writer craves to bare his soul and lighten his burden of hidden sin—yes, to admit that he hasn't always lived as a Christian, that he has played cards in low dives and done shameful things with floozies in foreign ports. He wants to make a clean breast of it before the world, to say, "There. You see me in all my sordid sorrow and moral wretchedness. Forgive me if you can." Well, I'm at that pass. I'm going to confess.

I like the French.

All right. I'll leave town. (Actually, come to think of it, I've left town.)

Yes, I've written harsh things about the French. The French like the French awfully well, and I figured that here was a teeter-totter that needed some balance to it. So I laughed at them. There was no malice in it. I was just being professionally disagreeable.

But now our tub-thumping patriots are whooping it up most frightfully against France. Why? Because the French saw no reason to blow up Arabs in a contrived war of dissembled purpose. Neither did I. Nor do I remember that the French are corporals in our army. Besides, if we don't support their opposition to the war, why shouldn't they oppose our support?

The patriots call the French "cheese-eating surrender monkeys." It's embar-rassing—though not because they insult the French. I just wish we had a patriot who sounded more than eleven years old.

I grant you that the French are imperfect. They live on a reputation they do not deserve. I refer to their famous intolerance of visiting Americans, which is a tourist attraction, listed in travel guides. One expects a Parisian to sight down his nose as if taking a measurement, and sniff, and be supercilious.

But no. You cannot trust a Frenchman.

In former years I often went to Paris for the Air Show. Always the French were tiresomely civil. I had expected the heathen rudeness one associates with moral crusaders. I considered bringing a case at law: I had spent all that money in expectation of gorgeous churlishness and didn't get any.

I waited everywhere for lightning to flash, for some spark to ignite the powder magazines of Gallic abrasiveness. Surely something would provoke them to vile manners. In particular, I had been warned that they would not suffer Americans who had not been born with a perfect fluency in French.

The rascals would not perform. My wife of the moment entered a drugstore in Paris to buy cough syrup. She thought she was asking for medicine, but was in fact asking for a doctor ("*médecin*"). The help were astonished as she went about peering at shelves, in the apparent belief that in France doctors were kept in little boxes. When the mistake was understood, the French laughed. They were friendly and helpful. It was low treachery.

Patriotism is more confusing than Japanese camera instructions. Russia, Ger-many, and France opposed our lunge into Mesopotamia. Which of these vil-lains has done America the most harm? Russia, I recall, forced us to spend trillions for defense that might better have gone for counterproductive social programs, and supplied our enemies in every war from Korea to Vietnam. Germany caused some little trouble in the Forties. But whom do patriots hate? France. The Russians after all can make no one feel inadequate. They wear baggy pants. Germans eat sausage. They polka.

Patriots make much of the dismal record of the French in matters military. Well, yes. It's hard to argue with failure. I note, however, that the French have Germany on their borders, a condition associated with military failure for everybody enjoying the same circumstances. Americans cannot always distinguish between military prowess and the Atlantic Ocean. In fact, a great many Americans cannot find the Atlantic Ocean.

The Yankee record in festive slaughter may not be quite as good as we puff it up to be. The United States came late to the parade of World War I after everybody else had done the fighting, and declared itself victorious. America won splendidly in World War II, drew in Korea, and lost in Vietnam. The United States has only a fairish record in wars against helpless countries: lost in Cuba, Somalia, Lebanon, Cambodia, and Laos, but won in Grenada, Panama, Iraq I, and, maybe, Iraq II and Afghanistan II. In our record of wars won we rank high in the standings and would make the playoffs, but on the percentages the British look better.

Now, I grant you that the French have done the usual irreparable damage to civilization that countries do when they can. Napoleon was a preening little scourge, yes. (He did show that the French can fight well when led by foreigners.) But—correct me if I'm wrong—did the French not produce Zola, Pierre-Auguste Renoir, Laplace, Galois, the lovely prose of Alexis De Tocqueville, and indeed about 12,000 shelf-feet of such like? For this, perhaps, they can be forgiven Simone de Beauvoir and those unnecessary existentialists.

If only patriots whooped who had heard of these people, we might have rather less whooping. And if you are going to eat cheese while surrendering, you might as well eat good cheese.

If the French have declined in war since Napoleon, they still have style. I wish we had some. Our current emperor always gives the impression that he has just finished eating a peanut-butter sandwich. His speeches might be the winning entry in a seventh-grade elocution contest in Texarkana. By contrast, you can look at almost any French minister without suspecting that he was dressed by his mother, and the merest of them radiates an air of worldly understanding and intelligence that would get him jailed in America. A French cab driver has more class than a congressman, and probably fewer gravy stains.

The French respect intelligence, whereas we are deeply suspicious of it. I'm not sure that intelligence has much place in diplomacy, other than to let one make bad choices in better prose. Still, misjudgment engaged in with class at least makes better reading for later students of history. Whatever their failings, the French do not cultivate boorishness as a compulsory credential of democracy, or lie systematically to their children, or endeavor to crush intellectual endeavor. We didn't either, once.

America once had a brash, rough, leather-breeches style with a cornpone but genuine appeal. The genius of America was the pawky outsider laughing at European pretensions, the lethal wit of Twain, Bierce, Mencken, and Hunter Thompson. The country wielded canny frontiersman like Davy Crockett, and enjoyed the cracker-barrel shrewdness of Andrew Jackson, who figured that Bourbon belonged in branch water and not on a throne.

Thing is, backwoods virility doesn't well make the transition to suburbia. The American unease with ideas didn't sit badly on Huck Finn, Daniel Boone, or, in the Heroic Age of American technology, the buzz-cut engineers working on Apollo. But put Tom Sawyer on Ritalin in deliberately crippled suburban schools to keep him from being a boy; teach him that to be manly is sexist and that to be educated is elitist; wean him from independence and self-determination but give him nothing to replace them; rigorously discourage intellectual enterprise—and you get the polar opposite of a Frenchman.

Europeans, and assuredly the French, like to believe that the tremulous age of Europe makes them proof against the jejune lurchings of the young United States. I see blessed little evidence of it. But there is something appalling in the boobish anti-civilization now eagerly embraced by America. Much of our noisy patriotism is not readily distinguished from the barroom tantrums of congenitally hostile louts. We have a president who probably thinks Haute Cuisine is something one feeds to horses. I'm not sure that, before we put our own house in order, we are a position to look down too scornfully on the French.

CHAPTER 49

The Camera State

A looming question: Is today's a'bornin' surveillance state in America an aberration? Or is it the unavoidable future of mankind? A spasm, like Prohibition, the Sixties, McCarthyism? Or an inevitable consequence of technological advance—something that must follow the spread of computers and networking as remorselessly as suburbs and shopping malls followed the automobile? Do we have a choice?

The technology exists today for a degree of control, of watchfulness, of spying even, unimaginable two decades ago. You can buy most of the hardware at a shopping mall. We need only use what we have: the internet, cameras, software, electronics. Step by step, sometimes inadvertently, not always realizing the consequences, we begin to use it. I don't believe that it is controllable.

Think about it. The capacity to store and search information, to transmit it over any distance, is today for practical purposes unlimited. A lowly mail-order pc is so powerful that it is difficult to grasp just how powerful it is. Technically, wiring the world is only slightly harder than wiring a country. The very innocence of it all makes it insidious. The tools of an iron control come into existence for practical reasons of efficiency and convenience.

Vast, multitudinous, and efficient data bases are already kept on us, innocently, by Visa, the Social Security Administration, telephone companies, banks, the police, and hundreds of others. They do it for reasons of convenience and efficiency. It is not possible to argue against these. Yet…when once these repositories of information are in place, linking them is technically easy. The Pentagon wants to do it.

We all know about data bases. I don't think many people know about some of the other, spookier things that exist today in the world of surveillance. For example, there are chips called RFIDs (radio-frequency identification devices). These, smaller than a grain of rice, transmit an identifying number when they pass an electronic reader. They are expected to cost perhaps five cents each in mass manufacture. Department stores want to use them for innocent purposes of inventory control. The readers can be inconspicuously built into almost anything. You won't know that you are being tracked.

They are so cheap, so easy, so useful.

The government is probably not going to force us to build these chips into things so that it can watch us. We are going to do it ourselves, for reasons of practicality and convenience. For example, RFIDs built irremovably into automobiles, so that passing police cars could read them, would make car theft far more difficult. The serial of a stolen car would go electronically onto a watch list. Put readers in toll booths, in stop lights, or in gas stations, and stolen cars would become virtually undrivable.

Who could be against stopping theft of automobiles? But the same chips would allow the government to keep records of where your car was, when. They could also be used to calculate your speed and, should it be excessive, call the cops or send you a threatening letter. We would never be unwatched.

How much surveillance are we willing to bear in order to prevent how much crime?

(There is, or was, in the Virginia suburbs of Washington a stretch of road where speed monitoring was done, though not with RFIDs. A sign flashed something like: "Slow Down! You are making 47 mph!" It was unsettling, as it was to start to cross an intersection against a light when no traffic was coming, and then to realize that a camera was pointed at you.)

Constantly being watched is intimidating, whether you are doing anything wrong or not. More and more we are watched, everywhere. In Washington's subway, if you stand near the trackway, an officious busybody in the kiosk above will admonish you over the PA system to stand back. Cameras. You begin half-consciously tailoring your behavior to the desires of the unknown chaperones.

Presumably, overt dictatorships such as China will simply impose whatever surveillance they wish. Can the galloping growth of surveillance in the United States be controlled? I think not (though I'd love to be wrong), for several reasons.

First, there is no way to object. We are not really a democracy. With an aggressive president, a legislative branch sinking into impotence, and an all-powerful and unaccountable judiciary, the public has little recourse but to do as it is told. The government will just do what it wants.

Second, fear is an effective way to get people to give up independence, privacy, and freedom. It is being used, and it is working. Tell people that they are in danger, that they are being attacked or about to be attacked or might be attacked. Tell them that the government needs to watch every detail of their lives to protect them. Throw in a bit of theater about bomb shelters, survival kits, and duct tape to give a sense of immediacy. Test the air raid sirens every Monday.

America frightens easily. We are afraid of second-hand smoke, terrorists, plastic guns, and little boys who point their fingers and say "bang." It isn't the attitude of Davy Crockett, but neither is it the America of Davy Crockett. The United States is perhaps the world's most timid nation. It will accept much in the name of security. Once people get used to the loss of rights, it will be almost impossible to get those rights back.

Third, the mechanisms of control go so painlessly into place. When the FBI was installing its software for monitoring email, there was a brief fuss, quickly forgotten. The software is still there. People got used to airport searches. Changes to obscure laws regarding warrantless access to records do not get attention beyond the beltway. The linking of data bases doesn't make a loud bang or produce a mushroom cloud.

Finally, how much do people really care about freedom? On average, not much. Give them three hundred channels on the cable, alcohol, food, sex, drugs, and rock and roll, and they will be docile if not always precisely happy.

Americans sometimes like to think of themselves as hardy yeoman, freedom-loving individualists, Fifth Century Athenians with squirrel guns. No. Increasingly the country consists of a bored suburban peasantry, politically inert, apathetic, in intellectual decline, oscillating from cubicle to sofa. As long as the government doesn't crash through their doors, which it almost never will unless opposed, the cameras won't bother them.

There may be no way to avoid the surveillance state. People may or may not be happy with it. It may or may not be particularly oppressive. I think we are about to find out.

CHAPTER 50

Horror and Susan Reimer. Take Horror. It's a Better Bet

Were I to offer thoughts on marriage to young American men today, in these the declining years of a once-great civilization, my advice would be as follows: Don't do it. Or, if you do, do it in another country. In America marriage is a grievous error.

And why so? Because of The Chip. The Attitude. The bandsaw whine of anger, anger, anger that makes American women an international horror. It's there. It's real.

You, a young man, may not recognize the Chip if you have never seen normal, warm, happy women. If you are twenty-something and haven't been out of the US, you haven't seen them. They exist by the billion—in Latin America, Singapore, Taiwan, Malaya, China and, last I looked, France and Holland. And of course not every woman in America carries the Chip. None of them think they do. Yet it is the default, the norm, what comes out of the box.

The following is a perfectly ordinary, everyday, bulk-lot example, suitable for poisoning a cistern:

"Other than a 29-inch waist and a full head of hair, there isn't much to recommend the twentysomething male...He is living an extended adolescence—an adult-olescence—and every immature, irresponsible, self-absorbed thing he does is reinforced by the latest issue of his favorite men's magazine." (Susan Reimer, a columnist for the *Baltimore Sun*. I bet she goes out a lot.)

Hers is the Attitude—and what they think of you. It is the defining trait of American women. Exceptions exist, and they have my apologies, but they are few and no, sport, your Sally probably isn't one of them. They're coiled to bite. As soon as problems arise in the marriage, they turn into Susan.

Susan Reimer is what is out there, guys: bitter that no one wants her (as who in his right mind could?), sure that no one is good enough for her, never having grasped that those who would be loved must first be lovable. Understand this: Susan is America. Some hide it better, springing it on you after the ceremony, but Susan is the rule.

The Susans do not like men. Sometimes they actually take courses in disliking men ("Women's Studies"). Yet they want to marry one and have babies. For them, the contradiction actually makes a kind of sense, because (and they know this, believe me) they will get the house, the children, and the child support. For you, it makes no sense. You will get raped in the divorce courts. You don't know how bad it is. Don't do it.

A prime effect of marriage is backbreaking financial overhead: the excessive house in the prestigious suburb, the pricey but boring cars, all that. But if you don't fall into the trap, if you stay single, keeping your expenses down means you can live in Mexico or overseas and enjoy existence. There is more to life than debt service. Although these are bad times for marrying, they are extraordinarily good times for being single.

Now, children. This is sticky. You may want them, or think you want them, or think you may want them. She does want them. My advice is to move to almost any country where English isn't spoken and women don't want their husbands to be the mothers of their children. Any country inhabited by the Chinese would do nicely.

Incidentally, remember that it is never now or never. Your prospects improve with time. At thirty-five or fifty you will be perfectly able to find a good woman if you know where to look. See above list.

Remember also that these are not good times for having children in America. It is almost irresponsible. The schools are scholastically poor, drug-ridden, given chiefly to political indoctrination, and hostile to male children. The universities are little better. Divorce is hell on children and their fathers, and nearly universal. The country lunges to police-statedom and isn't, I suspect, as stable as it might be. Worse, worst, there is Susan Reimer. Her name is legion, and she seeps everywhere, like the odor of unwashed socks.

Further, there is no social duty to have children. Some argue that the white population is in decline. Tough. If the country chooses to make having children undesirable, then let it decline. It is not your problem.

Now, you might well wonder, why are American women carrying the Chip? Practically, it doesn't matter: They do carry it, and will continue. Still, it is partly because from birth they are fed the notion that they have been oppressed, battered, cheated, deprived, harassed, used as sex objects, not used as sex objects, on and on. Being rational, you are perhaps inclined to point out that never has a female population been less any of these things, but don't bother. It will have no effect. The Chip is an emotional artifact to which they respond emotionally.

The bedrock of The Attitude is that everything is the man's fault. Wonders Reimer, "What is the answer, especially if the 20-and 30-year-old male is such poor marriage material?" She does not wonder, "If I am such a grindingly awful termagant that men on three continents are crossing their legs and feeling queasy over my mere column, and won't come near me except in a Kevlar bathysphere with a disinfectant system, maybe I'm doing something wrong. Gosh. I wonder what?"

Yet something more is going on, though one does not easily see just what. Note that in recent decades we have seen the invention by women of bulimia and anorexia, which no one had heard of in 1965. Men made them do it. At roughly the same time women began getting breast implants, which men also made them do, and then suing about it. In the same period they began having induced memories of being raped or satanically abused by their fathers. Men again. The psychotherapy racket grew like Topsy, a sure sign of deep unhappiness over something.

All of this is recent. You have to be fifty to remember women who were resilient, sane, psychically strong and, within the limits of an often sorry existence, content. But whatever the answer, guys, the problem isn't yours.

Spend a year overseas, however you have to do it. For smart, classy, just plain glorious women who often speak English, try Singapore. Argentina is splendid. Many places are. You would be amazed. See what's out there before you marry a gringa with her Inner Susan, who will one day burst from her chest like one of those beaked space-aliens in the movies, dripping venom. They're death.

CHAPTER 51

Why Goats Don't Nest in Trees

One of the funnier illusions of mankind is that our behavior is rational. This curious rejection of the obvious permeates the approximations of thought engaged in by politicians, professors, and those seeking federal grants so as to live well and improve us.

But no. Actually our behavior is largely built-in, with the software preinstalled at the factory and packed into a complex read-only file. We make the choices our instincts allow us to make, and thus have the freedom of choice of a bowling ball rolling down the lane. We seldom notice, because behavior in accord with instinct seems perfectly reasonable. Lemmings probably wonder why humans don't stampede over cliffs and drown themselves. (An idea worth looking into.)

"Instinct" is hard to define. Is the flowering of the sexual drive at adolescence instinctive, or is it a chemical response to new hormones? Is there a difference? Since we have decided to believe that the brain is a purely chemical entity, and ignore the obvious questions regarding consciousness and the mind, one might say that instinct cannot exist. Take your choice. Here I use the word to mean behavior that is built in, however effectuated.

If we have free will, it's only within built-in constraints. We are programmed from birth. A newborn wants to suck. Nursing isn't learned behavior. Babies just do it…The behavior of girl babies differs slightly but unmistakably from that of boy babies. They do not learn this from other babies. Thereafter every step of the way to adulthood we do very much the same things at the same time. Babies cry when they're unhappy. The Terrible Twos come and go with children who have never seen the Terrible Twos. Talking is learned, but learned at the same programmed time. Blind children have never seen anyone walk, yet they walk. It's built-in.

When the hormones of puberty hit, we become obsessively interested in the other sex. This too is scripted. Young males, if not restrained, begin butting heads over girls, remarkably like the males of other mammalian species. The girls begin competing with other girls. The boys do foolish and dangerous things and, when there are risks to be taken to gain access to the girls, the boys take them.

Sex, like fighting, is a major and irrational organizing force in our lives. We are always in heat, always looking or at least considering. People spend hours thinking about sex, reading books about sex, trying to find sex, looking at pornography or reading the mandatory stories about sex in women's magazines. Dogs, more sensible, become interested only when a female is in season. It must be an easier life.

The illusion of free will is more convincing when one considers the making of what appear to be choices. Learning to walk can be regarded as purely physical. Being a libertarian or a socialist seems more the result of ratiocination. But our politics are equally instinctive. We form groups and fight other groups. What appears to be intellectually determined usually isn't.

Teenagers begin their political existence by realizing that they understand everything far better than their parents do. They join crusades to retake Jerusalem or to save the world from the International Monetary Fund. They believe they are making principled choices. Their reasons are often persuasive: The young are not necessarily stupid, despite convincing simulations. They can learn much about the IMF, and weave arguments both subtle and sanctimonious.

But it's always something, and always at the same age. If it isn't the IMF, it's stopping the war in Vietnam, or saving the baby seals, or ending international finance capitalism. These causes may be good ones, but only accidentally.

When five hundred generations do the same things, one begins to suspect that the fix is in.

Deceptively, while the ends we pursue are predetermined, the means of achieving them depend on reason. Fighting wars for example is incredibly stupid. They waste huge amounts of money that could otherwise be spent on pork projects for politicians. Yet the design of an intercontinental ballistic missile is beautifully rational: the engineering elegant, the mathematics sophisticated, a thousand difficult technologies melded into a gorgeous baseball bat with a nail in the end. Our brains are the tools of our glands.

Thus the history of the species is a tale of war, rape, pillage, torture, and butchery. This is not curmudgeonly fustian (though I think highly of curmudgeonly fustian). It's how we have been, and how we are. We fight. We just do.

Savages everywhere that I know of regularly fought neighboring tribes for booty, women, or horses—or so they presumably believed. I think they did it because they were—we are—wired to do it. When people became a tad more civilized, they kept on fighting, butchering, and torturing. They just had better plumbing in their houses.

The Aztecs, a brutal military empire, invented open heart surgery to the astonishment of the Spanish and practiced it with abandon. They were propitiating the gods, see, to get good weather or something. The Spanish, a civilized people who burned heretics at the stake, were horrified by the Indian's practice of human sacrifice. Civilization doesn't temper barbarity. Later the 18th century French, a truly sophisticated society, wrecked Europe under that wretched little Corsican.

Horses don't behave this way. Different wiring. They run around in herds till they get slow and the wolves eat them, but they don't butcher each other. We do. It's built-in.

The race isn't improving with time. We can't: we don't know how to change instincts. In the past, armies put cities to the sword after capturing them. More recently we've done it before capturing them, because we could: Dresden, Hamburg. Sometimes there doesn't seem to be any reason at all, as in Pol Pot's liquidation of Cambodia. It's just how we are.

The instinct to conquer accounts for the unending wars of expansion, the empires that balloon like bubbles and collapse. It also accounts I think for the rise of commercial empires like J. P. Morgan's, or Microsoft. Bill Gates could probably get by on ten billion. Yet he wants more. Not *for* anything. Just more.

To me, the automaticity of our larger impulses militates against faith in progress toward a peaceable world. We like to think of ourselves as more advanced than, say, the ancient Persians, and technologically we are. But recently, as in all the intervening years, we have done exactly the same things they did, only our chariots now have turbines and high-velocity smooth-bores. We act the way we always act, because it's the only way we can act.

CHAPTER 52

Four Days and Three Maniacs in the Grand Canyon

Last September a couple of college buddies and I walked across the Grand Canyon, from the North Rim to the South. It was one of those trips we were always going to make, sometime, but hadn't. Planning had been elaborate. The Park Service wisely limits foot traffic, requiring permits that must be gotten far in advance. It's a nuisance, but keeps Disney out. Rob and I flew into Denver, where Dan lives, and drove the rest of the way.

The open road was a relief. The flight out had not been pleasant. The country was in the grip of its new institutionalized fear. The security police were being themselves. I had thought to bring a book on the Wahabis to read on the flight, but had imagined a security apparatchik deciding he had found a terrorist. I left it at home.

On the far side of the Rockies the land flattened out and lost the excessively lived-in appearance that begins to make Colorado look like the East. I realized that I hadn't crossed the deserts since I had hitchhiked them in the Sixties. Much had changed since then, and more since I had first seen the big empty lands while crossing the continent at age six with my parents. The deserts were still appallingly large despite the intrusion of the Interstates. Towns, though, were giving way to the homogenization and franchised conformity that cause

any part of America to look like any other. The West remains magnificent territory.

The Canyon was the same glowing caldron of reds and dusky purple that I
remembered from earlier trips, changing shades and hues with the dying sunlight. It is probably impossible to take a bad picture of the Canyon. At the
North Rim we checked into the lodge, ate, and hit the sack, suspecting that
four a.m. would come early. It did. We saddled up in chilly darkness, had
breakfast, and hoofed it toward the trail head. The last day would be a climb of
5,000 vertical feet, so we kept our packs light at about thirty pounds.

Going down, you don't see the Canyon. The trail descends through a narrow
side-canyon, a crevice, so that you find yourself traversing vast walls that loom
above and fall away to depths that an acrophobe would not want to contemplate. The rock face varies from green to tan to brown, weathered by thousands
of years of wind and rain. You walk for hours in a huge shaded silence. The
thought inevitably comes that you are in the presence of something above your
pay-grade. The Canyon was old when whatever partial molar and fragment of
jawbone, thought to be our ancestor, was gnawing flesh in the perplexity of too
much skull and not enough content. It will be around when we are long gone.
I doubt that we will be missed.

In my wandering years I passed through the South Rim, I forget just when or
why. Hitchhiking by its nature is anecdotal: You remember people and places,
but not how they are connected. At a place on the rim that did not seem much
traveled, I climbed down a face that was exposed enough that I probably
shouldn't have done it. Falls tend to be long in the Canyon. In the rock face I
found a small chamber, hollowed out I thought by hands. It was deep enough
to escape both weather and detection, and did not look natural.

I sat in it for some time and surveyed the Canyon, which wasn't doing anything. Since then I have wondered whether anyone else had been there since
some Indian, for whatever reason, had sat where I was sitting, and watched
for...what?

We continued down. A cold stream ran along the trail much of the way, tum-
bling and splashing and seeming to enjoy itself mightily. When the urge hit we

sat in it, buck nekkid if we chose, until the heat of the trail had dissipated. If life gets better, I'm unaware of it.

The lodge and campground of Phantom Ranch at the bottom were, like everything in the Canyon, well run and full of good people. Long-haul backpackers are extraordinarily convivial and decent. I don't know why. They seem to have a better idea than do most of what is important to them. Those who solo hike the 2000 miles of the Appalachian Trail, as several of these had, tend to be self-contained and able to fend for themselves. We ran into a couple of Chinese nurses from San Francisco and an Australian gal and her boyfriend to pal around with. They confirmed me in my liking for both Chinese and Australians.

We were booked for two nights at Phantom. The next morning Rob and I did a twelve-miler up the Kaibab Trail, across the plateau on the Tonto, and down Bright Angel. The climb out the next day would be a serious day's walking. We wanted our legs to be ready for it. Besides, we're crazy. For hours we went across rolling empty pink country, immense, pocked with blue-gray vegetation like frozen mortar bursts. A shriveled creek provided water and shade for lunch. Except for us and one idiot who had gotten lost—you can die in the desert—the world was deserted.

I decided that if God hadn't created the Canyon, he missed a good chance.

To be on the safe side we began the climb out at first light. Rob and I had a long history of week-long up-and-down hikes through the mountains of the East, with substantially heavier packs, but this was going to be pure, steady, serious ascent. We wanted to get the jump on it. The store on the South Rim carried a book called something like *Death in the Canyon*, of which there are some. I'm told that most involve out-of-shape people who proceed to cash in because of heart attacks and heat stroke. Still, it is wise to respect the geography.

It was a hump, but not a killer. A major help were Leki poles, things like ski poles, now almost universal in the back country. Their virtues are hard to quantify, but they improved balance, avoided twisted ankles, and shifted muscular effort to our shoulders. You go faster. As we ascended above the level of the plateau we found ourselves on endless sunny switchbacks overlooking the whole gaudy basin. The walls of the Canyon have well-marked strata. You measure your progress by which of them you have put below you.

It was a splendid trip. If you have the chance, do it.

CHAPTER 53

Ex-Pats, Here and There

Expatriates. You see them in back-street bars of Bangkok, Manila, Guadalajara, along third-world waterfronts, in up-country Thailand, anywhere living is cheap and rules scarce.

Some are old guys in their sixties and seventies with fading tattoos from other lives, lives that also fade into fewer and fewer living memories. Some are in their thirties and run little businesses, often legitimate. They are a bit rough-looking or maybe just eccentric, congenitally what they are and not concerned about what you think of them. You find them heisting a brewski in out-of-the-way spots, chaffing with the barmaids who may or may not have a sideline. They are the dropouts of the earth—the interesting expats, not the middle-management retirees who really belong in some dismal retirement colony in Arizona.

They are a breed overlooked by the world, which suits them fine. Some have pasts. You see jailhouse tattoos. A few are drunks waiting to die spitting blood—poor miserable sods who just couldn't get it together after the contract ran out on the oil rig and the wife ran with the kids, probably for good reason. Most are solid enough. They drop by the bars because that's where the social life is. Some own bars. Many have local wives and families. Some did once back in the States and figure they'll pass this time around.

They are men with stories, many of which wouldn't be believed in the uphol-stered countries of the earth. On the other hand, expats generally don't talk to upholstered people. You meet a lot of retired pilots, maybe for United and maybe for spook outfits like Air America, or maybe the personal pilot of some oil-sheikh out of Arabia. Some did things they don't talk about during the American lunge into Asia in the Sixties; after the war, the golf course just didn't appeal to them. Golfers don't always understand about Lucy's Tiger Den, the Grey House, the Blue Fox in TJ.

Their defining trait is that they don't fit in and don't want to. The bond broker for example who wondered, "What am I doing this for?" and stopped. He opened a dive shop in Mexico and never looked back. There are drug dealers who got smart in time; men who don't seem to have last names, or not the same one twice; guys who scout trinkets for the US import market. You bump into freelance writers living by their wits, credentialed by obscure publications which sometimes exist. Military men who retired on twenty and didn't want to work in the NAPA outlet; the former bouncer at a strip joint in Florida who somehow drifted abroad and saw no reason to go back.

The waters of anarchy run wide and fast through expatriate realm, though they don't gather up everybody. Some of the Americans are deeply attached to the memory of the US they left. For a few, patriotism has replaced religion as the psychic buoy for the otherwise unmoored.

Others are profoundly, by conviction or inattention, citizens of nowhere, loyal to no country. Maybe they've lived in so many places that whatever bonds they may have had have worn through; borders are to them just places where you get your bags inspected. Maybe they wearied of the socialism of Canada, the regimentation of the United States, and bailed. Some are angry that their countries haven't lived up to their desires. Others are bored with the question.

The world does not approve of deliberate statelessness. These men wouldn't care. There's not too much they do care about.

A few expats are bad-voodoo muck-skulkers. The *Federales* in Guad recently snatched a candyman on the lam out of Spokane: something like forty counts of homosexual child molestation. (He seemed like a nice guy.) But it's rare. More commonly men marry and play Leave It To Beaver, have kids or adopt the wife's, live happily and make sure she gets the Social Security when they die.

Almost universal among them is a profound desire not to be part of somebody else's parade. They want to be left alone. In the semi-developed countries favored by expats, governments usually don't care about you unless you break the law. Sometimes they don't care even if you do break the law, depending on the law. The big North American governments never stop supervising, admonishing, collecting data, requiring forms. Those who dislike it enough end up somewhere else.

The uncharitable in America bruit the notion that men expatriate because they want to enjoy sex with lovely young lovelies. That's part of it. For a man of fifty, a sloe-eyed sweetie of twenty-five beats hell out of an angry menopausing gringa with a law degree. Maybe it shouldn't be that way, but it is that way.

But much more than sex is involved. Women in the backwaters are often just plain agreeable. After the divorce back home, men learn. Some do, anyway.

There are interpretations and interpretations of the prostitution and semi-prostitution that one finds abroad. Hooking, an expat might tell you, if he cared, which is unlikely, gets a bad rap. Bar girls usually aren't bad people. The cynical among the expatriates, which is about all of them, say that hooking differs from other approaches to sex chiefly in that the latter cost more.

Deep down, a lot of men just don't want the admin overhead of the usual relationship: the breakup, the shrieking, the agony, and let's-get-counseling, and everyone feels like dirt. Relations between the sexes, they say, are always fundamentally commercial. Women trade sex for whatever they want, and men trade whatever they have for sex. In the US, when the whole mess becomes horribly boring, the husband insists that he's still in love to avoid admitting that he'd give anything to be in Bangkok. The woman eats bon-bons.

Remember that the expat lives there, unlike the crypto-sadistic Japanese sex tourist. He knows the girls in the bar, laughs with them, takes one home here and again. For her, it beats being sweated in a running-shoe factory. Most countries don't have the Puritan background America does.

I know lots of men who have married either bar girls or non-hooking local women. (Some don't know they have married bar girls.) Often it works well. The woman gets what she wants: a decent life, and a husband who doesn't knock her around. He gets what he wants: a pretty and pleasant young wife, food on the table, and a good mother if they have kids. He probably actually loves her because, praise God, she's not congenitally angry or in a law firm. They're happy. It's their business.

CHAPTER 54

Believing, Disbelieving, and Suspecting: Thoughts on Religion

We live in a wantonly irreligious age, at least at the level of public discourse. In America the courts, the schools, and the government seek to cleanse the country of religion. More accurately, they seek to cleanse it of Christianity. We are told, never directly but by relentless implication, that religious faith is something one in decency ought to do behind closed doors—an embarrassment, worse than public bowling though not quite as bad as having a venereal disease.

Which is odd.

I do not offer myself as one intimate with the gods, and on grounds of reason would be hard pressed to choose between the views of Hindus and those of Buddhists. I note however that over millennia people of extraordinary intellect and thoughtfulness have taken religion seriously. A quite remarkable arrogance is needed feel oneself mentally superior to Augustine, Aquinas, Isaac Newton, and C.S. Lewis. I'm not up to it.

Of course arrogance comes in forms both personal and temporal. People tend to regard their own time as wiser and more knowing than all preceding times, and the people of earlier ages as quaint and vaguely primitive. Thus many who do not know how a television works will feel superior to Newton, because he didn't know how a television works. (Here is a fascinating concept: Arrogance by proximity to a television.)

It will be said that we have learned much since the time of Newton, and that this knowledge renders us wiser on matters spiritual. We do have better plastics. Yet still we die, and have no idea what it means. We do not know where we came from, and no amount of pious mummery about Big Bangs and black holes changes that at all. We do not know why we are here. We have intimations of what we should do, but no assurance. These are the questions that religion addresses and that science pretends do not exist. For all our transistors we know no more about these matters than did Heraclitus, and think about them less.

Many today assuredly do know of the questions, and do think about them. One merely doesn't bring them up at a cocktail party, as they are held to be disreputable.

Yet I often meet a, to me, curious sort of fellow who simply cannot comprehend what religion might be about. He is puzzled as distinct from contemptuous or haughty. He genuinely sees no difference between religious faith and believing that the earth is flat. He is like a congenitally deaf man watching a symphony orchestra: With all the good will in the world he doesn't see the profit in all that sawing with bows and blowing into things.

This fellow is very different from the common atheist, who is bitter, proud of his advanced thinking, and inclined toward a (somewhat adolescent) hostility to a world that isn't up to his standards. This is tiresome and predictable, but doesn't offend me. Less forgivably, he often wants to run on about logical positivism. (I'm reminded of Orwell's comment about "the sort of atheist who doesn't so much disbelieve in God as personally dislike him." Quote approximate.)

Critics of religion say, correctly, that horrible crimes are committed in the name of religion. So are they in the name of communism, anti-communism, Manifest Destiny, Zionism, nationalism, and national security. Horrible crimes are a natural occupation of humanity. They are not the heart of religion.

The following seems to me to be true regarding religion and the sciences: Either one believes that there is an afterlife, or one believes that there is not an afterlife, or one isn't sure—which means that one believes that there may be an afterlife. If there is an afterlife, then there is an aspect of existence about which we know nothing and which may, or may not, influence this world. In this case the sciences, while interesting and useful, are merely a partial explanation of things. Thus to believe in the absolute explanatory power of the sciences one must be an atheist—to exclude competition. Note that atheists as much as the faithful believe what they cannot establish.

Here is the chief defect of scientists (I mean those who take the sciences as an ideology rather than as a discipline): an unwillingness to admit that there is anything outside their realm. But there is. You cannot squeeze consciousness, beauty, affection, or Good and Evil from physics any more than you can derive momentum from the postulates of geometry: No mass, no momentum. A moral scientist is thus a contradiction in terms. (Logically speaking. In practice they compartmentalize and often are perfectly good people.)

Thus we have the spectacle of the scientist who is horrified by the latest hatchet murder but can give no scientific reason why. A murder after all is merely the dislocation of certain physical masses (the victim's head, for example) followed by elaborate chemical reactions. Horror cannot be derived from physics. It comes from somewhere else.

Similarly, those who believe in religions often do not really quite believe. Interesting to me is the extent to which those who think themselves Christians have subordinated God to physics. For example, I have often read some timid theologian saying that manna was actually a sticky secretion deriving from certain insects, and that the crossing of the Red Sea was really done in a shallow place when the wind blew the water out.

Perhaps so; I wasn't there. Yet these arguments amount to saying that God is all-powerful, provided that he behaves consistently with physical principles and the prevailing weather. The sciences take precedence.

Now, people who seek (and therefore find) an overarching explanation of everything always avoid looking at the logical warts and lacunae in their systems. This is equally true of Christians, liberals, conservatives, Marxists, evolutionists, and believers in the universal explanatory power of the sciences.

That being said, at worst the religions of the earth are gropings toward something that people feel but cannot put a finger on, toward something more at the heart of life than the hoped-for raise, trendy restaurants, and the next and grander automobile. And few things are as stultifying and superficial as the man not so much agnostic (this I can understand) as simply inattentive, whose life is focused on getting into a better country club. Good questions are better than bad answers. And the sciences, though not intended to be, have become the opiate of the masses.

CHAPTER 55

Back South of the Rio Bravo: Home Again, Jiggety-Jig

Evening was well advanced when the lights of Guadalajara crept under the wing and I started peering out the window like a visiting space alien. Cities at night fascinate me. They look like glowing bacterial cultures in a huge Petri dish, tendrils winding off into the darkness from a dense center. I had been in Washington to sell a condo as a matter of simplification of life. Paperwork and labyrinthine taxes make owning anything you do not have to own more trouble than it is worth. The beast was sold. I was ready to get home.

I cleared customs and grabbed a cab. It was about a half hour to where I was going. The driver asked whether it was my first time in Mexico. I said no, I lived there. Ah, and what did I think of his country? Did I like it? People want you to like their countries.

The only possible answer was "Yes," which had the virtue of being true. I said I liked it because life was quiet. That is not why I like Mexico. It is why Mexicans like Mexico.

"*Tranquilo…muy tranquilo….*" he said with pensive approval.

They always say it. They have a capacity that I don't, for being what they are and living peacefully where they are. I am incorrigibly American, getting bored after six weeks of anything and wanting to head off for another continent or some jungle or other. People are more philosophic here. Many are content to spend their lives in the same town in the mountains, watching the storms roll in during rainy season and chatting with friends of decades in the plaza.

They seem happier than Americans, but it is a mixed blessing. I talk often to a Mexican woman, highly intelligent and cultivated. She agrees that Mexicans are more at peace, but believes them much less independent and adventurous than Americans. The reason, she says, is that children are coddled hereabouts and that family ties are so strong.

She has a point. Gringos wake up one morning and think, "I guess I'll start a computer company or, you know, learn to hang-glide, or maybe go live in Fiji." They don't stay at home very well.

She sees my daughters, about whom I tend to talk, as the perfect gringas. (They are.) Macon and Emily are forever hopping freight trains across Canada, or setting off into the city to be blues singers, or getting tear-gassed in Prague over something or other. Mexican kids don't. One might as well imagine Thoreau bungee-jumping.

The plaza was hopping, it being Saturday night. Swarms of kids charged about, parents talked, couples wandered around holding hands. Mexico is a country of plazas and churches. The bells ring, at least where I live, to mark the hour and to announce mass. Good bells cost money, which not every town has. The ones here sound like a Dempster Dumpster being repeatedly rammed by a cement truck. I live in the shadow of the church, and the constant whanging has inspired in me a certain ambivalence toward religion.

I unloaded my bags, grabbed some booty from them—CD burner so I can steal music and software, a lovely pocketable digital camera (Canon S400, sweet gadget), and a high-end scientific calculator that my realtor, a friend, had given me as a closing present. Much as I like Mexico, America is a better place to buy Japanese electronics. Clutching the Canon, I headed for Rex's bar on the plaza to catch up on the ongoing soap opera that is part of expat life.

People in the States often have curious ideas about Mexico. I get a lot of mail asking me, or telling me, about the perils of life here. The gravamen is to the effect that the *Federales* will at any moment scoop me up in the dark of night and throw me into durance vile, at a location unknown, without benefit of counsel, constitutional protections, or determinate date of dis-incarceration. This amounts to saying that Mexico anticipated Mr. Ashnamara's Patriot Act: While Mexico has adopted democracy, the colossus of the north retreats from it.

Now, if you want to get in trouble here, you can. Punch out a cop. You will get trouble. Money back if you aren't satisfied. Or take a flyer at rape, or traffic in drugs, or smuggle guns, or rob a bank. All will serve. Oh yes.

Or try to kill a policeman. Several months back a Mexican guy from Guad came to a local bar here. He found himself blocked by another car and began pistol-whipping the driver. (Isn't that what you would do?) He then shot at the police. It wasn't a career-enhancing move, though he did get a free funeral out of it. Public opinion was to the effect that if you beat people and shoot at the police, you take your chances.

Otherwise, you have to look for trouble. The Mexican government is not out to get gringos. Except for getting hit for the occasional bribe, the police are not a topic of conversation among expats. There's nothing to talk about.

Another thing Americans ask me about is politics here. It's pretty much like anywhere. Money disappears, deals get cut, bribes get paid. It could be Washington. Scandals bubble. Pemexgate, involving the petroleum industry. The Friends of Fox, about elections. Sheets that cost too much at *Los Pinos*, which is the Mexican Whitehouse. Some think Fox travels too much. (His airplane is sometimes called AirFox One.) None of it is a show-stopper. Fox is a politician, not a dictator, and a pretty decent guy.

Here, as in America, people think the government is insufficiently useful to merit attention. The Mexican commentators worry about abstention by voters as much as do American commentators. It runs at about sixty percent, says the radio, a bit more than in the United States, if memory serves. I had thought that electile dysfunction was a problem of aging democracies, but it seems young ones get it too: Them as figure they got nothing to vote for, don't.

A guy in a cowboy hat clopped past the plaza on a horse, his kid of maybe five sitting behind him. From Rex's Mick Jagger, old enough to have helped build the pyramids, hollered about his dearth of satisfaction. The air smelled of coming rain.

CHAPTER 56

Why Johnny Can't Add Like Rhajankerwhatsis

I wonder whether we don't need to wake up.

The other day I went to the web site of Bell Labs, one of the country's premier research outfits. I clicked at random on a research project, Programmable Networks for Tomorrow. The scientists working on the project were Gisli Hjalmstysson, Nikos Anerousis, Pawan Goyal, K. K. Ramakrishnan, Jennifer Rexford, Kobus Van der Merwe, and Sneha Kumar Kasera.

Clicking again at random, this time on the Information Visualization Research Group, the research team turned out to be John Ellson, Emden Gansner, John Mocenigo, Stephen North, Jeffery Korn, Eleftherios Koutsofios, Bin Wei, Shankar Krishnan, and Suresh Venktasubramanian.

Here is a pattern I've noticed in countless organizations at the high end of the research spectrum. In the personnel lists, certain groups are phenomenally over-represented with respect to their appearance in the general American population: Chinese, Koreans, Indians and, though it doesn't show in the above lists, Jews. What the precise statistical breakdown across the world of American research might be, I don't know. An awful lot of personnel lists look like the foregoing.

Think about this. Asians make up a small percent of the population, yet there are company directories in Silicon Valley that read like a New Delhi phone book. Many of our premier universities have become heavily Asian, with many of these students going into the sciences. If Chinese citizens and Americans of Chinese descent left tomorrow for Beijing, American research, and graduate schools in the sciences and engineering, would be crippled.

Jews are two or three percent of the population. On the rough-cut assumption that Goldstein is probably Jewish, and Ferguson probably isn't, it is evident that Jews are doing lots more than their share of research—and, given that people named Miller may be Jewish, the name-recognition approach probably produces a substantial undercount. I asked a friend, researching a book on Harvard, the percentage of Asian and Jewish students. Answer: "Asians close to 20%. Jews close to 25%—unofficial, because you are allowed to list by gender, ethnicity, geography, but not religion. Our last taboo."

None of this is original with me. In 1999, the National Academy of Sciences released a study noting that over half of U.S. engineering doctorates are awarded to foreign students. Where are Smith and Jones?

Why are members of these very small groups doing so much of the important research for the United States? That's easy. They're smart, they go into the sciences, and they work hard. Potatoes are more mysterious. It's not affirmative action. They produce. The qualifications of these students can easily be checked. They have them. The question is not whether these groups perform, or why, but why the rest of us no longer do. What has happened?

It is not an easy question, but a lot of it, I think, is the deliberate enstupidation of American education. Again, the idea is not original with me. Said the American Educational Research Association of the NAS report, "Serious deficiencies in American pre-college education, along with wavering support for basic research, were cited by the panel as major contributors to this problem."

Consider mathematics. In the mid-Sixties I took freshman chemistry at Hampden-Sydney College, a solid school in Virginia but not nearly MIT. It was assumed, assumed without thought, that students knew algebra cold. They had to. You can't do heavy loads of highly mathematical homework, or wrestle with ideas like integrating probability densities over three-space, or do endless gas-law and reaction-rate calculations, if you aren't sure how exponents work.

Remedial mathematics at the college level was unheard of. The assumption was that people who weren't ready for college work should be somewhere else. No one thought about it. Today, remedial classes in both reading and math are common at universities. We seem to be dumbing ourselves to death.

My children recently went through the high schools of Arlington, Va., a suburb of Washington. I watched them come home with badly misspelled chemistry handouts from half-educated teachers, watched them do stupid, make-work science projects that taught them nothing about the sciences but used lots of pretty paper.

The extent of scholastic decline is sometimes astonishing. So help me, I once saw, in a middle school in Arlington, a student's project on a bulletin board celebrating Enrico Fermi's contributions to "Nucler Physics." (Scripps-Howard National Spelling Bee champions: 2003, Sai Guntuyri; 2002, Pratyush Buddiga; 2001, Sean Conley; 2000, George Thampy; 1999, Nupur Lala).

It appears that a few groups are keeping their standards up and the rest of us are drowning our children in self-indulgent social engineering, political correctness, and feel-good substitutes for learning.

Some of our growing dependency is hidden. We do not merely rely on small industrious groups in America and on foreigners working here. Increasingly the United States contracts out its technical thinking to Asia.

If you read technically aware publications like *Wired* magazine (and how many people do?), you find that major American corporations have more and more of their computer programming done by people in, for example, India. In cities like Bombay, large colonies of Indians work for U.S. companies by internet. This again means that counting names at American institutions underestimates the growth of intellectual dependence.

The Indians, and others, have discovered the suddenly important principle that intellectual capital is separable from physical capital. To program for Boeing, you don't have to be anywhere near Seattle. Nor do you need an aircraft plant. All you need is a $700 computer, a book called something like *How to Program in C++*, and a fast Internet connection. Crucial work like circuit-design can now be done abroad by bright people who don't need chip factories. They need workstations, the internet, and engineering degrees.

This too we would be wise to ponder. Americans often think of India chiefly as a land of ghastly poverty. Well, yes. It is also a country with about three times our population and a lot of very bright people who want to get ahead. They're professionally hungry. We no longer are.

People speak of globalization. This is it, and it's just beginning. Where will it take us? How long can we maintain a technologically dominant economy if we are, as a country, no longer willing to do our own thinking? If we rely heavily on less than 10 percent of our own population while employing more and more foreigners abroad?

It's not them. It's us. I've heard the phrase, "the Asian challenge to the West." I don't think so. When Sally Chen gets a doctorate in biochemistry, she's not challenging America. She's getting a doctorate in biochemistry. Those who study have no reason to apologize to those who don't.

The Mathematical Association of America runs a contest for the extremely bright and prepared among high-school students. It is called the United States of America Mathematics Olympiad, and it "provides a means of identifying and encouraging the most creative secondary mathematics students in the country."

An unedited section of a list of those recently chosen: Sharat Bhat, Tongke Xue, Matthew Peairs, Wen Li, Jongmin Baek, Aaron Kleinman, David Stolp, Andrew Schwartz, Rishi Gupta, Jennifer Laaser, Inna Zakharevich, Neil Chua, Jonathan Lowd, Simon Rubinsteinsalze, Joshua Batson, Jimmy Jia, Jichao Qian, Dmitry Taubinsky, David Kaplan, Erica Wilson, Kai Dai, Julian Kolev, Jonathan Xiong, Stephen Guo.

Q.E.D.

CHAPTER 57

Uncle Hant, the Law, and Moonshine

'Tother day late in the afternoon I went down the holler to get Uncle Hant to explain to me about law and order. Hant knows nearly 'bout everything, more than anyone in West Virginia, even Bluefield. He makes the best shine for three counties, and sells it to yups from Washington. Hant can do pretty nearly anything. I guess he's one of them Renny's aunt's men.

I've always wondered who Renny was.

I followed the rail cut through the woods down toward North Fork. Since the mines went busted the trains don't come any more. The rails are rusty and weeds try to grow in the track bed. It was late in August and the air was warm and soft as a hound in the sun and bugs were hollering like crazy, trying to find girlfriends before winter came and they froze. I feel that way sometime too.

Hant was by the still, pouring stove polish into a barrel of shine. He's tall and scrawny and getting old now so he ain't as limber as he used to be. He still wears that old floppy hat that looks like a cow made it and he's got a jaw like a front-end loader. He says the hat makes him look authentic. Yups won't buy shine from you if you don't look authentic.

"Say, Hant, I come so you can tell me about law and order."

"Too much of it," he said, like there wasn't any more to say. He let the last bit of stove polish drip into that barrel of shine. He doesn't believe in wasting things.

"You want a drink, boy?"

"Not that pizen you make. I ain't that dumb."

I didn't go to school just to carry my lunchbox. 'Course, I'm not sure why I did go.

He sat on a stump, stiff, like a Buck knife folding and pulled a jug out of a bush. "I wouldn't give you any of that yup exterminator," he said. "This here's pure Beam."

"I reckon I will then." He passed the jug and I took a sup. "Hant, I saw this tow-headed gal on TV and she said we needed more law and order in West Virginia."

He looked thoughtful and hove the stove-polish bottle into the woods. He's always trying to find a way to give his shine a little extra kick. He tried wood alcohol but the yups went blind on the way home and ran into telephone poles. It was bad for business. The phone company said it would sue if he didn't stop. Then he tried LSD, but they kept trying to drive up roads that weren't there and kilt themselves. Brake fluid didn't work either. I hoped stove polish would do the job.

"Gimme that jug back," said Hant, who knew what mattered to him. "More laws? Never had much use for the ones we got. Maybe some people ought to leave other people alone." He took a three-gurgle hit and looked satisfied. Hant gets along fine without laws.

Hant don't actually exist. He's a Literary Device. We got lots of them in West Virginia. Mostly you find them in damp spots in the woods.

I said, "She allowed as how we ought to get rid of guns, and keep our dogs on a piece of rope when we walk around, and don't never smoke, and a bunch of other stuff that didn't make sense."

"Get rid of guns?"

You could see he was rolling the idea around in his head, trying to get the flavor of it.

"Then what you gonna shoot road signs with? Damn, you can't use a bow'n'arrow out a car window, leastways not over eighty mile an hour. I guess that lady don't got the sense God give a possum."

The county wasn't a good place to be a road sign. It wasn't a good place to be a cat, either.

"What the hell you want to keep a dog on a piece of rope for? Dog don't like it. You don't like it. Don't make sense. How's Jif, anyway? Still hid out?"

It's hard to keep Hant pointed in the right direction when you talk to him. He meant Jiffy Lube, my girlfriend. Her real name is Jennifer Imidazole Ferguson, but we call her Jiffy Lube.

"She's doing good. Sheriff says she can come home now."

A few weeks back she got in a fight with Jimmy Jack 'Callister at Red's Billiards and laid him out cold with a pool stick. The sheriff said he might have to give her a ticket if he could find her but he couldn't and he said the Statue of Limitations on smacking somebody as no-'count as Jimmy Jack was about two weeks.

"She said as how you didn't have enough shine for the yups last week and you might need another still."

He looked sorrowful. "That's me, a day late and a inch short. Maybe I'll put in another cooker."

"Hant, that television lady said we needed to shut down moonshiners."

I figured that would get his attention. It did too. He looked solemn as a undertaker that's wondering where his shotgun is.

"That ain't law and order," he said. "That's meddlin.'"

That's what it looked like to me. When Willy Bill Jenkins came back from Chicago, that's in Pennsylvania, he said you couldn't even have a dog if it didn't have some piece of paper, and kids gotta wear crash helmets if they ride their bikes and the law makes'em wear shoes. Now, I figure Willy Bill's stretching it some. I don't believe dogs can read, even in Pennsylvania. Still, it sounded to me like somebody needed to get smacked upside the head.

I saw why Hant was worried. His business is pretty good now. So many yups come out of DC that he pretty nearly needs a parking lot. He says drinking authentic shine gives a yup a sense of adventure so he feels like his life means something, which of course it doesn't. They pay forty dollars for that rust-cutter of his, leastways when he puts it in these authentic mountain stone jugs he gets in bulk from Taiwan.

I could see Hant wasn't going to tell me much about law and order, except it was people meddlin' where they didn't have any business meddlin.' I knew that anyway. Maybe that's all there is to say about most laws. I took another hit of that Beam and headed back. Hant's old three-legged hound Birdshot walked with me a ways. I scratched his ears for him. Birdshot's a fine dog. Don't meddle with anybody.

CHAPTER 58

We Done Been Ladened, But Good

Tell me I'm wrong. I gotta be wrong. Better be, anyway. But maybe we're getting had.

OK. Mr. Benjamin Laden did his trick with the airplanes and handed the United States its maybe worst one-day defeat ever, whoo-*eee*. It was gorgeous, specta-whoppular, made for television. For practically ever those buildings collapsed over and over on international TV. The Pentagon smoked dutifully. Arabs danced in the streets and a whole lot of people who didn't like the US sniggered in their sleeves because it wasn't the best time to irritate the country.

Now, when I say it was beautiful, I don't mean I approved of it. I don't approve when the wrong quarterback throws a perfect sixty-yard pass and the wrong receiver one-hands it thirty feet in the air and scampers into the hen zone like a cocaine-crazed hamster. But I still recognize a good play. New York was.

So George leads us hollering and shooting and blowing into Iraq and Afghanistan—well, sends some other people, but then he's one of our draft-dodging presidents, like Willy Jeff and Ron—and it worked better than lots of folks thought and pretty soon we owned both countries. For at least ten minutes. Historically, owning Afghanistan has been a low-margin enterprise as everyone from Phillip of Mastodon's kid through Elphinstone to the Russians has found out, but we're different.

I'm just not sure how. Maybe it's because we never find things out in time.

Tell me I'm wrong. I hope so. But it looks to me like we're getting out-brained again. While George orates at the teleprompter like a living, breathing bumper-sticker about how those Iraqi resistance people are all desperate and outside agitators and evil and hate freedom, it looks to me like the rascals know exactly what they're doing.

Anyone, even with his head in a towel, can see that the US doesn't have enough troops to squash Iraq if it doesn't want to be squashed. So the first order of business for the bad guys was to persuade other countries not to help: Isolate the US, make the war an American baby, turn it into an unending mess, and watch the gringos twist in the wind.

Now, George huffs about random violence. How random is it? Australia helps the US, and Australians get blown up in Bali. Italy helps the US, and Italians get blown up in Iraq. Turkey was going to send troops, and large bombs go off in Istanbul, coincidentally blowing up places owned by England, which also helped the US.

I guess that's random violence. No pattern at all. Countries that were going to send troops, like Japan and Korea and Turkey, suddenly have doubts. But probably the Arabs never thought of that.

So next the crazed desperate irrational resistance folk randomly target Iraqis who help the US, as for example police and others employed by Uncle Sucker. When someone else does it, we call it a "puppet government," but I suppose when we do it, they're independent Iraqi democrats under our control. Anyway, this discourages locals from co-operating with us; forces Christian soldiers allied with Israel to police a Moslem country, only incidentally stretching US forces ever thinner. It also robs the gringo regime of any pretense of legitimacy and, fascinatingly, keeps George from backing out. I mean, if he leaves without something that at least looks sort of like a government, he lost.

But I reckon the Arabs haven't thought of this.

Somehow it all points the same way—though purely randomly of course. Blowing up the UN and Red Cross and driving them out difficultates the pretense of progress and forces the US to take up the slack, stretching us ever thinner. Poor fire discipline, probably the result of military training aimed at appeasing the usual sensitives, results in shooting up weddings, kids, and women gathering wood. Hitting that civilian air-freighter with a SAM-7 threatens to make airlines stop flying to Baghdad, further isolating the country and making a graceful exit impossible. Blowing up the oil pipelines forces the US to pay for the occupation. All accidental.

Finally, the slow bleeding of American forces gnaws at the American public, oh yes, and makes the army lash out brutally, which enhostilates the Iraqis and—again—helps recruiting for the resistance. But this is all the unplanned result of random violence. Which is a good thing, or I'd think old Ben was sitting somewhere and laughing.

Now, tell me that after that we won't be forced to pull out. Maybe we won't. I'm wrong about a lot of things.

But…what if? Well, first of all America would never invade the Mideast again, leastways not for nearly ever. We'd be de-fanged. Nobody would be scared of us any longer. The A-rabs could do whatever they wanted. That would be it for the second American Century. Good move, George.

Now, I don't know where Ben is. I figure he's at Vail, waiting for powder, or a houseguest with some Saudi prince, or maybe grew dreadlocks and playing asphalt-court basketball in the Bronx. (With dreadlocks NSA couldn't recognize the top of his head.) You can't tell about Ben. But if what he wanted was to whip the US, and get it out of the Moslem world, and bring us low, why, I guess he'd figure he'd done it.

What would happen in Iraq, God only knows, but the rest of us can suspect. I reckon either it would get a Moslem gummint that hated us like poison, priced oil in Euros and sold it to China; or fall into pieces and everybody would invade everybody for years. What matters is Iran. If it developed nuclear hay-bombs the region's power balance would change whoo-bingo against Israel, which I bet the Israelis have thought about. And if we got run out of Iraq, I doubt we'd run into Iran.

Right now, Israel has the atomic trump card: No Moslem state is going to seriously threaten the Israelis because they know they'd turn into high-Geiger pork rinds. If Iran and the gang get the Big One, Israel will be under 24/7 threat of extinction. One on Tel Aviv would be the end of that adventure, like the fall of Acre. Maybe when a country has lots of nukes and a good air force, you don't really want to get its back to the wall.

But what do I know? Not much. What worries me is what maybe I'm going to find out.

CHAPTER 59

Unspeakable Crimes in Messico

I am sad to report that Mexico is the most criminal of countries. Let me illustrate.

Suppose that you were subject to, say, horrendous sinus infections or earaches. In America, by law you would have to get an appointment with a doctor, $75, thank you—when he had time, how about day after tomorrow, whereupon he would give you a prescription for amoxicillin, at fifteen bucks and a trip to a pharmacy. If this happened on a Friday, you would either slit your wrists by Saturday evening to avoid the torture, or go to an emergency room, however distant, where they would charge you a fortune and give you a prescription for…amoxicillin.

In Mexico, upon recognizing the familiar symptoms, you would go to the nearest *farmacia* and buy the amoxicillin. The agony would be nipped in the bud (presuming that agony has buds). The doctor would not get $75, which is against all principles of medicine. The pharmacist would not lose his license, as he would in the United States.

See? Criminality is legal in Mexico. That's how bad things are.

Another grave crime here is horse abuse. Often you see a Mexican father clopping through town on an unregistered horse—yes: the horror—with his kid of five seated behind him. A large list of crimes leaps instantly to the North American mind. The kid is not in a governmentally sanctioned horse seat. He is not wearing a helmet. The father is not wearing a helmet. The horse is not wearing a helmet. The horse is not wearing a diaper. The horse does not have a parade permit. The horse doesn't have turn signals. The father does not have a document showing that he went to a governmentally approved school and therefore knows how to operate a horse, which he has been doing since he was six years old.

In Mexico, if you want to ride a horse, you get one, or borrow one. If you don't know how to ride it, you have someone show you. Why any of this might interest the Mexican government is unclear to everybody, including the Mexican government.

You see. Here is the dark underside of Mexico. People do most things without supervision, as if they were adults.

This curious state of affairs, which might be called "freedom," has strange effects on gringos. Shortly after I moved here, I began to hear little voices. This worried me until I realized that I was next door to a grade school. Daily at noon a swarm of children erupted into the street, the girls chattering and running every which way, the boys shouting and roughhousing and playing what sounded like cowboys and Injuns.

In the United States, half of the boys would be forced to take drugs to make them inert. If they played anything involving guns, they would be suspended and forced to undergo psychiatric counseling, which would in all likelihood leave them in a state of murderous psychopathy. Wrestling would be violence, with the same results.

Here you see the extent to which, narcotically, Mexico lags the great powers. The Soviets drugged inconvenient adults into passivity. America drugs its little boys into passivity. Mexico doesn't drug anyone.

In fiesta season, which just ended, everybody and his grand aunt Chuleta puts up a taco stand or booze stall on the plaza. Yes: In front of God and everybody. These do not have seven-page permits. They are just there. If you want a *cuba libre,* you give the nice lady twenty pesos and she hands it to you. That's all. There is in this a simplicity that the North American instantly recognizes as dangerous. Where are the controls? Where are the rules? Why isn't somebody watching these people? Heaven knows what might happen. They could be terrorists.

If you chose to wander around the plaza, drink in hand, and listen to the band, no one would care in the least, in part because they would be doing the same thing. If you didn't finish your drink, and walked home with it, no one would pay the least attention.

In America this would be Drinking in Public. It would merit a night in jail followed by three months of compulsory Alcohol School. This would accomplish nothing of worth, but would put money in the pockets of controlling and vaguely hostile therapists, and let unhappy bureaucrats get even with people they suspected of enjoying themselves.

Mexicans seem to regard laws as interesting concepts that might merit thought at some later date. There is much to be said for this. The governmental attitude seems to be that if a thing doesn't need regulating, then don't regulate it. Life is much easier that way.

If a law doesn't make sense in a particular instance, a Mexican will ignore it. Where I live it is common to see a driver go the wrong way on a one-way street to avoid a lengthy circumnavigation. Since speeds are about five miles an hour, it isn't dangerous. The police don't patrol because there isn't enough crime (in my town: the big cities are as bad as ours) to justify it. It works. Everybody is happy, which isn't a crime in Mexico.

I could go on. In Mexico, legally or not, people ride in the backs of pickup trucks if the mood strikes them. This is no doubt statistically more dangerous than being wrapped in a Kevlar crash-box with an oxygen system and automatic transfusion machine. They figure it is their business.

Here is an explanation of Mexican criminality. The United States realizes that a citizen must be protected whether he wants to be or not—controlled, regulated, and intimidated in every aspect of everything he does, for his own good. He must not be permitted to ride a bicycle without a helmet, smoke if he chooses, or go to a bar where smoking is permitted. He cannot be trusted to run his life.

Have you ever wondered how much good the endless surveillance, preaching, and rules really do? In some states your car won't pass inspection if there is a crack in the windshield. There are—I don't doubt?—studies measuring the carnage and economic wreckage concomitant to driving with a cracked windshield. Presumably whole hospitals groan at the seams (if that's quite English) with the maimed and halt.

Or might it be that the rules are just stupid, the product of meddlesome bureaucrats and frightened petty officials with too much time on their hands? Maybe it would be better if they just got off our backs?

Nah.

CHAPTER 60

Disordered Mind Loose in Bangkok

Bangkok—

I love this place, and have for a long time. One reason is memories. I first came through in the seventies, en route to Calcutta and Delhi from, I think, Phnom Penh. That may not quite be right. Things went fast then and places and times blur. I stayed in the Thai Song Greet on Rama IV, it probably was, a fifty-cent-a-night flop that would have outraged a New York alley cat: plank bed, ghastly john, hotter than a blown big-block and with no ventilation in the grisly heat of Southeast Asia.

The first floor was a noodle restaurant of sorts, meaning a small room open to the street with a mama-san and a wok in what looked like the sub-basement of a medieval prison. It wasn't a place your mother would have recommended, but I was poor. Back then many of us were cutting our journalistic teeth, men some of whose names you might know, and we did what we needed to. Anyway, guys are dirtballs.

In the restaurant I met an aging hooker while slurping noodles. She had been unemployed since the drawdown had closed the American bases. She was sitting at a back table and drinking Mekong whiskey alone. Not a good sign. Lousy whiskey, too. I was maybe twenty-seven and thought forty-five was practically dead. Nice gal. I popped for another pint of Mekong as she was down on her luck and we talked. She wanted to attach herself to me, reasonable enough considering her alternatives. Next morning I left without saying goodbye. I hoped things would go well for her, but it wasn't likely.

Today the city is bigger, clogged with traffic, buzzing and sputtering with motor scooters, the air loud with the wing-ding-ding of two-cycles and thick with pollution, and just flat wonderful. I don't know why it's wonderful. Most people hate it. Thais hate it. Seven out of every three cars in Asia are registered in Bangkok. Traffic doesn't move. If glaciers ever come down from the north, they will overtake the clog, and freeze passengers like those people buried in the ash of Pompeii. In places drivers have built houses and raised families while trying to out-wait the congestion. Some have developed new cultures and applied for sovereignty.

The Sky Train, Bangkok's elevated train, is a godsend, and comparatively new. I hadn't used it before. It is fast, air-conditioned, and runs across the city at an altitude of maybe thirty feet. In an emergency you could use it to airdrop food to people starving below in stalled traffic. It runs along two main drags, Silom and Sukhumvit, with convenient stops.

It is a wonderful place to admire young Thai women, who run strongly to willowy, well-dressed, and naturally classy. They are much of why men expatriate here. As a friend put it, "Beats hell out of cellulite, nine yards of attitude, and lousy manners," which is hardly fair to all American women but captures the trend.

These days on visits I stay with expat friends. The American expats here are different from those in Mexico. The latter are retired bureaucrats who really have no business being in a poorish country, much concerned with leash laws and turning the Mexicans into copies of themselves. The Thai guys are largely ex-military, many left over from the war, veterans of spook outfits like Air America. After years in Asia they didn't want to become cubicle warts. The office doesn't compare with flying a chopper into Indian country under an Asian moon, running hot and black and waiting for little green sparks to arc toward you. Many have gone native, taking Thai wives, often upcountry, and blending in.

A curious expat network has sprung into being with assistance from the internet. It helps. Guys in Thailand who read my column wrote and said Hey Fred, let's heist one if you come this way. An old Special Forces buddy from back then, now in LA, emailed me to say You ought to look up so-and-so, I'll email her that you're coming. Another reader is a friend I hadn't seen for thirty years, when he ran UPI Saigon and I was a greenhorn stringer freshly loose on the world. We had lunch. Another is a guy I knew in Phnom Penh during the war who fell in love with the country and spends half his time there. I missed him this trip but won't next time. The net makes it all possible.

Now, to most people Thailand means the sex trade. The assumption is that you are going to Thailand to get laid and that if you so much as breathe the air you will seroconvert, and half the population is dying of AIDS. Mostly this is nonsense. Yes, there are massage parlors where a dozen women sit behind plate glass with numbers pinned to them ("Four, please."), specialty houses for the S&M trade, and plenty of action for gay men. But all of this is available in any big American city. In Thailand it is just more open.

Thing is, few foreigners get beyond the three red-light districts: Patpong, Nana Plaza, and Soi Cowboy. I usually hit all three in memory of youthful crime, but they aren't likable places, being garish, loud with vile disco music, and generally disagreeable. And often full of katoys, Thailand's famed transvestites.

The Thais are slender, delicate in appearance (though I wouldn't want to dispute the issue with the Thai army), and have little body hair. The result is a convincing TV. Visiting gringos don't always know about katoys. In Nana I saw a fiftyish Yank talking to a lissome Thai lovely, a tad tall for a local lass and keeping her chin down to hide her Adam's apple. Welcome to the City of Surprises, I thought. In about an hour and a half. It wasn't my problem.

Get away from Nana and Patpong, and the Thais are as likeable a people as you will find, being courteous, friendly and, while not puritanical, no looser than anyone else. As religions go, Buddhism is more civilized than most. The art and architecture are remarkable. This is a splendid country and, I think, a country with a future. There is an energy here that I don't see south of the Rio Bravo, in Arab lands or sub-Saharan Africa.

I was going to tell you the story about the howling mathematician, but we're out of space. Later. Meanwhile I'm going to ponder a cosmic mystery: Why did I buy a round-trip ticket? Something must be deeply wrong with me.

CHAPTER 61

Scamming Blacks, Again

Do blacks realize the contempt in which the government, the universities, and what is frequently called the "liberal establishment" (though it is hardly that) hold them? That the transparent premise of virtually all racial policy is that blacks are irremediably helpless?

I recently saw a news story saying that a black girl at the University of Colorado, I believe it was, felt "uncomfortable" because the social atmosphere wasn't to her taste. There weren't enough black faces, or black clubs, or black this and that. Her attitude was, "Do something. The universe owes me any adjustment that I demand to my tedious minor problems. How I suffer. Take care of me."

Now, why was this a national story? I don't care about her discomforts. Does she care about mine? Discomforts by definition are minor.

Ah, but a governing principle of American politics is that blacks cannot manage their own lives, solve their own problems, or compete with others. It is a position embodying a profound contempt, a smug disguised condescension that might seem excessive in a colonial missionary serving bushmen.

Think about it. As we all know, a wide disparity exists between the academic achievement of black students and white. If government federal or otherwise regarded blacks as being able, it would do the obvious: provide rigorous schooling in the necrotic black regions of the cities, demand from blacks everywhere the homework without which one learns little, supply highly qualified teachers, and expect reasonable decorum.

Government does none of this. It will do many other things for blacks. It will provide food, housing, medical care, i.e., charity, things that keepers of a zoo would provide. It provides jobs on easy terms. It never does anything that implies an expectation of performance.

By inescapable implication government expects nothing of blacks except failure—not in the schools, not at work, nowhere. Law after policy after regulation aims at hiding poor performance and bad behavior, or at punishing whites for noticing it. If you consistently don't expect people to perform, the implication is that you think they can't perform. They can come to believe it themselves, no? And then where are you?

And there is the now-tiresome matter of affirmative action, which can be summed up in four short sentences. It is for losers. If you are good enough, you don't need it. If you need it, you aren't good enough. If you don't need it yet take advantage of it, you are a freeloader. The offer is insulting, and acceptance evidence of a lack of self-respect.

Yet blacks have come to depend on it as Eskimos depend on fish. In examinations for promotion in police departments, admission to universities, federal employment, everywhere, the question is not which candidates are best but which candidates are black.

What must it be like? I'd love to get a degree from CalTech in applied mathematics, but I'm not smart enough. I can't imagine being accepted on affirmative action and then pretending—sitting in class knowing that I was being given grades I didn't earn, knowing that everyone else knew. I'm close to shameless, but not that close.

One might say, arguably but not unreasonably, that blacks come from an intellectually deprived background and need extra help to catch up. The idea might be plausible if there were the slightest evidence of an expectation that they ever would catch up. There is not. Have you heard a politician suggest a cut-off date for affirmative action, such as January 1, 2005? Special privilege is now

demanded by blacks as an entitlement and accepted by the government as per-
petual.

Again, there is the implication of contempt. Those you believe permanently to
need help are those you believe to be permanently helpless.

The universities treat blacks as prizes, not as students. A school with average
boards of 1200 will accept a black applicant with boards of 1000. Now, if the
school actually cared about the student, it would recommend that he go to a
school with average boards of 1000. He then really would be an equal, the
other students would recognize it, and he would have every opportunity to
graduate.

Instead the universities admit badly unqualified blacks as diversity trophies, as
ambulatory bumper stickers exalting the virtuousness of the faculty. This
implies contempt, does it not? One thing it does not imply is intellectual
respect. The black kid is outgunned, he knows it, and he knows the other students know it. A little less charity and a little more respect might help. Respect
and affirmative action are mutually exclusive.

What effect does the unmentionable pervasive scorn have on society? One
result is the widespread assumption among whites that blacks are incompetent. For example, I won't let my children (or me) within shouting distance of
a black doctor. I don't care about his color. I know how great the affirmative
action is, how great the pressure not to fail blacks. Sorry. I'm not going to take
the chance. Nor are a great many people. Black doctors know it.

Is this fair to the black doctor who advanced on his merits? No. But it is
responsible parental behavior.

What does affirmative action do to people who live by it? I can only imagine.
What is it like to work in an office of whites and perhaps Asians who quietly
look down on you? (Asians assuredly do.) The human response is either to
work like a dog to show the white thus-and-suches (which is the Chinese, Jewish, Vietnamese, and Japanese reaction), or to fall back into sulky, marginally
cooperative, you-can't-make-me-ism. And this too many blacks have done.

244	A Brass Pole in Bangkok

The effect on whites? A very quiet, angry hostility that would not exist if blacks were held to normal standards. Yes, there are exceptions. I don't think there are many.

Another effect in a country built on calculated division, and on control of public discourse, is a certain *schadenfreude* in watching politicians who have overstepped the unspoken bounds. From time to time a white pol slips and says something that upsets blacks, as almost anything does. People wait. The next day he will be on television whimpering and apologizing and saying he didn't mean what he obviously meant and writhing like a puppy that has wet the rug. It is amusing.

Blacks of course can safely say far worse of whites without consequence. But does this not demonstrate the belief that they can't be expected to meet usual standards of comportment? If I were black I might wonder whether I weren't being taken for a ride by people who really didn't have much use for me.

CHAPTER 62

❀

Universities and Athlete's Foot.
'Bout equally Useful

Today we'll destroy the universities and drive professors into the streets to starve. They will perhaps pull themselves along by their fingernails and feed on remnants of discarded hamburgers. This will reform western civilization. (This is a full-service column. It doesn't mess with the petty stuff.)

Universities are sorry institutions. First, they cost too damned much. Thirty thousand a year is a bit steep to launch the tad into a career of half-literate commercial brigandage and rapine.

Second, they're pretty much worthless. How useful, for anything at all, are watered-down courses taught in pseudo-academic zoos dedicated to propaganda and the competitive collection of uneducable minorities? How useful are inflated grades, remedial arithmetic, and college credit for independent breathing? Or subjects like "Post-Modernist Perspectives On Lesbian, Bisexual, and Simply Puzzled Learning-Disabled Single Mothers from a Guatemalan Hamlet"?

Most of these wretched schools are no longer worthwhile—don't do what they ought, do what they shouldn't ought, and cost a devilish lot. They get away with it because they have a monopoly on the award of diplomas, which we think we need.

Now, what are universities for? What do we expect them to do, besides charge too much and provide a place to drink beer? First, to teach the student things; second, by awarding a degree to provide to others a reasonable assurance that the student has indeed soaked himself in the precious marinades of learning. They no longer reliably do either.

How can we accomplish these ends without the price tag and the baffled Guatemalan single mothers?

The trick is to separate education, and measures thereof, from the possession of a diploma. You ask: How? Curiously, I have the answer: By the equivalent of home-schooling at the college level.

First, I suggest the establishment of a more thunderous and definitive parallel of the Graduate Record exams. (We'll come to "establishment by whom" in a moment.) These would measure competence in the material both of high school and collegiate education. For example, I'd have them give a score in arithmetic (can you divide fractions?), algebra (can you handle exponents?), as well as in mathematics at the college level. Remember, high schools have been enstupidated as much as the universities.

This would separate the possession of knowledge from the possession of a diploma. Now, could employers be persuaded to accept scores on this beast of an exam instead of the usual fraudulent credentials? (Despite the merits of schooling as an improver of our very own selves, most of us still have to get jobs.)

Maybe.

Employers are very much aware of the dismal output of the schools. A friend in the State Department tells of the disappearance of the ability to write clearly. Companies complain that high-school graduates often barely read and can't do simple arithmetic, that graduates of universities frequently are little better.

If I were running a tool-and-die operation, and a kid aced a real test of arithmetic, algebra, and clear English (I might want to promote him) I wouldn't care whether he had been within rifle range of any particular school. Similarly, if I were hiring an office manager or a teacher of Latin for a good private school, I'd prefer high GREs to a doctorate in Education. The former assure reasonable knowledge; the latter, hopeless incapacity.

The second step is to end the monopoly of professors on teaching. Like their schools, they are enormously overrated. Some can teach, and some can't. They are no better at it than any number of other people easily found. A PhD is chiefly an award for wanton patience and lack of initiative and, in most fields, amounts to a union card, intended to prevent competition.

Example: There is where I live in Mexico a woman, literate and intelligent, who imparts Spanish to North Americans. She could teach Cervantes to a lawn chair. If she were a college professor, I'd rate her as one of the five best I've known. She couldn't teach in an American university because she doesn't have a PhD. She's not in the union.

Ah, but she can teach in her living room. If academic achievement were measured by a standard test instead of by diplomas, students who wanted to learn Spanish could study with her, and demonstrate that they had learned Spanish. Where they had learned it would, and should, be irrelevant. If they didn't want to learn Spanish, they could go away.

Any city has talented people who would teach if they could. Community colleges usually have a heavy sprinkling of good people. Absent the dictatorship of the degree, people could assemble any education they chose, good, bad, liberal arts, specialized, whatever—and demonstrate it—for a bunch less than thirty thousand green ones a year.

Current universities would of course remain, the Ivies for networking and suchlike preemptive brown-nosing, and downscale schools for drinking yourself into a coma. But the test would still be, for those who chose to use it, the measure of accomplishment.

Note, incidentally, that the function of professors is not primarily to teach, but to select the material and to insist that students show up for class. Sure, sometimes the prof offers useful explanation or discussion. The study of spoken languages requires a teacher. Yet there are few subjects that a bright and determined student couldn't learn with a textbook and a library. Other sorts of student shouldn't be studying at all.

A crucial question: Who would write the universal test? There's the rub. If the present professoriate got anywhere near it, they would intellectually disembowel it, translate it into Ebonics, and stuff it full of crypto-Marxist blather with the enthusiasm of a taxidermist given to excess. I would suggest a committee of people who had worked in their fields but could prove they had never taught.

Universities would of course fight the idea fang and claw, in hideous English. But they couldn't do anything about it. The law does not require that anyone attend college. The academic union can decide who may award a degree, but it cannot stop people from taking a test, or from showing the result to whomever they chose. The government can prevent a superb teacher from describing himself as being accredited, but it cannot stop him from teaching.

One thing is sure: As long as the degree, however worthless, is the measure of merit, we will get more propaganda, lower standards, and less cultivation. Have you noticed that signs on bathrooms today no longer say "Men" and "Women," but have little pictures? I used to think they were for foreigners.

CHAPTER 63

Fooling Around in Laos

Vientiane, Laos—

The Mekong flows brown and ugly past the beer stalls and restaurants across the street from the Lane Xian hotel, a slightly decomposing pile but comfortable enough. The country is green, perhaps not hopelessly backward but nearly so, and rattles with motor scooters. The people are small and brown. When female, they are often quite pretty. Westerners are not uncommon: A pretty fair current of backpacking tourists comes through, often en route to Luang Prabang. Laos is the sort of place writers invariably call "sleepy," so I won't.

It is a backwater, and was during the years of the war in Vietnam. Today it contains preserved traces of those receding times, like fossilized tracks of forgotten dinosaurs.

I met a reasonably English-speaking young Lao woman in a stall on the river and recruited her as tour guide. I liked her. She was studying to the extent she could in a school of business in hopes of getting into hotel work. Waitressing in a Lao beer chute is a dead end. Our deal was that I'd pay for the cab on forays into the countryside, correct her English, and buy lunch. She would be factotum.

During a temple crawl she mentioned in passing that life had been difficult for her family after they had lost her father. How had that happened, I asked unwisely. He died fighting the Americans, she said.

Oh.

Maybe it is better not to go back to where your wars were. Perspective corrodes causes unless they are very good ones. I'm not sure ours were. Three decades have passed since we were bombing the Laos. It is hard to remember why they were a threat to the United States. The Lao communists won, at least in the sense that they kept the country, and nothing bad happened to the US. The communists won decisively in Viet Nam, and nothing bad happened to the United States. They won in Cambodia, and nothing bad happened to the United States.

I, my guide, and two taxi drivers were looking at another temple, which Laos has lots of, when I asked about the French. They were gone, said one of the drivers with approval. After them came the Americans, he said, who were also gone, and then the Russians, who too were gone. They clearly thought that gone was the proper condition for all of these groups.

I don't think that Americans quite grasp that countries don't like having foreigners bomb them. We tend to justify our wars in terms of abstractions: We are attacking to defeat communism, impose democracy, overcome evil or, now, to end terrorism. The countries being bombed, devastated, and occupied usually think they are fighting invaders who have no business being there. The distinction is lost on many. I know aging veterans who to this day do not understand why the Vietnamese weren't grateful that we had come to help them fight communists.

Southeast Asia is full of the moldering offal of deceased foreign policy. In Siem Reap in Cambodia a couple of weeks ago I was delighted to find a thriving tourist economy based on the ruins of Angkor. The schools were full. Hotels went up. Yet you still see one-legged men. For years, Cambodia's chief crop was land mines.

I lost acquaintances to the Khmer Rouge after the fall of Phnom Penh and tend to be disagreeable when I think about it. Perhaps I should reflect stoically on the necessity of breaking eggs to make omelettes. The wisdom of this is more apparent to those who are not eggs.

In Cambodia the United States, exercising its god-given right to meddle catastrophically anywhere it can reach, had destabilized a puzzled country of thatch huts and water buffalo and facilitated the arrival of Pol Pot. The Americans then went back to California to surf.

The communists, exercising the mindless brutality common among them, had then killed huge if uncertain numbers of people for no reason, and wrecked the country. This showed that the Russians and Americans could cooperate when they wished. Call it non-peaceful co-extermination. Or call it synergy or convergence or conservation of parity. The Khmers died.

On the train from Bangkok to the Thai-Lao border I had shared a compartment with a Lao, perhaps in his sixties, from a comparatively rich family. He had spent thirty years in business in Paris. We became casual friends and he invited me to dinner at his house, where some fifty of his relatives were having a Buddhist commemoration of something or other. Members of the family had returned for the event from several countries.

They were hospitable and spoke I have no idea how many languages among them. The children were well mannered, the food excellent and accompanied by that traditional Lao drink, Pepsi. I supposed that they were the enemy, or had been, but wasn't sure why. I sometimes think the State Department needs to get out more and the CIA, less. The notion of devout Buddhist atheistic communist businessmen scoured around my mental craw but I could never get a handle on it.

While eating breakfast at the Lane Xian, I was surprised to hear Spanish. The two fellows at the next table were Cubans, doubtless in Vientiane because of party solidarity or something equally as tiresome. I chatted with them briefly about nothing in particular. They were friendly, having the notion that the American government hated Cuba but that the American public did not. To a considerable extent this is true. The analysis is complicated by the inability of many to distinguish between Cuba and Castro.

I don't understand our embargo of Cuba. When the Russian empire was trying to turn the island into a military base aimed at the United States, the embargo made sense. Now it doesn't. As nearly as I can tell, it continues because of the petrified vindictiveness of cold warriors without a cold war. It's funny: We don't like Castro because he oppresses his people, so we maintain a now-pointless embargo that also oppresses them.

If you get to Laos, the reclining Buddha a half hour from Vientiane is worth the trip. The little countries of the region were not always backwaters, or not so backwaterish anyway. In brief respites from killing each other, which they did as relentlessly as everyone else, they made some remarkable things. If you are in the business of building hotels, you might put one hereabouts. The country could use the money. I can recommend a young lady to help you manage it.

CHAPTER 64

Fred Throws Hat in Ring, Head Gets Cold

I guess I'm going to run for president. Destiny calls me, like a malevolent telemarketer selling aluminum siding. The flame of civilization gutters. The trend lines all point downward. People stranger than Caligula bay at the moon and await their electoral chance. The nation yearns for Fred. I can smell it. The times are ripe for—yes—The New Frederalism.

It's just like Nostradamus said, who I thought was a football team. We lunge from bad to worse. George's numbers are dropping faster than a prom dress. The incumbent's bizarre habit of collecting Moslems takes its political toll, even on a catatonic electorate fixated on the lobotomy box. He now has two countries full of them, Iraq and Afghanistan.

I don't get it. Why collect Moslems? Why not Faberge Eggs instead, or early Plastic Man comics? You don't have to bomb Plastic Man comics and they don't shriek from minarets at odd hours. Hear that *whuffwhuffwhuffling* sound? That's Hillary flapping her wings offstage. Barely offstage. If George gets a bit more gummed up in his various overseas tar babies, she's going to run like underdone eggs. The president will be dog meat. If we are lucky.

You see. The country needs me. Desperately.

Whether I need the country is another question, but, well, noblesse oblige. No blesse, no bleege. No pain, no gain. Sorry. I'm getting giddy at the thought of the White House. I may run under an assumed name, though.

I'm trying to think of a campaign slogan. Help me. The heart of any presidential campaign is a bumper sticker that doesn't use too many of the hard letters of the alphabet, like Q and Z. Something like "Timbuktu and Frederick Too," which has rhythm without being too intelligible. Or "A Fred in Every Pot"? Been done.

Maybe, "We Have Nothing To Be Afred Of But Fred Hisself." That works unless people think about it, a remote likelihood. What do you figure?

My advisors in moments of sobriety tell me that I need a platform. It means a list of things that you lie about planning to do—or principles that you stand for, on, or behind. For a platform you want fifty-weight insights that would slow an oil leak in a '48 flathead. Things like, "Our children are our future." (Though has anyone tried, "Our children are Upper Permian stem reptiles"?)

Then there's, "I stand behind the youth of America." Barney Frank did that, though, and it didn't get him anywhere. But then, he was gay and I'm not. Or "We have to get the country...*going* again." Of course, anyone with the brains of a tent caterpillar can see that it has already gone. That's the problem. "If elected, I'll get the country to come back." Not too decisive. What if it didn't want to?

How about a simple slogan, elegant, yet evocative and to the point?

"Fred Says Shoot the Sumbitches!"

Anyway, my platform. Maybe I should be more specific. "If elected, I will spray anthrax on the teachers colleges." Does that sing, or what? It would raise the national IQ by thirteen points. My first thought was to spray anthrax on the rest of the country, on the theory that a place that puts its young in the hands of low-normal gape-mouthed social shims merits some vile thirteenth-century disease. But then what would I be president of?

But what will I be president of anyway? This is getting tricky.

Sorry, I keep worrying about my slogan. Maybe "Elect Fred! Win Free Prizes!" Reckon?

Half the population doesn't vote, probably because they're on the couch, eyeballs sewn to the propaganda modem like buttons on a sock puppet. I want to inspire them, to give people an incentive to vote, something profound and rooted in the deep wells of the national psyche, something to hope and yearn for.

"Elect Fred and Get Half-Priced Burgers!"

Maybe "Fred! Better Than Ebola." Could seem speciesist. "Filiviruses are people too"? I'm not sure that "A Country Deserves What It Tolerates" would have broad appeal.

I'm assembling my campaign staff. As I understand it, you need three speechwriters, a makeup artist, a gestures coach, five pollsters and a focus-group geekess. Why you need a candidate isn't clear. With a staff like that you could elect a styrofoam cup or a park bench. Which we may have done.

The way it works is that the pollsters and focus groupers, who are the big fish on the staff, ask people, "Do you think the candidate is masculine enough, or does he need a squirt more compassion? Does he need to ratchet up the decisiveness, or does he need a wholesome admixture of flexibility? Eye of newt, or wing of bat?"

Then the gestures people and writers dial in the stats, having calculated the standard deviation and a regression to the mean. The candidate adopts a pole-axed stare: Unblinking eye-contact with a teleprompter is thought to indicate candor and forthrightness. He says Something Firm, or Something Soft, depending on the correction to his moral heading suggested by the poll's results. Then the pollsters sally forth to again take the temperature of the electorate.

This works, even though the flickering screens, to which the electorate has its eyes in direct corneal contact, have explained for a week how the candidate is adjusting his image, like the suspension on a NASCAR rocket that's a bit loose on the turns.

Perhaps "Vote Fred! For God's Sake, Look at the Other Candidates!"

Actually, campaigns could be done in software. If computer graphics can make a convincing dinosaur, why not something with a simpler nervous system, as for example a president? Seriously, think about it. The survey numbers could go straight into RAM. Then you would specify the target audience for a given pitch: men, women, veterans, derelicts, parasitic minorities, illiterate teenagers, all the underpinnings of democracy.

The software would generate the best candidate for the particular demographic: For women, a vaguely gay guy with melting features that you just know wants to talk about feelings. For men under thirty, the same: People always want to vote for candidates like themselves. For older men, rock-solid guys who smoked themselves into cancer. Marlboro Man, Humphrey Bogart. You could have sliders for sincerity, sensitivity, testosteronal vacuity.

"Fred! Good as Any, Better'n Some." Reckon?

Perhaps a little intellectual appeal, though disguised. "Save the Prairies. *Faut-il Bruler* Sod?" or "Buying is Prior to Essence. Support Your Chamber of Commerce." But I think I'm getting wacked-out with the strain of strategic planning. It isn't easy to lead the residue of a great nation into whatever dark and twisted future it faces, flittering with bats. I'm going to the nearest bar and consult with James Beam. He understands.

(Note to paleontologists: I know, I know.)

CHAPTER 65

Istanbul: Days That Were

In the late Sixties the main path for the young gripped by wanderlust ran from India, where it picked up a lot of Aussies, across Asia to Istanbul. There it forked. One branch went to Egypt and the Middle East, the other to Europe. Istanbul was the hub. In jeans and boots, with backpacks and shoulder bags, kids arrived from Bombay and Katmandu, from Sydney and Brindisi and New York. Most were between eighteen and twenty-five. They wanted to see far places and astonishing things, and simply did it, as kids will. They had little money. They didn't care. They pooled to buy decomposing minibuses and casually set off across Persia.

In Istanbul their—our—habitat was the Sultan Ahmet district, in the shadow of the grand domed mosque that loomed against, when I was there, grey wintry skies. Dirty ice squeezed from between stones of winding streets and a whiff of wood smoke hung in the air. Dark-faced and vaguely dangerous looking men who in fact weren't hurried by in thick coats. You were Somewhere Else. It was magic.

Many of the male wanderers wore beards. These were the freak years, and anyway shaving is a nuisance on the road. They were motley: college girls from Barnard, a black smooth-talking DJ out of Jersey, drugged-up spindrift from the hippie havens of Europe and North Africa, a guy from somewhere east with a parrot. Some were truth-seeking tumbleweeds pursuing enlightenment, others just adventurers. There was an artist from Ohio who showed us photographs of a blue fiberglass sculpture he had made of his ex-wife's backside. It wasn't obscene, just rounded. All of us were caught in the craving for new things that besets late adolescents if they're worth a damn.

I was a bit of an oddity—pretty much out of the Marines by then and traveling with a shot-up squid named Len Vanderwood who had been in PBRs in the delta and gotten ambushed. He did all sorts of heroic things, like chopping the paravanes and using a Browning .30 like a fire hose, which only happens in the movies but Len didn't know it. We were exotics among hippies, poets, and seekers. On the other hand they had crossed Afghanistan in VW buses, passing through towns where both you and your girlfriend could get raped and sometimes were.

Most were just kids with an itch, and stayed at the Yucel Hostel, pretty much the standard European gig: a buck-fifty if you had a sheet bag in a bunkroom with five other people. They would travel for a year, remember it forever, and go back to Belgium to be doctors. A few were different.

These stayed at the Gulhane Hotel. The Gulhane was for the lost, the doomed, for people too low-caste to sleep under bridges. You went up narrow dark stairs and came out on the roof where sheet plastic covered a two-by-four framework to form a skeletal barn in the January cold. You could stay there for twenty-five cents a night. It was a good price for kids who had sold their passports to buy drugs and had nowhere to go. Len and I went to see it in a spirit of anthropological curiosity.

Your two bits bought you squatter's rights to a decomposing grass mat on the floor, on which to lay a sleeping bag. Maybe a dozen people stayed there. There was no electricity. From a crossbeam at either end a hash pipe dangled on a cord. At night the inmates sat in circles beneath the hash pipes, jacketed against the chill, staring at what appeared to be pie pans of bluely burning alcohol.

The pipe went around. When it burned out, etiquette was that whoever then held it filled it from his stash. The flames danced, shadows leapt strangely, especially after a while in the circle, and some freak from North Africa tweedled on a soprano recorder. He couldn't quite play it, but neither was it unmelodic. The camaraderie of those who knew it was cold outside gripped us, a conspiracy of warmth. We told stories of Goa and Marikesh, of mortar flares hanging ghastly in clouds over the ugly thumb that was Marble Mountain.

From time to time, so help me, a Turk from the hotel came through and called, "Hasheeshkabab, twenty-five cents." Lamb, dog, road kill, morgue meat, I don't know. It was well spiked with the herb.

The lost too had their place in the order of things. I wished them well.

We were the first drug generation. Ritalin was the preferred amphetamine, not yet being used to subdue schoolboys. Kids gobbled it and for a couple of days were very intense. If you got close to them you heard a faint "*bzzzzzzzzz*" and smelled hot insulation. A plaque of hash the size of a Heath bar cost three bucks. Most of us experimented for a few years, enjoyed the sense of shared misbehavior, got bored, and quit. A few ended up at the Gulhane.

The scam of the times was selling traveler's checks. You sold them to a South African for forty percent of their face value, unsigned. His operatives then forged them for face value. You went to the American Express office and said that you had lost your checks. They replaced them. A long line of kids waited at the Amex office to report lost checks. It was no more moral than shading your deductions, cheating on your wife, or downloading music.

Yenner's, if memory doesn't lie, was the roasted-meat den near the Pudding Shop. It was dark and blackened by smoke, like a medieval torture chamber but without the cheer. You knew immediately that it wasn't Kansas. The roasts were savory, greasy, and smoky. A clothesline ran diagonally across the room. On it in those pre-internet days travelers left notes to each other, held by clothespins. One I remember: "Will the girl in the green dress I met on the bank of the Ganges ask for me at the Youth Hostel? Mike."

That's how it was. Wherever you were going, somebody had been there, and knew what to do. Calcutta? Sure, try the hostel on Sutter Street. (I did. Coming out one day, I saw a naked man with no feet rolling down the sidewalk to beg from me.) Israel? Ask them not to stamp your passport because then you can go to Arab countries. In Delhi the Pahar Gange section is really cheap, the Venus hotel is fifty cents a night. You won't find it in a tourist guide.

I don't know where kids go today. I just hope it is as good.

CHAPTER 66

The Mess in Potamia

Our foray into the Middle East appears pregnant with largish consequences. I wish I knew which consequences.

The attack on Iraq was indeed shocking and awesome. If the United States can now subdue the country, and bend it to chosen ends whatever they may be, America will presumably be the dominant power in the world for decades to come. Syria and Iran will take note and behave prudently. Everyone will understand that the US can enforce its will almost anywhere and impose such political solutions as it thinks wise.

On the other hand, if the US cannot hold on in Iraq, no one will fear it for a long time. Instead of gaining influence in the Moslem world the US will lose any it had. Iran for example will understand that it can do whatever it likes. America will shrink from overseas involvement as it did after Vietnam. The occupation will be seen less as the beginning of the new American century than as the end of the last.

Which?

Further, the presidency of Mr Bush, and his place in history, are at stake. He knows it, which will either make victory possible or defeat ugly. He has invested too much of both pride and political capital to pull out. Coitus interruptus is not much of an electoral strategy. If he prevails, he will perhaps be seen as a smaller Churchill, a clear-sighted man who by tenacity and unsuspected wisdom transformed the Middle East. If he loses I suspect that he will be remembered as the worst president we have had, the man who single-handedly neutered America in the world.

Which?

I don't know. But one thing is sure. He won't retreat unless forced.

Now, can Mr. Bush prevail? I don't know. I'm not in Iraq. I neither speak nor read Arabic. However: If, as the White House has argued, the Iraqi resistance consists of outside agitators and a few followers of a detested dictator, the US can probably wear them down. If the population of Iraq supports the resistance, or is coming to support it, then the occupation is in all likelihood doomed.

Which?

The power of the American military will be largely irrelevant to the outcome.

The military is small, heavily reliant on technology, and designed for attacking point targets and organized military forces. For these purposes, it is good, and in fact has no competitors. It is, however, poorly designed for occupying large countries with armed and hostile populations that choose to adopt guerrilla tactics.

The way to defeat American forces is to avoid giving them clear targets, stretch them thin, steadily inflict enough losses to alienate public opinion in the US, and keep the war dragging on. You don't defeat the US in the field. It can't be done. You defeat it in America. When a war loiters about inconclusively (if it does) and the body bags trickle home, eventually the country wearies, the press turns against the war, the president's numbers fall, politicians of the other party make elections into referenda on the war, and (in this case perhaps) Hillary smells blood in the water.

Oddly, the occupying army itself often becomes the ally of the resistance. For example, the guerrillas destroy a truck in a supply convoy in a town. The soldiers return fire wildly, killing several civilians including, if the guerrillas are lucky, a child. The burning truck gives the resistance credibility: they are defeating the invaders. The killing of the civilians arouses hatred and aids recruitment.

Killing GIs eventually forces the occupiers into fortified encampments, making political ends harder to achieve. It also (reasonably enough) causes the GIs to hate the population. The soldiers are very young, in a country whose ways they do not understand and whose language they do not speak. Many of its people want to kill them. This makes troops angry and quick on the trigger. They therefore tend to treat the population roughly, which is exactly what the guerrillas want.

The occupiers often find themselves in circumstances in which there is no right answer. If at a checkpoint they do not search a woman in baggy clothes, it may well turn out that she was carrying a large amount of Semtex. Something blows up. If they do search her, the population will hate them. Body-searching the women of a conservative society doesn't get you party invitations. Kicking in doors in the night and holding women at gunpoint poses the same difficulty. If you don't do these things, you don't catch the resistance. If you do, you recruit for them. And probably still don't catch them.

It is a hard kind of war to win. A while ago, the media reported, GIs accidentally killed nine Iraqi policemen. Other American troops (said the papers) killed civilians when, hearing celebratory shots fired into the air, they opened up on a wedding. If these accounts are correct, they suggest very poor fire discipline. To the US command these were "incidents." To families of the dead, the killings were reasons to seek revenge. And of course all Iraq knows. The guerrillas could ask for nothing better.

Now, is the resistance growing or diminishing? I don't know. Having been around both reporters and military PAOs, I know better than to trust either too blithely. Still, it sounds as though the Iraqis are getting organized and getting better. They seem to be gaining in sophistication.

A few weeks back, for example, the media reported that the Iraqis had attacked a convoy and then ambushed the rescue forces. This was a standard Viet Cong tactic. Another was to put two remotely detonated mines close to each other.

The first one gets the convoy and, a bit later, the second gets the medical teams. Coming soon to a theater near you.

What now? So far as I can see, the best possible solution now is that the US win, establish some reasonable government, and leave. I'm doing more hoping than expecting, but maybe. (Of course, I run to pessimism. This would be a splendid time to be wrong.) But if—if—things get worse and fighting grows, the odds would seem good for a long war by an increasingly desperate president, and then a humiliating retreat, leaving a helpless Iraq next to a healthy Iran. It sounds like a recipe for chaos. If you go to Baghdad, rent.

Meanwhile Hillary makes backseat noises: Oh, no, I'll never, no, not that, keep trying....

CHAPTER 67

Lie Back and Enjoy It

I-Already-Feel-Safer Department: In the *Washington Times* I discover that some ditzbunny in the legislature of Annapolis, Maryland, wants to outlaw plastic guns. Yes. She's going to get rid of them rascals. It's because it will end crime.

Quoth the *Times* "Alderwoman Cynthia A. Carter, Democrat, [now that's a surprise] said the law would ban all toy guns except for clear, brightly colored plastic guns." Honest. She's doing this. "If someone commits a felony with one, they [sic] will not only be charged with the crime but also with using a toy gun," avowed she, semi-literately.

Oh, good, Cynthia. You're encouraging criminals to use real guns, so that they won't be hit with the plastic penalty also. Of course a chief reason for using plastic guns has been that, if caught, the criminal could say with reason that he wasn't threatening life. How very astute, Cynthia. In your credit I'll say that when it comes to thinking, you have one motingator set of hormones.

The good lady will also fine parents of children caught playing with plastic guns. "Anything that can be done to deglamorize guns is a plus," said Ellen O. Moyer, mayor of the city that is home to the Naval Academy.

Cynthia is a co-mother of the Political Redskins Effect, which is the aesthetic appreciation of really good catastrophe. I used to follow the Skins when they were having a good year. When they had a mediocre year, I slacked off. But when they had disastrous years, when the running backs went in the wrong direction and the quarterback threw only interceptions and every other play was a fumble—I followed them again. It was fun to see how bad they could be. I longed for more-humiliating mistakes, for impossible errors. Maybe it was sadistic, or traitorous, or maybe just a joy in parody.

I've come to feel the same way about American society. Slow decline is draining, but spectacular collapse invigorates. It's no longer anything to be upset about. The season's lost anyway, no hope of the playoffs, so enjoy it. It's entertainment. I fire up the computer every morning in hopes of finding some new and unexpected form of daft behavior, a new chuckle, some form of social self-parody that I never dreamed of.

My political philosophy these days is to favor the funniest candidate and the most absurd policy, just to watch what will happen. Don't delude yourself that this is an easy course. The principle of Greater Comedy does not make for casual choices.

If Hillary ran against George, for example, I'd be hard pressed to choose. On responsible terms, Hillary would easily be my choice. She would socialize the country, but George is Stalinizing it; she's lots brighter, less embarrassing, and doesn't want to be Arabia's mother. She doesn't want to put a camera in my bathroom.

But in terms of amusement, George wins. Hillary is just an old-line big-government Democrat, and boring. She would take the country in bad directions, but not interestingly bad ones. George and his buddies are turning the United States into the first state of total electronic control. It's a first-rate show. Face it: Watching the destruction of the world's greatest free government is much cooler that watching the snoring growth of federal departments.

Another recent headline: "Sayreville, New Jersey-AP—You can't pretend your finger is a gun—even if you're in kindergarten.

"So says a federal appeals court in ruling that a New Jersey school district did not violate a kindergarten boy's free-speech rights by suspending him for threatening to shoot his friends during a game at recess."

Now *that's* what I like: Forty-weight solemn clownishness, the kind you could calk a roof with. A kid of maybe six points his finger, gets suspended, and it becomes an issue of freedom of speech to be decided by a federal court. Only in America do courts concern themselves with the unfurling of a kindergartner's finger. (Personally, I think that kindergarteners ought to be fitted with sensors in case they point fingers when alone. Yes, digit monitors. All sorts of things can be done with fingers. I bet nobody else ever thought of that.)

It is well that Americans do not care what others think about them. As best I can tell, Mexicans find our behavior puzzling if not lunatic, and the French think it deliciously amusing. The Canadians follow the American lead and often are even nuttier. The Russians probably watch with a sense of looming nostalgia. They've been there, but without the humor.

Anyway, for those who prefer to enjoy the spectacle instead of opposing the inevitable, I suggest that the best course is to promote a coalition of male Republicans and female Democrats. These reliably display the most amusing traits of their sexes.

The Republican men, as for example BushCroft and Rumsfeld, bring to the table a peculiarly male arrogance and sense of godhead. Female arrogance tends to be social; male, military. Male insecurity takes a form slightly different from that of the female: I suspect that those occupying the great double-wide on Pennsylvania Avenue worry that maybe size does matter, and they need to do something quick. They easily persuade themselves, in the absence of any real system of values, that their duty is to sweep away the smoldering ashes of the Constitution to make room for more microphones.

The female Democrats should manage the social burlesque. Being viscerally obsessed with security, security, security in a world that seems to be mysteriously but disturbingly somehow wrong, they will pass Niceness Legislation. The analysis will be emotional rather than rational. They won't know this. When the ill-conceived proves unworkable, they will insist on tighter controls on little boys, more bans on second-hand smoke, more intrusiveness in a flailing attempt to impose Niceness.

What I figure is, there's probably an alien Space Base somewhere, maybe on Jupiter, full of people with hairy green tentacles coming out of their heads and several eyes. And they're shooting Degradation Rays at the Earth. First they did Russia, which was already pretty degraded and didn't have far to go. Now they've got the US. They're beaming the footage back to wherever they live as a reality show.

Nothing else really explains what is happening. It's three-ring national apoptosis, the long leap from the Golden Gate. Whom the gods would destroy, they first make outrageously funny. We're there, and it's a splendid show.

CHAPTER 68

Tyin' the Big Ugly in La Cristina

The afternoon when Ron and Sara proceeded to become one flesh, and an artifact of globalization, as well as married to the gills, their fool dog Toby was eating avocadoes in the yard again, which in a dog means he don't got the sense God give a Democrat. But he's agreeable, which is more important than intelligence in a dog. And most people. Especially Democrats.

You don't know Ron and Sara. Ron is what Yankees call a Good Ol' Boy, with capital letters so they can feel lofty, and worldly, and knowing. Yankees are idiots. Anyway, "Good Ol' Boy" means somebody with judgement and a Southern accent. (Yankees are a mess. It's hard to believe, but some of them think "red" is a word of one syllable. The schools went down something terrible after Gettysburg.)

When Dixie plays, Ron stands with his hand over his heart, which shows he has his values straight. He eats avocadoes too, like Toby, only he usually peels them. He understands trucks. And politics. And 'gators, the which are all over Florida.

Nobody is sure how Ron caught Sara. Everyone agrees that he married above himself. It's not that Ron isn't upstanding and admirable. It's just that a first-rate Mexican woman is hard to compete with. I know three gringos married to Mexicanas, and one more who might be if she recognized my virtues. In every case, the man is doing better than he ought. (I just hope Mexican women don't read this. If they found out what scoundrels we are, they'd probably marry each other. Like feminists.)

Anyway, Sara looks to be pure Aztec, and might weigh ten pounds if she were holding a twelve-pound dumbbell. She's smart as a whip. I don't mean your modern dumbed-down socially promoted whip. I mean one with high boards and a degree from Tulane. She's a nurse. She's funny, and real nice, and no crazier than the baseline for the sex.

Now, their backyard where they were getting married is broad and green, and littered with avocadoes that Toby hasn't gotten around to yet, with shade trees and a rooftop flat place that's wonderful for watching the brawling-ass lightning storms they have around here. And huge sunsets that look like a Chinese lacquer lamp with a light bulb inside. There's a casita out back for visitors.

It isn't high-end housing because Ron and Sara can't afford it. It's just pretty and comfortable with a fireplace and gorgeous view of the mountains and the brawling-ass lightning storms and quiet and peaceful, and I guess I'm starting to wonder why it isn't high-end housing. Didn't cost enough, I guess.

People started showing up in early afternoon. I was sitting in Ron's office with Ron, who had the willies. It wasn't doubt. He didn't have any. It was just that marriage is like quadruple-bypass surgery and you haven't seen the doctor's diploma but he's holding a Buck knife and an ice-cream scoop. Outside, folks appeared in droves: Ron the Mechanic, Don the dirt-floored Kentuckian with the maxed-out dune buggy, Lex Luther and the Toad Queen, Tommy and Luz, La Fantasma, Crazy Fred the Alleged Writer (a bad influence, I can tell you), and a whole lot of Messicans.

It may be that some beer wasn't in the yard. The rest of it was.

Now, you've got two kinds of gringos here. The first kind live in gated retirement communities to keep Mexico out. I think the locals hope the gates will keep them in. I do. They don't mix with the country. After ten years, they are still saying, "Grah-shuss."

And you've got Ron, who doesn't need gates. You could drop him in a remote town in China and a week later he'd know everybody worth knowing and have a sweetheart of a girlfriend and be holding barbecues. He fits here. Besides, Mexicans are basically Southerners with a pronunciation problem. It's why I like them.

So I sat under the trees and ate ribs and scratched Toby's ears and chatted with Sara, who looked nervous but hadn't yet gotten into her wedding paraphernalia. Don the dirt-floored Kentuckian came over and we talked dune buggies. What they do here is take the motor off a VW bus, mount it on a tube-frame buggy chassis with a serious roll-cage, do things to the engine that would surprise the hell out of German engineers who thought it was a family car, and stick big tires and a heavy transaxle on it. The result looks like the automotive equivalent of Spiderman.

Boy babies in Georgia have been known to be born with a ¾ Isky in one hand. The South is a place that understands muscle cars. And Don's dune rocket was every bit of that.

But we're trying to get these folks married. Sara disappeared, Toby started chasing somebody's toy poodle as if he didn't know he'd been fixed, and Ron showed up in a tux. Nobody else much noticed because after all weddings seem kind of normal if you aren't in them, and there were lots of ribs and beer.

A nice lawyeress from Chapala was there and ready. Mexico believes in separation of church and state, as distinct from persecution of the church by the state, so they needed a JP. Somebody banged on a glass with a fork and said, hey, we're here to do this so shut up and let's do it. Everybody shut up because it was the right thing to do and anyway they liked Ron and Sara.

Sara popped out of the house looking like a million pesos that hadn't been devalued for a while. As a color scheme, Aztec on white works just real well. I grabbed my digital chimera and prepared to immortalize the moment for such posterity as mattered. Which includes readers of this column, and that's why the picture is there.

I guess it worked. They're still married and say they like it, and I go over every couple of weeks to eat ribs and visit. Alexia, who is Sara's daughter from a previous marriage, is smart as her mother, which is a pretty high benchmark, and makes A's in school. Sara's a wicked cook and a tremendous gal. Toby is hopeless. What can you say about a dog that eats avocadoes? But, well, he's an agree-able beast. That's better than a lot of people.

CHAPTER 69

❀

Dwarf Tossing: The Search for Oppression

I'm going to fill a dark awful basement with radioactive cockroaches. Yep. Big nasty ones like skateboards on legs, that go *click-click-click* when they walk. And maybe poisonous. I'm going to starve them for a week.

Then I'm going to catch all the coercive priss-spigots in the world, the ones that want to ban second-hand smoke and dwarf-tossing and beer. I'll smear the rascals with bacon fat, so the roaches won't know what they're eating, as otherwise they might not.

Then I'm going to toss all those greased busybodies into the basement. And whoop. And dance. Ha.

In the *National Post* of Canada, I find that one Sandra Pupatello, a member of that afflicted nation's Parliament, has her knickers in a bunch over dwarf-tossing. Upset, she is. No end.

Now, dwarf-tossing is a sport, like baseball. The Aussies invented it. (I think.) A great big guy picks up the dwarf, or maybe a couple of great big guys, usually in an agreeably unruly bar full of second-hand smoke, and beer, where people say dirty words, and toss him as far as they can. Like the shot-put.

I'm puzzled. Why is this terrible? And why is it any business of Sandra's?

From the pupatellian whoop, and yellin,' you might believe what the dwarves aren't tellin': that they're being forced into indentured tossedhood—shanghaied, or drugged, or hit on their heads and dragged into dark alleys, thereafter to lead degraded lives of being tossed till closing, and then kept in wall lockers, and fed scraps.

No. It is voluntary. In fact Bradley, a Torontovian dwarf otherwise known as Tripod, said, "I'm doing this because I want to. I'm an adult and can make my own decisions."

Well, no, he can't. The dread lady is going to make them for him. It's because she's his mother. She's everybody's mother.

I want a DNA test.

You might also gain the impression that the dwarves, victims of course, were being hurled against broken rocks, or boards with nails in them, or perhaps into industrial grinders. Savagery. Sadism. Oppression (especially). Broken and bleeding little people.

Again, no. Cushions. It is a non-destructive sport. Silly, perhaps. Silly almost certainly. But not vicious.

I once knew a couple of dwarfs casually. One did some kind of library research in Washington, and the other didn't. Relying on an exhaustive statistical sampling of both of them, I have elaborated Fred's Law of Dwarves: They're like everybody else, only short. They can make their own decisions without help from some overwrought Carry Nation with an Adolf wish.

Used to be, crusaders wanted to stop abuses, such as wretched treatment of migrant labor, or the sweating of children in shoe factories. It was a good idea. Mostly it worked. Then the reformers ran out of victims, and needed to find some more. So, like pigs snuffling for truffles, they started hunting for new and largely imaginary victims.

Soon fat people were victims. Homosexuals were victims. Women who gave birth like a slot-machine jackpot were victims. The shiftless were victims. The unhappy and bored and rained-on were victims, and people with warts. Their rights had to be protected.

The reformers had discovered predatory moralism. It gave us Prohibition and organized crime. The focus shifted from helping the downtrodden to brow-beating everyone else. Virtue is the instinctive weapon of the vaguely angry. They wield it like a cosh.

Do they ever. Sandra says, "We've worked diligently over generations to change attitudes towards people who might be different in some way."

The dripping sound you hear is Ms. Pupatello. She's leaking forty-weight med-dlesome tediousness. "We"? Who is "we"? Who asked her to change our atti-tudes? (Maybe in Canada they elect politicians to change attitudes.) What attitude precisely needs to be changed?

Mother Pupatello has found a new twist in the social rope: Coercive third-party civil rights. She wants to impose unwanted rights, and then enforce them. Dwarf-tossing, which is voluntary behavior between consenting adults, becomes a violation of rights, though no one involved thinks it is, and nobody asked Mommy Sandra in the first place. (Who, by the way, is in violation? The dwarf willingly engages in the tossing. He's violating his own civil rights. We should jail dwarves.)

The punitive imposition of rights not asked for grows common in North America. Note the banning of dodgeball in the public schools as violence, and the attempt to keep boys from roughhousing. Why? Kids want to play dodge-ball. If they didn't, they wouldn't. We aren't talking compulsory dodgeball. And boys like to wrestle. It's why they do it. (Anybody thought of that?)

But teachers don't like to roughhouse. So, following the totalitarian instincts of prigs and prudes and the self-consciously inadequate everywhere, they make sappy passivity a human right. Then they inflict it on kids who would rather have scarlet fever.

It's rule by parsnips, I tell you, by smugly hostile hop-toads with damp fingers.

Smoking in bars works the same way. If you don't like smoke, tell the owner. Then go to another bar. If enough people want smokeless bars, somebody will start one, or lots of them. But don't tell me I'm a victim of second-hand smoke, when I didn't ask your opinion in the first place, and then protect me from something I don't mind.

(No, I don't smoke, never have, but I like smoky bars. People who smoke are more interesting than people who don't. And reformers would never come to a smoky bar because they'd be afraid they'd get cancer. I'd be afraid they wouldn't.)

But maybe there's hope. Says an AP story out of Tampa, a dwarf named Dave Flood is suing to have Florida's anti-tossing law overturned. He appears on a radio show as Dave the Dwarf, and opines as follows:

"They assume because you have some physical handicap, you can't make decisions for yourself...I don't have a mental handicap. I don't like the government telling me what I can and cannot do."

But the position of the reformers, though they would never admit it, is precisely that the very short *are* mental defectives. They can't manage their lives, so priss wads have to do it for them.

Ms. Pupatello needs a cat.

Now, if the tossed guys aren't offended (and if they were, they'd just quit), and the customers aren't offended, who or what is offended? Answer: Ms. Pupawhatsit's delicate sensibilities. Of which more and more of us are indeed the victims.

I'm changing my mind about the giant radioactive cockroaches. It's an animal-abuse issue. I mean, I'd hate being kept in a dark basement and having puritans dropped on me.

CHAPTER 70

Adolf, Patriotism, and Really Stupid Mail

In my daily snowstorm of email I find furious appeals to patriotism, usually addressed to large lists of recipients. The writers invoke The Founding Fathers, urge fealty, and counsel solidarity with all the whoop and holler of a camp meeting. I'm puzzled. Why is patriotism thought to be a virtue? It seems to me a scourge.

Judging by my mail, patriotism has little to do with a fondness for one's country. Yes, many Americans like America. They reflect affectionately on Arizona's painted deserts and the wooded hollows of Tennessee, on the music of Appalachia and New Orleans, the rude vigor and brashness of a remarkable people, the rich accents of Brooklyn and Mississippi, all the things that give a sense of home and attachment in a large world. But they do not want blood. They speak quietly. Apparently they are not patriots. They do not use the word.

The email patriots are different. They growl and threaten, and seem less to appreciate their country than to hate others. They remind me of nothing so much as bar-room drunks looking for a fight. Their letters seethe with bitterness and begin with denunciations of liberals and the communist media (by which they mean any that fail to agree with them). They don't eat French fries. They hate. They would make, and in fact did make, excellent Nazis.

The difference between patriotism and love of country seems to be the difference between an inward-looking fondness and an outward-looking hostility. The email patriots regard any disagreement as treachery and softness. To doubt the wisdom or necessity of a war, any war, is treason; any inclination to think for oneself is evidence of being in the enemy's camp.

This is everywhere the rule. There were Japanese who thought that attacking the United States was not a conspicuously bright idea. They were squelched by patriots. GIs loved duty in Tokyo.

Malignant patriotism explains the attack, by a large heavily armed industrial power, against a weak and bedraggled nation so helpless as to be conquered in weeks. I refer of course to the Nazi assault on Poland. The Wehrmacht, like the Imperial Japanese Army, was awash in patriotism. It is in large part why they fought so well. No emotion is more usefully manipulable by governments with misbehavior in mind.

The connections among patriotism, military service, Christianity, and morality are tangled and fascinating. The first two appear to me to be incompatible with the second two. Consider Heinz, a German youth joining his armed forces in, say, 1937. Enlisting was then, as now, a patriotic thing to do. Heinz was probably a decent sort. Most people are. He probably had little interest in Poland, a minor creation which posed no threat to Germany. He liked beer and girls.

Then, come September of 1939, he found himself butchering Poles. The war had nothing to do with defense. The German attack was savage, unprovoked, and murderous. And why was Heinz killing people he didn't know? Because his government told him it was his patriotic duty. Which is to say that being in the Wehrmacht meant forfeiting moral independence to a dark, squatty, effeminate blond Aryan superman. Oh good.

It is curious. If Heinz had decided to kill Poles as a free-lance, he would have been called a mass-murderer, hanged, and had a movie made about him. If as a soldier he had decided not to kill Poles, having no reason to kill them, he might have been shot as a mutineer. But when he killed them unreflectingly because he had been told to, he became a minor national hero and, if extraordinarily effective in the killing, received a medal.

Fortunately for Adolf, refusals on moral grounds to kill the enemy, any enemy, are rare. In human affairs, morality is more than window-dressing, but not much more. Lust, hormones, and the pack instinct take easy precedence. Thus armies seldom say en masse, "No. We think it the wrong thing to do."

When the war goes badly, patriotism becomes compulsory. Heinz, driving toward Stalingrad, did not have the choice of changing his mind. Deserters tend to be shot. Enormous moral suasion serves to quell reluctance to die. Going against the herd is unpleasant. Governments understand this well.

Patriotism often needs propping, and gets it. Conscription serves to make fight those who otherwise wouldn't. (The ancient Persians used whips to force unwilling soldiers to go forward. Firing squads work as well, and do not tire the arm.) Societies punish draft-dodgers, except in the case of Republican presidents, and revile conscientious objectors as cowards, traitors, and homo-sexuals. Deserters particularly suffer heavy punishment, because if soldiers in a long nasty war could escape without penalty, most would.

Heinz, being German, was probably a Christian. Soldiers often believe them-selves to be Christians. There is remarkably little in the New Testament to encourage aggressive slaughter, yet Christian countries have regularly attacked everybody within reach. (So of course have most other countries.)

Heinz cannot serve two masters. Either he puts the authority of religion above that of government, or he kills anyone he is told to kill. As a rule he compart-mentalizes, accepts official justifications, and obeys.

Why does a coalition of Christian nations send troops at great expense to the Middle East to attack a Moslem nation offering little threat at the time? I refer of course to the Crusades. (Well, not much threat while Constantinople held.) The answer is simple: Humankind has a profound instinct to form warring groups. Crips and Bloods, Redskins and Cowboys, Catholics and Protestants, liberals and conservatives. Because a thin veneer of reason floats like pond scum on our instincts, we invent tolerable rationalizations: We must take the Holy Lands from the infidels. God says so.

In Chicago, young males form nations, which they call by such names as the Vice Lords, the P Stones, and the Black Gangster Disciples. They have ministers, pomp and circumstance, hierarchy, and intense loyalty to the gang. They wear uniforms of sorts—hats with bills pointed to the left or right, chosen colors—and they fight for turf, which is empire measured in blocks. The gangs of Chicago are international relations writ small.

Patriotism is most dangerous when mixed with religion. Both give high purpose to low behavior. Worst are the fundamentalists, the Ayatollahs and born-agains, the various Christian Wahabis and Islamic Cromwells. A fundamentalist believes that any idea wandering into his mind comes from On High. Actually he is making it up. He confuses himself with God, which is not a good thing when he is a bit loony to begin with. Fundamentalists usually are.

Usually wrong, but unfamiliar with doubt. I can't think of a better ground for policy.

CHAPTER 71

Achieving Bovocracy

The Supreme Court, our unelected and irrefutable legislature of nine, now ponders, or pretends to ponder, the legitimacy of racial discrimination in collegiate admissions. How comforting. One assumes of course that, with unrebuttable presumptuousness, they will merely dress their prejudices in constitutional-sounding awkward English. Still:

What is one to make of racial preferences?

First, some de-twaddling. The question before the Court is said to be whether race may be a factor in admission. This is not at all the question—and we all know it. The question is whether blacks should enjoy special privilege in admission.

Suppose that a college, using race as a factor, decided to give unqualified whites preference over qualified blacks. The federal government would bring its full punitive force to bear on the malfactorous institution. No matter how one may try to disguise it, no matter the weasel-wording and clouding and evasion, the issue, always, is special privilege for a particular race.

I know it. You know it. The Supreme Court knows it.

Second, the dispute has nothing to do with racism against blacks. The white population would, if polled, overwhelmingly support a policy of neutrality with respect to color. The bone in contention is special privilege. Nothing else.

Third, the prevalent policy of preferential racism is not intended as a temporary measure. There is never any talk among its advocates of phasing it out. They want it forever.

Regarding the Court, remember that high office does not of itself confer high competence or principled intention. I do not know how the Nine think, whether they have any particular principles, or even have real contact with the country they rule. One may wonder when any of them last rode a subway or put air in his own tires. They may, or may not, have any idea what they are doing.

Still, if I were among them, I would reflect on affirmative action (can there be a phrase more redolent of the used-car salesman?) thusly:

First, its continuance would illuminate the awful truth that the government is not an impartial institution of the people, but the special tool of some people. To put it clearly: My own government discriminates against me on grounds of race, and does so by law. It is a form of corruption worse than nepotism or croneyism. Nepotism, though it occurs, is disapproved. Racism is the legal bedrock of American politics.

How much damage does racialization do to the social fabric? I don't know. Certainly it gnaws at the loyalty to institutions that gives cohesion to a nation. People decide, as commonly happens in corrupt countries of the third world, to ignore the national government as being at best unresponsive or, in the case of affirmative action, hostile. They shift to local focus. They worry about friends, about their own, but cease to feel attached to the nation, or at least to Washington.

Come almost any election, we have gnashing of hands and wringing of teeth because people do not vote. Why should they? They know that policy is decided not according to the popular will, not according to cherished principles of equal access and opportunity, but according to race, creed, color, sex, and national origin. Resentment flows, lubricated by a sense of futility.

Another result of racial government is that blacks become—are—the focus of a widespread, federally suppressed contempt of which they are quite aware. The inevitable observation is that affirmative action is for losers. If you are good enough, you don't need it; if you need it, you aren't good enough. It's that simple.

Whites know about the large degree of racial privilege dispensed by the universities. Blacks know they know. While some blacks gain, others lose. A black doctor who has earned his degrees will find himself avoided by white patients, not because he is black but because he may be a Bakke case.

Racial preferences inescapably imply inferiority: All blacks with degrees will be presumed to have been given them because of pigmentation. It isn't fair. It is, however, reasonable, given that there is no safe way to check credentials or, having checked them, to act on the results. Might it not be better to hold blacks to normal standards and thus hold them in normal respect?

And doesn't racial preference set blacks up for failure? Consider. Suppose that I, a shiny white blue-eyed devil without too much hair, scored reasonably well on the SATs. I would be accepted only at schools with reasonably good SATs, not by Yale. If I were black, Yale would affirmative-action me. I would then find myself over my head, competing against far better students. The professors might pass me because of racial compassion, or I might hide in Black Studies, but the other students would know what was happening. So would I.

Is this what we want?

The peddlers of affirmative action make the point that universities engage in "legacy" admissions—that is, they give preference to children of alumni, especially those who have buildings named after them. Usually these students are white. Is this different from racial preference?

Yes. The country will not be wracked by division because an under-brained Rockefeller gets into Yale. Nor, crucially, is there a vast federal mechanism working on behalf of students named Rockefeller.

Of course another approach to admissions is possible. One might, if one could not be fired, ask why the government should meddle at all. Right now, universities are eager to collect black students. Why not let them? If a few universities chose to admit only highly qualified whites, or only qualified students, why not also let them? The government being incapable of impartiality, why not try something else? (We could call it, say, "freedom.")

Maybe we should stop kidding ourselves. Little pretense remains that reason or morality has much to do with government. Everything is done by groups. It is said to be unconstitutional to burn a cross, yet constitutional to burn a flag. Why? Because the first offends blacks; the second, conservative whites. (Personally I couldn't care less about burning either.) Enormous pressure forced VMI to admit girls, yet Wellesley, admitting only girls, gets nary a hard word. Are black colleges forced to become 85% white? No. We believe in high principle, but only for some people.

It never stops. "Deadbeat dads" are persecuted, pilloried, denied passports, imprisoned. Women who give birth to twelve illegitimate kids by several dozen fathers, none of whose names they can remember, are victims. Why? We all know. It is because we are a government not of men, not of laws, not of principle, but of sacred cows.

CHAPTER 72

Pancho Tequila

The night Pancho Tequila nearly poisoned my daughter in the Mexican port city of Manzanillo is one that will make me forever remember Ninja, or at least her legs.

Macon, nineteen, had come to learn scuba. She wanted to dive because she was afraid to be underwater and had a phobia about fish. Her response to fear is one of bull-headed aggression. She doesn't like being afraid. It annoys hell out of her. She goes at a fear like a bulldozer at a stump.

She took diving lessons with friends of mine at Neptune's Diving. After her first pool session George, her instructor, was not sanguine. "I don't know, Fred. Maybe she should take up golf. She doesn't...I don't know."

I didn't know either, but I suspected.

On her first checkout dive, kneeling in sunny rippled sand at twenty feet, she was running on guts alone. Second dive, more comfortable. Third, wandering around looking at fish (Yes, those: the hated enemy).

By the end of the week, with me watching like three hawks, she was doing 80-foot canyons at Carrizales, afterwards hollering, "Oh, *wow!* Dad! That was neat! Can we find some really *big* fish?"

That evening some of the dive crowd went to Colima Bay, a boisterous night spot where the poisoning nearly took place. They were celebrating because it was Wednesday, or maybe because it wasn't. I was celebrating a daughter. Meanwhile, Ninja…

Let me back up. Ninja was a woman I'd been on several dive runs with. She was smallish, looked Asian but spoke good Spanish, dove like a dream, and did full-contact karate for a hobby. And kinda cute. Very cute, actually. We'd agreed to meet that night to dance.

The crowd got there, but no Ninja. Colima Bay is your standard glass-ball disco—dark, with rotating ball hanging from the ceiling covered with mirror fragments, splashing reflections everywhere, and music at 12,000 decibels and lots of sober people, all of them somewhere else. We got a table in the thumping murk and ordered exotic fish dishes because that's what they eat in Manzanillo. The young Mexican males all wanted to dance with Macon. She's blonde. In that room full of dark hair and coffee-colored flesh, she stood out like Rasputin at a convention of·Quakers.

Further, she was in her shrapnel phase, with funny-looking pieces of metal stuck in portions of her anatomy. It's what kids do. She looked as if a bomb had gone off in a barbed-wire factory and she should have been several blocks farther away. It's hip. The Mexican kids wanted to be hip too, so they flocked around.

(Once Macon called me from San Francisco and said solemnly, "Look, dad, you aren't going to like this, but, well, I just got two tattoos on my face. And my brain pierced.")

Still no Ninja. I was disappointed. "Ninja?" said one of the dive mob. "She goes to the gym to work out for a couple of hours in the evening. Maybe she'll show later." Oh.

Instead, Pancho Tequila showed up. He was about three feet tall, a genuine midget, wearing a sombrero several yards in diameter and crossed cartridge-belts on his chest. Pancho had a magnificent moustache you could have hung clothes on. He looked like the Cisco Kid, only somebody had hit him on the head with a rubber mallet and shortened him by half.

Except the cartridges were shot glasses. Pancho worked for the house. His job was to wander around and pour shots of tequila down the guests. Since there was no charge, there was no resistance. He noticed Macon, who looked like a sunflower. He bore down on her with a clear intent to tequilate.

I didn't care about the kid's getting a shot of tequila. She was legal in Mexico. She had spent a year in serious art school in San Francisco before deciding that she wanted an education, and had lived in the Tenderloin. She was pretty and could do charming, but for fragile innocence, for shy vulnerability, she was up there with boot soles and tank treads. But we were still in the daddy-daughter state when she hadn't told me all the crazy things she had done, and I was pretending I didn't already know.

Thing was, her mom did something about Substance Abuse. If word got back that I'd taken our precious offshoot to a den of Mexican dwarves wielding tequila and branding irons (stories like this one, well, mature with age), I'd be dogmeat. I wondered what rentals might cost in Tierra del Fuego.

At midnight Ninja showed up, causing me to catch my jaw in both hands. She had looked nice on a dive boat, with salty hair and a shorty wet-suit. Gussied up with a tad of makeup…yeesh. I thought gentle and sophisticated things like, Hoo-*ahh*! and took deep breaths.

Two o'clock rolled around and the place was starting to rock. Little blips of colored light raced around like rabid moths and the music actually began to sound good. Better living through chemistry. Macon was happily dancing with some kids she had found. They couldn't understand each other, but it just seemed to give them something to talk about.

Then Ninja hopped onto the bar and started gogo dancing. So did I eventually, or so Macon tells me. I guess it seemed the best thing to do. Nobody seemed to care, certainly nobody male. Ninja was all plum glitter and nice legs. Thus began Macon's notion that her dad dated hot-ticket gogo dancers in weird foreign bars. It wasn't quite true, but most of the best thing in life aren't. The young are perennially surprised to find that their parents already know about sex.

In a moment of temporary exhaustion we were sitting at the table again and here came Pancho Tequila with, of all things, a watering can. Or maybe a tea-pot. I'm not too technical on domestic apparatus. Anyway it was made of clear plastic and full of (are you ready for this?) tequila punch. Pink.

Pancho would just pull some victim's head back and pour punch into his mouth, gunk, gunk, gunk, for as long as seemed to him a good idea. Which varied. It was scary. With some brands of tequila, you can get cirrhosis just by reading the label. Pancho was engendering a lot of cross-eyed people.

I'm not sure what else happened. Things didn't seem to get any clearer as the night wore on. My impression was that something was wrong with the air-con-ditioning and it began to emit blurry air. Not my fault. Actually, I wasn't there. I just heard about it later. That's my story anyway. Plum, though, will always be one of my favorite colors.

CHAPTER 73

Ethnic Purgation. Of Me

In the *Washington Post*, the trade journal of the coming vacuum, I discover a story on "Whiteness Studies." These, at what used to be the University of Massachusetts, are yet more un-courses that grow like mold on the wreckage of American education. They endeavor to make white students ashamed of being white. Useful, don't you think?

An implement wielded to this end, saith the *Post*, is the Privilege Walk. In this the students or, more accurately, indoctrinees, are asked to take a step forward if they can answer "yes" to such questions as "Can you get a bank loan whenever you want?"

The *Post*: "You looked behind you and became really uncomfortable," said Naomi Cairns, a 24-year-old junior who stood at the front of the classroom with other white students. Asian and black students she admired were near the back. "We all started together," she said, "and now were so separated."

Which discomfort was of course intended. Whiteness is bad. In fact anything associated with achievement is bad.

The questions must have been carefully crafted to separate whites from Asians, who are smarter than whites, more industrious, less criminal, generally more successful, and consequently wildly over-represented in the better schools.

But…embarrassment over qualifying for a loan?

"Can you get a bank loan?" might be phrased otherwise. For example, "Has your family, by virtue of proven honesty, sense of responsibility, and the economic fecundity that comes of study, competence, and hard work, demonstrated that it would not be foolish to lend you money?"

The Privilege Walk is transparently designed to punish whites for having historically been intelligent, studious, and productive; for having contributed most of the things enjoyed, often at the expense of white taxpayers, by the shiftless, dull-witted, improvident, and parasitic.

Now, I like the idea of a Privilege Walk, but I believe we ought to make it an Earned Privilege Walk. What do you think?

"Take a step forward if the following statements apply to you:

You got into the university without benefit of affirmative action.

No one in your family has a criminal record.

You have read three books this year you didn't have to read.

You have ever read any book you didn't have to read

You have ever read any book.

You are majoring in a hard science, mathematics, or engineering.

You had 600 math boards or better.

You had 600 verbal boards or better.

You study more than an hour a day."

Since Whiteness Studies is explicitly aimed at segregating the races, how about this:

"Your racial or ethnic group invented (take one step for each): Computational fluid dynamics. Tensor calculus. The harpsichord. The theory of finite automata. Cardiac surgery. Restriction Fragment Length Polymorphism. Writing. The wheel. Counting past ten. Fingers. (OK, OK, I'll give you that one.)"

And:

"You can spell 'polymorphism,' 'automata,' and 'ten' (one step each)."

The result would be an interesting electrophoretic trace. Anyone want to try it?

Next topic: In the *Washington Times*, I find this lead: "The District's schoolchildren rank as the worst readers in the country and only slightly better in some grades than non-English-speaking children in the territories of Guam, the Virgin Islands and American Samoa...Only 10 percent of D.C. fourth-and eighth-graders last year were at or above proficient in reading ability."

Having lived for many years in and about Washington, I can decrypt the foregoing story. "Children" means "black children." The few white kids in school in the District generally go to private schools, read competently, and produce the Merit finalists. Whites are uninvolved in the city's scholastic catastrophe: The government of Washington is black through and through, has a high expenditure per student ($9,650 says the *Times*; the average salary of teachers is $48,651), and can therefore have any schools it wants. This being so, the presumption is that it is satisfied with what it has.

Newsweek: "An astonishing 47 percent of Detroiters, nearly one out of two adults in this predominantly black city, are functionally illiterate. (By way of comparison, the figure for Vietnam is 6.7 percent and 1.7 percent for Croatia.)"

Do you suppose they should have done their homework? Whites however should be ashamed because they can get a loan from a bank.

Black America is a vast, hidden, changeless disaster kept afloat by welfare and pretense. Nobody is even trying to do anything practical about it. While this goes on, the therapists of the University of Massachusetts beat their breasts conspicuously and waste the time of students. Do you sometimes suspect that some people are more useful than others?

Next: The stories are dying down now about Benton Harbor, Michigan, which blacks spent two days burning. It was the usual story: a black with a suspended license ran from the police, wrecked his motorcycle, and killed himself. The population began igniting things. It happens every few years with either blacks or Latinos rioting. Cincinnati, Miami, DC at least twice, Los Angeles, Crown Heights, Newark, St. Pete, on and on, city after city torched, the stories played down, no consequences for the rioters, and the expectant wait for the next conflagration.

Racially, things aren't working. Yet we have Privilege Walks. The Eloi play while awaiting the Morlocks.

Next: I saw a political talk show in which a Mexican-American politician talked about the Latino population in Texas. He didn't sound hostile to whites. He was, however, pro-Mexican. He said (I may have the number slightly off) that sixty-some percent of kids under 18 in Texas were Mexican. In ten years, he said, when they reached eighteen, and voted, "there is going to be a huge political change." Yes. Specifically, Mexicans will own the state. (This is exactly what he meant.)

How bad this will be, if at all, depends on how relations develop. An ominous trend however is that Latino kids are dismal students and drop out of school. Other tensions loom. Latinos congregate in cities and, where they outnumber blacks, will displace them in elected office. There will be consequences.

Finally: A friend in California, an economist, tells me that whites begin to flee the state to avoid the taxes needed to provide social services for immigrants. Unfortunately Mexican doctors, engineers, shopkeepers, and taxi drivers do not swim the river. America gets those who can't make it at home. The ethnic cleansing of California, should it continue, will be fascinating.

Whence the productivity, the leadership for America's declining years? Latinos won't provide it, blacks can't, whites are gnawing their own veins, and there aren't enough Asians. But we at least have Whiteness Studies.

CHAPTER 74

Golf, Women, and Kidding Ourselves

All sorts of people are running around shrieking and pulling out their hair because a lady golfer played in some golf contest for men. I'm trying to figure it out. Mostly I'm coming up dry. Maybe I'm just a country boy, and slow, and can't understand things that don't make any sense at all. It takes a professor to do that.

Anyway, the papers were hooting and hollering about how she was going to do real well and it was a new world and she was going to end the hedge-of-money that men had in sports. Of course she didn't. It was because men are bigger and stronger and like to smack things—golf balls, each other, bartenders, they don't care. A possum knows as much. So I guess people stuck their hair back on and tried to think about something else.

What I don't understand is how come people in this country, except about five with good sense, can believe things they know aren't true. Probably even door-knobs know that some kinds of folk are just better at some things. People know it too. We just don't believe what we know.

It's a talent Americans have. Most of our social policy is based on things we know aren't true. We think if we say a raccoon can sing like Elvis, if we believe it real hard and tell everybody it's true and put anybody who knows better in jail for a hate crime—why, then that raccoon will launch into Blue Moon Over Kentucky and maybe Heartbreak Hotel.

And when things don't happen that can't, we wonder why they didn't, even though we know.

I saw on the box once that this German rifle club, that was all men, let a woman join. Next thing you knew, she won the club's championship. The men were all surprised and upset and wouldn't give her the prize. Those pole-axed-looking blonde anchor-personesses on TV got riled up and said as how it was just men not being able to admit that a woman beat them and it wasn't fair.

I reckon it wasn't. She did beat them. If they let her in, and she won the match, then I guess it was her prize. It's not a really difficult idea.

What I don't see is why the club should let women compete against men in the first place. Sure, it sounds like high principle and real fair and American, like Superman. But I notice that all this fairness is one-sided. If men wanted to shoot in ladies' clubs, or play in the women's golf tournaments, every feminist and all her litter-mates would go crazy. *Na-a-wwww,* that wouldn't be fair.

It seems like women want to compete with the men when they think they can win, but want protection from male competition when they can't, which in sports is usually. Now that's fair. Like a trapdoor.

I'm not at all sure that if women wanted to shoot, which they mostly don't, they couldn't do as well as men, or better. I shoot sometimes at ranges. A lot of women come in with their boyfriends to try it. Most do pretty well, and a fair few are wickedly good right out of the box. (My eldest daughter, for example. I'm glad she wasn't armed during adolescence.)

Suppose women decided that shooting was more fun than when Aunt Sally sat on the ants' nest, and got real good, and always beat the men. What then? I figure we'd still need to have a men's team and a woman's team so the men would have a chance. But I wouldn't think I had a right to shoot for their prize money when they couldn't shoot for mine.

Now, it used to be that women didn't think they had to compete with men. When I was in high school, everybody knew the boys could beat the girls at basketball. It was just how the world was. Nobody ever thought about it. I didn't figure I was somehow better than Gloria because I could out-rebound her. Boys and girls were different things, like birds and algebra. Nobody was mad about it.

When boys and girls did compete, like when Susie and Art were seeing who was going to be valedictorian, Susie was trying to beat Art, not the male race. When girls made better grades, which they generally did, the boys didn't feel oppressed and talk about how their self-esteem was a quart low and the teachers were against them. Girls just did better homework. It was how things were. Of course, the boys had better scores on standardized tests.

Now it's different. Women are always challenging men at things. When a lady golfer wants to play against the men, that's exactly what she's doing: Saying, "Gals can smack that little ball as well as guys, and I'm going to prove it." It's not individual. It's challenging men as a subspecies. Or at least that's how the media package it.

Of course if women challenge a man, or all men, the men *do* start thinking in terms of who's better, when left to themselves they wouldn't have. That's what competition is for: to see who's better. And if the woman loses, which she's mostly going to in sports, then women are going to feel humiliated and quietly mad. Why do it?

Of course the competition is implicitly rigged. The rules are different. If the men win, they get no credit and don't crow about it. If a woman wins, the feminists will gloat and generally be as disagreeable as they know how, which is very. The curious thing is that men don't want to compete against women in the first place. For men, that used to be one of (many) pleasant things about women: They were people you didn't have to compete with.

It looks to me as if those feminist gals have gotten women to measuring themselves by how close they come to being men. It's funny how much feminism resembles a rejection of everything feminine, almost like vicarious male-chauvinism. A woman who works sixty-hour weeks in some depressing law firm is a hero (feminists don't like the feminine "heroine") but a woman who raises her children is an embarrassment. Which is more important? Continuing the species? Or having another lawyer?

I don't get it. Like I say, I'm slow.

CHAPTER 75

The Two Cultures

I spoke recently to a gentleman, now getting on in years, who had spent a career in the slum schools of a big American city. He was bright, tough, and realistic, one of the very few gringos hereabout in Mexico who speak good Spanish. Though white, he had grown up in a housing project and so knew well the culture of the bottom of society.

Most of what he said of his experience tracked with the descriptions of slum schools that are found everywhere—dropout rates in excess of fifty percent, unconcerned parents, the usual. We need not recapitulate them here.

He made the interesting point that most education has no purpose other than to prepare the student for further education. Algebra in high school, for example, readies the student for the study of chemistry in college, but is otherwise useless, as one never uses algebra in daily life. Other examples may easily be imagined. Roman history has no relevance to anything that a black teenager in downtown Chicago might do in life; it does however prepare one for the study of further Roman history and of Shakespeare, which also have nothing to do with the teenager's future life.

He thought that instead of academic subjects, students should be taught to read, do arithmetic, balance checkbooks, be good parents, take out a mortgage, care for their health, and suchlike practical matters.

He had a point. The majority of students don't need to know history, mathematics, physics, or literature, do not want to know them, and in fact do not know them. Few are interested. Most children of the urban slums, if one can believe the studies, will pass their entire lives without reading a book. Why try to teach them what, for them, are hideously boring subjects that they won't learn, and in any event will never think of again?

Why indeed? Much of the public, probably a majority, lacks either the capacity or the interest required for an academic education. Nor do they need the knowledge conveyed by liberal studies. They do not need to know how to write clearly, since they never will. Virtually everything they learn after graduation will come either through television or conversation. An eighth-grade vocabulary suffices. They don't need to know the multiplication tables since, on rare occasions when they need to know the product of two numbers, a calculator will serve.

In fact they do not know these things. It is well documented that the schools teach little. Poll after study after test shows that astonishing majorities of Americans cannot find England on an outline map, place the Civil War in the correct century, name the major countries involved in WWI, or recognize the Bill of Rights. Poor teaching and dumbing-down account for some of this dark night of the mind. A lot, I think, springs from trying to teach people what they don't want to learn.

Why waste their time and the public monies?

All of this strikes me as reasonable. Yet I find myself becoming annoyed when I think about it. I come from the minority culture that does not regard education as preparation for watching television and punching a time-clock. I saw algebra as worth learning because, yes, it was necessary for chemistry and calculus later—but also because it was just plain interesting, and further because it is an important element in the intellectual development of mankind. I'm glad I studied it. Later in life, when for mysterious reasons I became interested in differential geometry and classical mechanics, a fluency in algebra and calculus allowed me to read them.

For some, reasons exist for learning things beyond tying one's shoes and reading traffic signs. People who do not know history live in temporal isolation; those who do not read literature, in a small mental world.

The gentleman from the big city saw no purpose in diagramming sentences. For his students, no. But for others, there is a purpose: Those who do not understand the mechanics of their language cannot appreciate such writers as Spenser and Milton and T.S. Eliot, as Twain and Mencken and Milne. Writing is an art as well as a means of communication. Art means imagination within rules. You have to know the rules.

Nor are the grammatically inept at all likely to be able to learn to read or speak another language. The reason is less that they have no idea what an indirect object or past subjunctive is than that they are incapable of seeing the language apart from its content. ·

It is true, as the gentleman suggested, that most people have no interest in languages or literature. But I do. So do countless others from cultivated families. How do we reconcile the existence of the two cultures? Of groups who want from the schools things almost diametrically opposed?

The beginning of wisdom would be to recognize that there are two cultures, and to let each study what it chooses. No?

I should not be allowed to impose algebra on people who will never do more than count on their fingers; they should not be allowed to enstupidate the schools to which I send my daughters. (Yes, they may be intelligent. But they are an enstupidating influence to the extent that they are uninterested.) As far as I am concerned, the lower classes (which is largely what we're talking about) can study anything they want, or nothing at all. I don't care. It's their choice. But leave my schools, my language, and my civilization alone.

I'm not being heartless. Should the intellectually uninspired ask my advice, I would happily give it. If they wanted to study Sophocles or digital design, or bird-watching or golf-ball repair, I'd be delighted to supply the teachers. Anyone from any class with the ability and desire should be mildly encouraged to learn. Vocational training should be available for those who want it. But if people choose not to study, I don't care.

Why require anything of them beyond basic literacy, and let them out after the eighth grade? They aren't going to learn anything else anyway. (Again, this is documented reality.)

For those who want an academic education, I say establish separate schools, and make attendance at all schools voluntary after the eighth grade. Those who wanted to learn nothing more would simply drop out, to the great benefit of serious students. The force of parental suasion would keep those students in attendance who ought to be in attendance.

Finally, decouple jobs from degrees. Hiring should be dependent on the results of a test, given by the prospective employer, of preparation for the particular job. This would empty the universities of students with no academic drive—a splendid idea.

How's that for PC?

CHAPTER 76

Green Kid Loose in America:
How We Were

I'm going to tell you about the time I was seventeen, ran away from home, and went hitchhiking through the South. And how I ended up in jail for vagrancy in Myrtle Beach with a beefy feeble-minded suspected rapist. Really, though, this is about how a kid found himself loose in the world for the first time and learned about independence. Even more really, it's about how countless kids took to the road in the freak years.

In case you were wondering. I mean, you might be. How would I know?

During high school I lived aboard Dahlgren Naval Proving Ground, on the Potomac River in what was then rural King George County, Virginia, where my father was a mathematician. Dahlgren existed to fire enormous guns downriver, including sixteen-inchers that rattled our windows most wonderful. The county was Huck Finn territory. People farmed and crabbed in the Potomac for a living. The country boys spent their time driving disintegrating wrecks at unwise velocity, lying about how much poontang they hadn't come close to getting, wandering through the woods with rifles and shotguns, and swimming in Machodoc Creek. It was what boys were supposed to do. We did it.

I wanted to go on the road, a drive that I've never shaken. I had a literary bent as well as a rifle and a decent jump shot, and had read Kerouac. A sense of urgency was upon me. I was getting old. Running away at seventeen was almost reasonable; at thirty-five, I sensed, it would be ridiculous. After my junior year at King George High I began surreptitiously packing a duffle bag with what I thought people needed in the wilds of América: Canned food, a jungle hammock, my prize Panasonic multi-band radio, and a razor I only barely needed.

I wasn't running away from anything, but toward something. I just didn't know what. Nor was I sure where I was going. South. That was easy because Route 301, then the major north-south artery, was maybe three miles from my front door.

Various subterfuges served to keep my parents from suspecting. Fortunately, like all teenagers I knew far more of life and the world than did my parents, which made it easy to fool them. For at least three years I believed that my preparations weren't plain as leprosy on Miss America.

I'd never hitchhiked at all. Starting on a June night from the crossroads of 301 and Route 206, I hung my thumb out. My first ride was a black guy, queer as a three-dollar bill, who kept going down back roads and showing me a notebook of photos of a fag party. I understood at last and said no thanks. A nice enough guy, he said ok and took me to Fredericksburg. Then the drunk in the '61 Fury who between Warrenton and Roanoke nearly drove head-on into a gasoline tanker. Then…

I thought these were adventures. Actually they were the everyday coin of the roads, known to all long-haul thumbs. I just didn't know that yet.

But that's not what this is about.

A few days out, on a rainy night somewhere in the coastal flatlands, I found myself beside a deserted rural highway. At this point I'm not even sure what state it was. The region had been cleared a couple of years back and was growing over in pines not much taller than I was. They glistened with recent drizzle that threatened to start again. The only thing of human provenance was an Esso station glowing a hundred yards away in an otherwise empty night. I had the world pretty much to myself, which I would learn to like. I think a lot of us did.

I was alone, but not unhappy. A couple of years later I would find that being solo on the big roads worked for me. I wasn't antisocial but...self-contained. I went far enough into the pines not to be seen and, with a little fumbling in wet needles, the jungle hammock was up. I walked over to the Esso station to get a couple of cokes.

I don't remember anyone working there, though someone must have been. The blue-white glow of the pump island bathed everything, and the bottles clunk-lunked out of the drink machine. There was no traffic, just dark woods and Standard Oil.

It was...my world. I was accustomed to the woods, had lived for a summer in a jungle hammock at a camp in Maryland, and had spent high-school vacations working at Kriegstedt's Esso on Route 301. It fit me somehow.

Back in the pine flats I climbed into the hammock after stuffing supplies for the night inside. A jungle hammock has mosquito-net sides that droop so that you can keep light objects in them, as well as a rain tarp and a double bottom so that the rain doesn't soak through. I was just in time. The drizzle picked up, not a rain but a pitpitpit on the tarp. The night was chilly but I had a sleeping bag.

I lay there with an open can of tuna fish on my chest, an orange soda gripped between my legs, and a roll of crackers in the mosquito netting. It was mighty satisfying. Cold rain an inch away engenders appreciation of a dry sleeping bag. It gave me a feeling that I was getting away with something. Having eaten, I plugged the earphone into the radio. Even then I knew it wasn't wise to call attention to myself at night.

For I don't know how long I tuned into the web of stations that covered Dixie, the late-night country stations listened to by a thousand truckers on the empty highways beyond midnight. Night on the radio is a curious world of affable DJs talking to people they understand and almost know. The cab of an eighteen-wheeler becomes almost a living room. So does a hammock.

What sticks in my mind was a delight in self-sufficiency, in being warm and dry on a wretched night out in the great sprawling expanse of America, making it on my own. Soon it would be commonplace. I and thousands like me would stand by the highways, rocking in the windblast and whine of the big trucks, living out of backpacks, dropping into an arroyo with a bottle of Triple Jack when we got tired of waiting. Not yet. It was a stripling' s first time out. And it was great.

I guess we didn't get to Myrtle Beach. Another time.

CHAPTER 77

White Males Arise

Being as I am an aspiring dead white male, I believe I could weary of hearing harsh words about what guttersnipes we are, and sludge, and sharpers, and impediments to civilization, and rapists and slave drivers and Marines: yes, and just no damned good. For one thing, I think we are a splendid lot. For another, I notice that most of the yapping comes from life's camp-followers—from those who didn't and can't and aren't likely to. Yet they seem perfectly willing to live in a world that white European males built. It is not a dignified performance.

Now, graciousness is a trademark of this column. And a good thing, too, as otherwise I might say, "Them as can't compete can shut up. Talk to me when you have credentials. Now bugger off." But no. I won't say it.

I may think it though.

Permit me a suggestion to those who appreciate us not. (See? I'm trying to be helpful.) I address it to race hustlers, to bilious feminists of immoderate inutility, which is all of them, and to the gelding professors of the Ivy Leagues.

Look around you and see whether you can find anything, with a moving part, that isn't the work of white European males. You might start with your refrigerator, which you probably don't understand. What about your hair dryer? You do know how an electric motor works?

Yes, I know what the grade-school textbooks say. The electric motor sprang from the work of the Guatemalan Native-Peoples thinker Rigoberta Tloxyproctyl who, while planting cassava with a sharp stick, discovered the npn junction, foresaw the integrated circuit, and founded Intel. Previously she had invented the amniote egg.

From the same books you would conclude that the central figure of the Civil War was not Robert E. Lee but Sojourner Truth, that the Iliad was written not by Homer but by Marge, and that civilization had been invented by grub-eating, pre-literate if you are optimistic occasional cannibals of color in the Amazon basin who barely understand the engineering underlying the loincloth. (If engineering is what underlies loincloths. I've never looked.) Mendacity is no substitute for achievement.

Now, I suspect that these uprooters of white maledom don't appreciate their blessings because they don't understand them. Familiarity breeds a sense of understanding, but not understanding itself. If miraculous things are always there, it's easy to regard them as just part of the world, like bananas in the tropics.

Consider. If you showed a television set to a bushman in New Guinea, and asked him how it worked, he would say, "*Hoo*! Bad juju, boss. Heap spirits dey in it, talk talk." He would have the judgement to be astonished by what is, after all, astonishing.

Now imagine asking the same question of Al Sharpton, or Gloria Steinem or, let us say, the head of Harvard's Department of Micronesian Lesbian Studies, Carnita Tlacuache-Lombriz.

She: "Uh, well, waves. You know. In the air. Oppression, people of color, capitalism…."

Me: "*Yes*, Ms. Tlacuache-Lombriz! *Splendid!* You are on to something. But can you be more precise? What kind of waves? Surf, perhaps? Tidal waves, or little bitty shiny waves? As in a millpond."

"Well, no. Some other kind of waves. I think. Oppression, people of color…."

You would find that she knew as much as the bushman. She knows the same amount about her watch, refrigerator, automobile, microwave oven, and stereo. They are, to her, low-hanging fruit, or what money is to Democrats: something that is just there.

All of these things, note, are products of what such as Steinem call "white male linear thinking." (It used to be called "thinking," until people noticed the albedo and steroid chemistry of those who usually did it.)

Here we come to part of the reason for their bad behavior: These folk are genuinely, blankly, appallingly ignorant of things around them. To Ms. T-L, for example, a computer is a commodity, like soap. It's just there, has buttons, usually works.

And she is right. A computer *is* a commodity. But she has no idea why it is a commodity, or why this too is miraculous. She doesn't know, or avoids reflecting, that her laptop rests on an towering edifice of physics, chemistry, and electronics, of which she is supremely innocent, resting on mathematics and theory also elaborated by tens of thousands of—yep—white males whose books she has never heard of.

To the white male (ok, slightly geeky) mind, a computer is something quite different. It is a stack of intricately interlocking abstractions. At the bottom (somewhat arbitrarily) you find solid-state physics with its band theory and lattices and dopants and a lot of formidable physical chemistry; a level higher you have transistors, address buses, interrupt hierarchies and row latches; next, DMA and video controllers and file-allocation tables; then software, optimizing compilers and top-down programming.

These for the most part are not easy ideas. When they are easy, as programming is, the response of men is to write programs so complex that they have to think about them in teams. Overwhelmingly these things arose from...white males, mostly European.

Other men (white, European, and mostly dead) of phenomenal brilliance developed the underlying math and theory: Gauss, Newton and Leibniz, LaGrange, Shannon, Hamilton, Galois, perhaps Minsky if you think finite automata actually have anything to do with computers, and Turing, none of whom Ms. T-L has heard of either.

Given that she probably couldn't solve a quadratic if you gave her a band saw and a large staff, she can't understand what it is that she doesn't understand. Nor, one may suspect, can Al Sharpton, nor those goofy alleged teachers who are always nattering on about how little boys need to be drugged.

But let me approach the matter from another angle. I propose (again trying to be helpful) that those who don't like white males try spending a week without the things that white males have foolishly provided for them, thus allowing them to complain in comfort.

Ms. T-L could begin by taking her fillings out. (Dentistry is not low-tech. Try making a drill burr spin at 350,000 rpm or whatever the current figure is.) Then she could denude herself, preferably after warning bystanders, since everything she wears was made on machines designed by evil white males, using metallurgy and engineering demonically invented by other evil white males. Next she could toss everything electrical and mechanical. She would soon find herself sleeping in a hollow log and eating bugs.

Which would be marvelous. I suggest January. In Fairbanks.

CHAPTER 78

In Praise of Mexicanas

Living in Mexico as I do, I often hear from North Americans that gringos move to Mexico chiefly for the women. Well, yes. The women are certainly an attraction. Indeed they are. The North American tendency however is to confuse women with sex. American men in the United States usually see Mexican women as LBFMs, "little brown, er, sex machines," faceless, indistinguishable, and cheap. So do American women, though with resentment instead of longing.

Permit me if you will a different view of Mexicanas.

To my eye, they are almost quirky in their distinctiveness, strong, content with being themselves, and psychically stable. They are also women, delightfully so, vibrantly feminine. They are wonderfully amorous without being loose, uninhibited, frequently beautiful, and they are...ladies. They do not drink themselves silly in bars and shriek obscenities.

They can also be savagely jealous, to the point of removing body parts. But for this I respect them. Any woman worth having has every right to expect her man to keep his pants up except in her presence. He owes to her what she owes to him. Fair is fair.

It is not easy to explain to an American readership under forty what is meant by being a woman. We are accustomed to androgynous, litigious, Prozac-sucking shrews who would inspire erectile dysfunction in an iron bar. Yes, there are exceptions and degrees, but here is the main current. (If there is anyone with less respect for women than the average squalling dyke feminist, I haven't met it.)

Feminists of course say that femininity cannot be distinguished from subservience. But it ain't so. The Mexicanas I know are not subservient. They work harder and bitch less than we do. They are not weak. They do not need support groups, Depacote, Paxil, Welbutrin, or classes in self-esteem (which idea they find puzzling or ridiculous). They are self-sufficient adults.

There is for the Mexicana a difference of centrality. Her focus is on her home, her man, and her children. She sees her job as a way to support her family instead of, as happens northward, the other way around. Her home is more important to her than her office. Making partner at Dewey, Cheatham, and Howe is not her reason for living. Should the man share these sentiments, as gringos with Mexican wives seem to, there flows a warmth and steadfastness that changes the tenor of life. The time at home, talking, doing yard work, dancing to the boom box, or screwing their brains out, counts more than whatever else might be out there.

For gringas, Mexican women are tough competition. The embittered single American women in my town do not understand why, believing that men only want young Mexican bodies. Everything, they assume, must be sex.

Yeah. Sure.

Now, young and beautiful has its charm. Men do not, as a rule, seek out the aged. But—and I know many of these men well—what draws them is the warmth and womanliness of the Mexicana. In Mexico you don't marry one of the guys. You don't marry a child-support bomb waiting to explode without visitation. You don't marry a hundred pounds of irrational anger looking for an excuse. You marry a woman. The difference...my God, the difference.

Often, though by no means always, the age difference is substantial between gringo and lady, from ten to twenty-some years. The easy interpretation is that she wants money, and he wants sex. No. For one thing, the economics of marrying for sex, as distinct from paying fifty bucks a shot for agreeable lovelies at the Galleon in Guadalajara, is absurd. In terms of money, renting makes much more sense than buying. Sex is not why the men marry.

Further, there is such a thing as being too cynical. (Wait. I said that?) Yes, money is the only effective aphrodisiac, anywhere, as any man knows who has been in the Philippines with a paycheck. Drive a flashy car in Washington and leave hundred-dollar tips and you will have women all over you. But:

The Mexicanas married to my friends here do not want jewelry, clothes, or big houses. They certainly do not want to go to the United States. None wants to give up her job and be supported. They want security, love, loyalty, and not much else. It works for me. It works for a whole lot of guys.

The men? I know them, know them well. I know them sober and in their cups. They do not talk about how good Maria is in bed, what a great piece Conchis is. They talk about how much they love their wives or girlfriends, how fortunate they are to have found them.

I'm one of them. And I mean every word of it.

The Mexicana has a strength that Americans of the era of the Depression had, but somehow lost. The wife of a friend of mine was working as a nurse when an earthquake struck her town. Mexico does not have the money to provide the services upon which Americans rely. She spent over a month in a makeshift tent in a field, during rainy season, with a suckling child. (Her husband had abandoned her. Mexican men are not always as impressive as their women.)

It was tough. She didn't like it. Neither did she crumble under it. Life is life. In the crude but succinct Anglo-Saxon, shit happens. Deal with it. Net psychic trauma: None. Prozac consumed: None. Hours of grief-counseling required: None. Symptoms of PTSD: None. Importance of all of this to Sara: Not much. They were cold and wet for a while. Gee. Golly.

She is not an exception. The Mexicana to whom I am undeservedly yet miraculously linked came from a poor family in Guadalajara. She worked her way through university in letras. Then she set about teaching Spanish to foreigners, mostly Americans, to earn a living.

When those buildings went down in New York, her students disappeared. I cannot conceive why. The condition of real estate in Manhattan has no obvious connection with learning Spanish in Guadalajara. How pitifully frightened of nothing can people be? Violeta was suddenly, utterly, and in the short term irremediably without work or money. She also had a daughter of nine to care for.

For a long time it was beans, tortillas, and water. Mexico does not have the social safety net that Americans rely on. So they stayed home and read. Violeta got through the Decameron and four volumes of Borges. The daughter, whom I know well, will read anything, probably to include lawnmover manuals in languages she doesn't speak. Were they depressed, I asked? No, they said. What purpose would that serve? Anyway, they got to read a lot of books.

Use of Prozac: Zero. Psychotherapy: Zero. Psychic scars: None. Shit happens. They dealt with it.

Yes, women are high among the attractions of Mexico.

Viviendo en México, oigo frecuentemente de hombres estadounidenses, que a los gringos les gusta vivir en México porque les interesan las mujeres. Pues, sí. Las mujeres son muy atractivas para los gringos. No cabe duda. Sin embargo, la tendencia de la gente norteamericana es confundir las mujeres con el sexo. Los gringos en Estados Unidos suelen ver a las mexicanas como "LBFMs," pequeñas maquinas cafés de sexo, anónimas, indistinguibles, y baratas. Las gringas comparten este punto de vista, aunque con resentimiento en vez de deseo.

Permítanme ofrecer un concepto diferente de las mexicanas.

Para mis ojos, son casi excéntricas en su individualidad, fuertes, contentas con sigo mismas, y psicológicamente estables. Son verdaderamente mujeres, deliciosamente así, maravillosamente femeninas. Son entusiastamente amorosas sin ser fáciles, modestas pero sin inhibiciones, frecuentemente hermosas y...damas. No se emborrachan en cantinas y gritan obscenidades.

Pueden ser salvajemente celosas, hasta remover partes del cuerpo masculino. Por eso las respeto. Cualquier mujer que vale la pena tiene el derecho de demandar que su pareja mantenga el pantalón levantado excepto en su presencia. Él le debe a ella lo que ella le debe a él. Lo justo es lo justo.

Es difícil explicarles a lectores estadounidenses de menos de cuarenta años de edad lo que quiere decir "ser mujer." Nosotros estamos acostumbrados a litigiosas, semi-marimachas chupa-Prozaques que podrían causar disfunción eréctil en una viga de hierro. Sí, hay excepciones y grados, pero aquí está la corriente mayor.

Las feministas por supuesto dicen que la feminidad no se puede distinguir de la servidumbre. (Si existe cualquier persona que tenga menos respeto por las mujeres que la típica feminista lesbica, lo que es decir simplemente la típica feminisa, bramando y ladrando, no la he conocido.) Pero no es así. Las mexicanas que conozco no son serviles. Trabajan más y se quejan menos que nosotros. No son débiles. No necesitan "grupos de apoyo," ni Prozac, ni Welbutrin, ni Depacote, ni Paxil, ni clases sobre el autoestima (idea que encuentran confusa o ridícula.) Son autosuficientes adultas.

La mexicana tiene una idea de lo importante muy distinta a la de la gringa. Se enfoca en el hogar, en su hombre, y en sus hijos. Para ella, su trabajo existe para mantener a su familia, no al revés. Su casa le importa más que su oficina. Lograr una posición esplendida en una compañía de abogados no es su razón para vivir. Si su hombre comparte estos sentimientos, lo que es común entre gringos que se casan con mexicanas, el resultado es un cariño y estabilidad interior que cambian el sabor de la vida. Para ellas, el tiempo pasado en el hogar, platicando, trabajando juntos en el jardín, bailando al boombox, o cogiendo como conejos, cuenta más que su carrera.

Para las gringas, las mexicanas son competencia casi insuperable. Las gringas amargadas de mi pueblo no lo entienden, diciendo que los hombres quieren nada más los jóvenes cuerpos de las mexicanas. Creen que todo es el sexo.

Pues, joven y hermosa tiene su encanto. Los hombres por regla general no buscan a las ancianas. Pero—y conozco bien a estos hombres—lo que los atrae es el afecto emocional y la feminidad de la mexicana. En México, un hombre no se casa con "uno de los muchachos." No se casa con una bomba de divorcio, a punto de estallar y robarle sus niños. No se casa con cien libras de enojo irracional que nada más espera un pretexto. Se casa con una mujer. La diferencia...Dios mío, la diferencia.

Muchas veces, pero no siempre, hay una diferencia considerable de edad entre el gringo y su mujer, entre diez y veinte y pico años. La interpretación normal entre las gringas es que ella quiere el dinero y el quiere el sexo. No. En primer lugar, el costo de casarse para el sexo, a distinción de pagárselo a una chica bonita en los prostíbulos de Guadalajara, es absurdo. En términos económicos, rentar es mejor que comprar.

Mas, es posible ser demasiado cínico. (¿Cómo? ¿Yo dije eso?) Sí, el dinero es el único afrodisíaco efectivo en cualquier lugar, como sabe cualquier hombre que a estado en las Islas Filipinas con su pago en el bolsillo. Si conduces un coche caro en Washington y dejas propinas de cien dólares, tendrás muchas mujeres detrás de ti. Pero:

Las mexicanas casadas con mis amigos no quieren joyas, ni ropa, ni casas grandes. Es cierto que no quieren ir a los Estados Unidos. Ninguna quiere abandonar su trabajo y ser mantenida. Quieren la seguridad, la lealtad, el amor, y no mucho más. Funciona para mí. Funciona para muchos hombres.

¿Los hombres? Los conozco, los conozco bien. Los conozco sobrios y ebrios. No hablan de qué tan buena está María en la cama, ni de lo bueno que es su cuerpo. Hablan de qué tanto aman a sus esposas o novias, de qué tan afortunados son de haberlas hallado.

Soy uno de ellos, y lo digo en serio.

La mexicana tiene una fuerza que los norteamericanos de la época de la Depresión tenían, pero de alguna manera han perdido. La esposa de un amigo estaba trabajando de enfermera cuando un terremoto destruyó el pueblo. México no tiene suficiente dinero como para darles a los damnificados los servicios de los cuales los gringos dependen. Ella pasó más de un mes en una tienda de campaña, mal construida, en una cancha de fútbol, dando pecho a un bebé. (Su esposo la había abandonado. El hombre mexicano no es siempre tan admirable como la mujer.)

Fue difícil. No le gustó. Pero no se derrumbó sicológicamente. La vida es la vida. En el crudo pero conciso anglosajón, "shit happens" ("Que puta vida.") Manéjalo.

Neto trauma psíquico: Nada. Prozac consumido: Cero. Horas necesarias de psicoterapia: Cero. Importancia de todo eso a Sara: No mucho. Fueron frías y mojadas por un rato. No fue gran cosa.

Ella no es excepcional. La mexicana a quien estoy milagrosamente ligado, sin merecerlo, viene de una familia pobre en Guadalajara. Logró graduarse de la universidad en letras por sus propios esfuerzos. Entonces empezó enseñarles el español a los extranjeros, mayormente estadounidenses.

Cuando los edificios se cayeron en Nueva York, sus estudiantes desaparecieron. No puedo imaginar por qué. La condición de bienes raíces in Manhattan no tiene relación obvia con aprender español en Guadalajara. ¿Qué tan temerosa puede ser la gente sin razón? Violeta se encontró súbito y por el momento irremediablemente sin dinero ni trabajo. Y tenía una hija de nueve años.

Por mucho tiempo comieron nada más frijoles, tortillas, y agua. México no tiene la red de seguro social que los Estados Unidos tiene. Se quedaron en casa y leyeron. Violeta terminó El Decameron y cuatro libros de Borges. La hija, que conozco bien, leerá cualquier cosa dentro de su alcance, probablemente incluyendo los manuales de instrucciones de cortacéspedes, en lenguajes que no habla. ¿Estaban deprimidas? les pregunté. No, me dijeron. ¿Para qué habría servido la depresión? De todos modos, leyeron muchos libros.

Prozac consumido: Cero. Psicoterapia requerida: Cero. Cicatrices psíquicas: ninguna. Shit happens. La manejaron.

Sí, las mujeres están entre los atractivos más fuertes de México.

CHAPTER 79

NASA Caught Lying

Being the rabidly nationalistic patriot that I am, I heard with delight that NASA had landed an $820 million dollar golf cart on Mars. Always get the best, I say. The planet has always seemed to me a reasonable place to play golf. I bow to no one in my mindless enthusiasm for technotrinkets. And I quietly gloated a bit that America had done it and not, say, Vanuatu or Papua-New Guinea.

Then I thought: Wait a minute. Mars is a gazillion miles away, probably whole whoppaparsecs or gigawhatsisses. Mostly you can't even see the place. NASA says it shot a golf cart all that way and hit the right crater? After the thing bounced all over the place wrapped in inner tubes? The federal government did it—that couldn't make a functioning doorstop?

Nah. Buncha engineers just wanted funding.

When I was eight I used to throw rocks at the hub caps of passing cars. Those cars were all of twenty feet away, not going over forty, and I had a pretty good arm for a tad. I almost never hit those hub caps. Of course after every rock I had to hide in the woods till the driver stopped looking for me. Still, I couldn't do it.

Neither can NASA. You can't hit something that far away, going that fast, in all whicha directions, with a golf cart. It ain't doable. Any fool can see that if he thinks about it, and probably if he doesn't.

And those pictures they always show after they spend $820 million, or more likely put it in a Swiss bank—they really do look just like Arizona. They're always grainy, because grainy pictures look authentic. Besides, if the resolution was any good you might see jeep tracks, or a distant sign saying, "Pepi's Miracle Cat Tacos."

I have another question. Why do we think Mars even exists? Have you ever been there? Know anyone who has? Have you ever even seen it? Sure, maybe some teacher pointed to a dot in the sky and said, "*Yay*-us, brother, thass Mars. Fulla them little green rascals. Got canals all over the place too. Go fishing."

Nah. Red speck. Could have been a red balloon with a flashlight inside it, or just about anything. We think Mars is there because people tell us it is, people who got told by other people who didn't know anything about it either. Sure, astronomers say they see it all the time, but they get the money. An astronomer would see Mars if you put a bag over his head.

Those pictures mean nothing. I've seen pictures of an island full of dinosaurs that look more real than some of my old girlfriends. They stomped around and ate people, and if you showed them to a four-year-old kid and told him they lived in Africa, he'd never think to doubt it. Isn't it so? I mean, a dinosaur is no stranger than, say, a four-foot iguana, or a Pacific tube-worm living inside an underwater volcano, or Michael Jackson, or Democratic social policy.

Fact is, NASA could show us a piece of Nevada with a shopping mall and a K-Mart, tell us it was Ganymede, and we'd rejoice because we'd Discovered Life. That's assuming you believe there's life in shopping malls. We'd believe it because we believe anybody in a white coat. Then we'd have to give the space people a billion or so more so they could send a complicated prongy space thing to fingerprint everybody on Ganymede and search for weapons of mass destruction.

Tell you what: I don't think the solar system exists. The only part of it you can see is the sun, except in Los Angeles, where you can't. Long time ago, that fellow Galileo hollered that he'd found planets, and a bunch of moons, Ganymede and Io and Callisto and Europa, sailing around Jupiter like they had something in mind. (How did he know those were their names? Was it written on them? None of this adds up.) We believed it, and then we believed in Pluto which is so far away that if it was there, you couldn't tell.

The truth is that we have nothing more than fifth-hand evidence for most of the things we believe in. None of it would stand up in a court of law. Atoms, for example. We all know that they are really, really tiny things that have electrons flying around them like disgruntled hornets when you shoot their nest with a BB gun. The definition of an atom is that it's too small for you to know it's there. Which means we don't.

Attorney: "Mr. Reed, how do you know that these...er...atoms exist?"

Me: "Well, this teacher I had said she read in a book that some scientists wrote about some experiments she said some other scientists did, she thought, a long time ago, somewhere she'd never been."

Other attorney: "Objection. Hearsay."

Me: "But it was in a book...."

Other attorney: "So are Grimm's Fairy Tales."

Scientists don't really know anything. In chemistry they have this thing called Avocado's number, which is how many atoms there are in a mole. Seriously. Six-point-oh-two-three-times-ten-to-the-twenty-third atoms per mole. It makes no sense. What size mole? Obviously a huge ubermole with great hairy forepaws like scoops (the only kind I get in *my* lawn) has more atoms than a dwarf mole or a baby mole. Why moles and not, say, flying squirrels?

But what I want to know is, who counted those atoms?

Now, you're probably thinking, "Fred, be reasonable. Physicists know this stuff." No. They're crazier than Rasputin's loony brother, who used to stand on his head in a corner and sing the Marseillaise.

They have what they call the Wave Equation, invented by some disturbed German. The Wave Equation is full of second partial derivatives, and del-square, sigh, and all the orphan constants in the world. What it says is that you can never be sure where atoms are.

Aha! Then how can you count them?

The wave equation says—honest, they told me this—that an electron can be here now, and over there later, but it can't ever be in between where the plot crosses the x-axis because when you square zero you mostly get zero. (Unless you went to school recently, in which case it's up for grabs.) You believe that? I don't.

What I think is, NASA made up the solar system. It was to get grants. When the Feddle Gummint wants money, it makes things up—the Maine, the Gulf of Tonkin, nerve gas, Mars, the universe. It always works.

CHAPTER 80

Sunsets and Mosquito Hawks

Of a late afternoon long ago I sat in the clearing above the swamp, headwaters of Machodoc Creek, where my parents lived in Virginia's Tidewater. I was reading. The air was thick with summer and almost silent, except for the occasional bird and bug going about their affairs and the distant cough and roar of big trucks gearing their way up the hills on Route 301. Dragonflies flittered about in light that began to slant through the trees. Odd. Usually they kept to the wetlands below the hill.

Something fell on my pages and thrashed awkwardly about. A bug of some sort, but not one that I had seen, and it seemed to have trouble walking. Above, the dragonflies flashed and hovered. I dumped the stranger on the grass and kept reading. Shortly another of the curious creatures fell on my leg. It couldn't walk either.

Suddenly I understood. The ants were queening—hopeful chitinous maidens taking wing to mate, and the dragonflies eating them, nipping off the juicy abdomens and dropping the rest on me. That was why they had left the swamp.

I knew dragonflies well. As a boy in Alabama with a BB gun, I had hunted them, and moccasins, in the wet region near the Valley Gin Company, which didn't make gin but took the seeds out of cotton. The town was Athens, then small and almost rural. The air there was alive with snake doctors, as dragonflies were locally known, though elsewhere they are called mosquito hawks or the devil's darning needles—fast, muscular insects, with huge compound eyes like radomes. They are fearsome to look in the face and, for small prey that fly, agile death. They glittered iridescent blue and green in the sunlight. I could never hit them.

In Virginia, ant parts rained down. The world, I reflected, seemed friendly only because people were too large for most things to eat. The world we live in bears little relation to the smaller world roundabout. In our pretty clearing with the smell of warm vegetation and the babble of birds was a realm of nightmare mechanical monsters, unnoticed because small. I have seen ants tear apart a wounded hornet, a mantis eating a struggling bug held in brawny green forearms. It is well for us that mantises don't weigh three hundred pounds.

I sometimes think I am the only man who doesn't understand wherever it is that we are.

As the light failed and I could no long see my page, I wandered across the bean field to where the old road, once a wagon track, ran between high banks into the woods. A flaming sunset had come over the sky, rolling off forever in what looked like ocean waves or burning dunes. The air smelled of damp earth and leaf mold. Night came early in the road cut. The first bats began to flicker through branches dark against the flames.

The droning announcers of the endless nature shows on television, full of the confidence born of limited understanding, tell us that bats and cockatoos and locusts are the necessary consequent of blind chance, speaking in the next breath of Mother Nature's intentions. For them everything is simple. Starlings are drab so that nothing hungry can see them, and cockatoos are gaudy so they can find each other to mate. Yet I note that starlings seem to mate prolifically if drably and, given what cockatoos sound like, it is hard to see how anything could fail to find one that wanted to be found.

I think those big birds are too pretty to be accidents. Those of religious nature have attributed such things to any of several thousand gods, some more attractive than others. They, like the acolytes of evolution, are perfectly sure of the rightness of their views. I am not sure of anything. Alone in a darkling wood, with things all about flying and hunting and growing in a vast ungraspable dance, I suspected that I was in the presence of something above my station. Just what, I couldn't say, nor of what intentions or provenance. I didn't think it was much concerned with me. It wasn't physics.

Recently I found the noted astrophysicist Stephen Hawking quoted, perhaps correctly, as saying that humanity may be on the verge of understanding everything whatever. Physicists often say such things, speaking of string theory, singularities, and the 3K background radiation—words redolent of insulation and sixty-cycle hum. If one may differ with a cosmogonist, I suggest that we understand almost nothing. And without the slightest disrespect, I note that the brightest of a large population of hamsters is, after all, a hamster.

I suppose that people believe that they understand this mysterious universe because it is more comforting to think that one understands than to worry uneasily that one mightn't. The faithful, Darwinian and otherwise, persuade themselves that they have The Answer. The fury of their defense of their creeds suggests a nagging doubt. Others focus on the here and now and deny the question. Few say, "I don't know."

The sky glowed in gorgeous oranges and reds like a Chinese lamp lit from within and slowly burned out to blues and ashen black. Yes, I have heard of water vapor and indices of refraction, but I don't think that was what was happening, or not all that was happening. In the marsh below things would be coming out to eat.

I wish explanations explained better. There is a peculiar wasp that kills tarantulas, buries them, and lays eggs on them. I have tried to imagine how an infant wasp, crawling unschooled from where its mother left it as an egg, knows how to find a tarantula, where to sting it, and how to bury it. One would think the world would be a confusing place to such a newborn with no experience of it and only the outline of a nervous system. Yet they do it unerringly. More is going on here than I think we know.

My idiot dog Deacon showed up and set about whuffling in the black undergrowth. He was an agreeable if foolish brute, and appeared to be the product of illicit coupling between a German shepherd and a boxcar. Why he whuffled, I don't know. I didn't need to know. He did what is proper to his place in things and I, what is proper to mine. He sniffed, and I supervised the sunset. It suited us.

About the Author

According to Fred, who is an occasionally reliable source (though he says his heart isn't in it):

I was born in 1945 in Crumpler, West Virginia, an unincorporated coal camp near Bluefield where my maternal grandfather was the camp doctor, and steam locomotives chuffed spectacularly in to load coal at the tipple. (When someone got sick on the other side of the mountain, the miners would put Big Pat, as granddad was called, in a coal car and take him *under* the mountain. He had a robust conception of a house call.) My father was a mathematician, but then serving in the Pacific aboard the destroyer USS Franks. My paternal grandfather was dean and professor of mathematics at Hampden-Sydney College, a small and (then, and perhaps now) quite good liberal arts school in southwest Virginia. In general my family for many generations were among the most literate, the most productive, and the dullest people in the South. Presbyterians.

After the war I lived as a navy brat here and there—San Diego, Mississippi, the Virginia suburbs of Washington, Alabama, what have you, and briefly in Farmville, Virginia, while my father went on active duty for the Korean War as an artillery spotter. I was an absorptive and voracious reader, a terrible student, and had by age eleven an eye for elevation and windage with a BB gun that would have awed a missile engineer. I was also was a bit of a mad scientist. For example, I think I was ten when I discovered the formula for thermite in the *Britannica* at Athens College in Athens, Alabama, stole the ingredients from the college chemistry laboratory, and ignited a mound of perfectly adequate thermite in the prize frying pan of the mother of my friend Perry, whose father was the college president. The resulting six-inch hole in the frying pan was hard to explain.

I went to high school in King George County, Virginia, while living aboard Dahlgren Naval Weapons Laboratory (my father was always a weapons-development sort of mathematician, although civilian by this time), where I was the kid other kids weren't supposed to play with. I spent my time canoeing, shooting, drinking unwise but memorable amounts of beer with the local country boys, attempting to be a French rake with only indifferent success, and driving in a manner that, if you are a country boy, I don't have to describe, and if you aren't, you wouldn't believe anyway. I remember trying to explain to my father why his station wagon was upside down at three in the morning after I had flipped it at seventy on a hairpin turn that would have intimidated an Alpine goat.

As usual I was a woeful student—if my friend Butch and I hadn't found the mimeograph stencil for the senior Government exam in the school's Dempster Dumpster, I wouldn't have graduated—but was a National Merit Finalist.

After two years at Hampden-Sydney, where I worked on a split major in chemistry and biology with an eye to oceanography, I was bored. After spending the summer thumbing across the continent and down into Mexico, hopping freight trains up and down the eastern seaboard, and generally confusing myself with Jack Kerouac, I enlisted in the Marines, in the belief that it would be more interesting than stirring unpleasant glops in laboratories and pulling apart innocent frogs. It was. On returning from Vietnam with a lot of stories, as well as a Purple Heart and more shrapnel in my eyes than I really wanted, I graduated from Hampden-Sydney with lousy grades and a bachelor-of-science degree with a major in history and a minor in computers. Really. My GREs were in the 99th percentile.

The years from 1970 to 1973 I spent in largely disreputable pursuits, a variety that has always come naturally to me. I wandered around Europe, Asia, and Mexico, and acquired the usual stock of implausible but true stories about odd back alleys and odder people.

When the 1973 war broke out in the Mid-East, I decided I ought to do something respectable, thought that journalism was, and told the editor of my home-town paper, "Hi! I want to be a war correspondent." This was a suffi-ciently damn-fool thing to do that he let me go, probably to see what would happen. Writing, it turned out, was the only thing I was good for. Using my clips from Israel, I argued to the editors of *Army Times* that they needed my services to cover the war in Vietnam. They too let me do it. Editorial bad judgement is a valuable resource.

I spent the last year of the war between Phnom Penh and Saigon, leaving each with the evacuation. Those were heady days in which I lived in slums that would have horrified a New York alley cat, but they appealed to the Steinbeck in me, of which there is a lot. After the fall of Saigon I returned to Asia, resumed residence for six months in my old haunts in Taipei, and studied Chi-nese while waiting for the next war, which didn't come. Returning overland, I took up a career of magazine free-lancing, a colorful route to starvation, with stints on various staffs interspersed. For a year I worked in Boulder, Colorado, on the staff of *Soldier of Fortune* magazine, half zoo and half asylum, with the intention of writing a book about it. Publishing houses said, yes, Fred, this is great stuff, but you are obviously making it up. I wasn't. *Playboy* eventually published it, making me extremely persona non grata at *Soldier of Fortune*.

Having gotten married somewhere along the way, I am now the happily divorced father of the World's Finest Daughters. Until recently I worked as, among other things, a law-enforcement columnist for the *Washington Times*. It allowed me to take trips to big cities and to ride around in police cars with the siren going *woowoowoo* and kick in doors of drug dealers. Recently I changed the column from law enforcement to technology, and now live in Mexico in Jocotopec, near Guadalajara, having found burros preferable to bureaus. I now share my existence with Violeta Gonzales, who was what God had in mind when he created women but just hadn't quite perfected the idea until recently. My hobbies are crawling South America, scuba, listening to blues, swing-danc-ing in dirt bars, associating with colorful maniacs, and writing seditious col-umns.

My principal accomplishment in life, aside from my children, is the discovery that it is possible to jitterbug to the Brandenburgs.

978-0-595-39390-9
0-595-39390-X

Printed in the United States
64703LVS00003B/110

9 780595 393909